Jack Webb

THE BADGE

arrow books

Published in the United Kingdom by Arrow Books in 2006

5 7 9 10 8 6

Copyright © Mark VII, Ltd, 1958
Introduction copyright © James Ellroy 2005

Jack Webb has asserted his right under the Copyright, Designs and Patents Act,
1988 to be identified as the author of this work.

First published in the United Kingdom in 1958 by Mark VII, Ltd
First published in paperback in 2006 by Arrow Books

Arrow Books
The Random House Group Limited
20 Vauxhall Bridge Road, London, SW1V 2SA

Addresses for companies within The Random House Group Limited
can be found at: www.randomhouse.co.uk/offices.htm

The Random House Group Limited Reg. No. 954009

www.randomhouse.co.uk

A CIP catalogue record for this book is available from the British Library

Penguin Random House is committed to a sustainable future for
our business, our readers and our planet. This book is made from
Forest Stewardship Council® certified paper.

Printed and bound in Great Britain by Clays Ltd, St Ives plc

ISBN 97880099499732 (from Jan 2007)
ISBN 0 09 949973 8

Typeset by SX Composing DTP, Rayleigh, Essex

For Lew, who started the whole thing anyway

Contents

INTRODUCTION

Some books influence a writer. They impart a great story and induce a sense of narrative awe. They teach style, structure, and the power of language. They attack the writer's unconscious and make him wonder how he can do this himself. They show him the mechanics of character development and display the mystique of milieu.

It all runs abstract. Books attack the inner brain and leave their virus there. Books rarely shape a writer's curiosity *whole*. Books rarely give him sustained subject matter and a time and place to re-create anew. I'm anomalous that way. I got lucky at the get-go. It was one-stop imaginative shopping. I found all my stuff in one book.

It was March '59. I'd just turned eleven years old. I lived in L.A. I shared a dive pad with my dad and our un-housebroken dog. I was a fucked-up child of divorce. My mother was murdered in June '58. I was nine months into an ambiguous bereavement. I was a big-time reader. My mother's death corrupted my spirit and got me permanently hooked on crime. I exhausted the canon of kids' crime books and turned to adult fare. My dad got me a birthday gift. It was Jack Webb's book *The Badge*.

I knew Jungle Jack from the TV show *Dragnet*. He played Sergeant Joe Friday and directed most episodes. *Dragnet* was taciturn drama and ripe LAPD propaganda.

The fuzz talked terse. Craven criminals withered and whimpered and ratted each other out. Cop nomenclature cascaded. 'R & I,' 'Bunco Squad,' 'strong-arm 211.' Stern detectives with flat tops. Sweaty hoodlums with goatees and 'gone' attire. A criminal universe writ large – but circumscribed within L.A.

I read the book. It was the TV show unchained. Censorship restricted television content. Publishing strictures were much more loose. Jack top-loaded *The Badge* with sex and scandal. He hot-wired me to L.A. crime forever.

There's the 'Black Dahlia' murder. It's L.A. '47. Betty Short – *muerta*. She's been tortured, bisected, and dumped in Leimert Park. It's an unsolved sex crime – just like my mother's case. Betty Short claims me. She merges with Geneva Hilliker Ellroy. She engages my kiddie lust. She bops with my mother symbiotically. She spawns my lifelong dialogue on misogyny. I write my novel *The Black Dahlia* many years later.

The Badge got me hooked. I just followed Jack Webb's lead.

There's pint-sized hood Mickey Cohen. He's jungled up with mob mouthpiece Sam Rummell. Brenda Allen's running whores. The '48 county grand jury is coming down hard. Mickey's goon Neddy Herbert leeches lead. It all goes blooey.

This tsurus ended up in my novel *The Big Nowhere*. *The Badge* got me hooked. I just followed Jack Webb's lead.

There's Stephen Nash. He's an ex-heist man. He's a hophead. He's a hell-bent homo high on hate in '58 L.A. He slashes a ten-year-old boy under the Santa Monica pier. He's gap-toothed, he's flappy-mouthed, he's vicious, he's vile. He's on death row with Donald Keith Bashor.

Demon Don hot-prowls pads in Westlake Park. He peeps. He burgles. He's out for cash and gash. He rapes one woman. He beats two women dead. LAPD snags him in a rolling stakeout.

I featured Nash and Bashor in two recent novellas. *The Badge* got me hooked. I just followed Jack Webb's lead.

This book taught me. This book gave me heroes and fiends. This book gave me the Los Angeles Police Department – a magnificent and complexly defined monolith that rocks to its own progressive and often iron-fisted beat. L.A. has been called 'The Big Wrong Place.' It's got the best police force and the most garish crime. The '40s and '50s were L.A. at its boomtown best. This book takes you there.

This book *left* me there. I'm riding and writing out a life sentence. Jack Webb crapped out in 1982. He was a juicehead, a chain-smoker, a steak-and-fries man. He kicked too fucking soon. I was a kid writer then. I never got the chance to thank him. I never got the chance to say, 'You got me hooked. I just followed your lead.'

– James Ellroy
January 23, 2005

Foreword

By now, it's no secret.

I have been involved in a documentary radio and television detective series for some eleven years now. A feature-length motion picture was made. It played throughout the world. The television episodes . . . nearly 300 . . . have been translated into German, French, Spanish, Japanese. The half-hour films are currently being run off in England, Canada, Australia, Latin America, Africa. And youngsters in Dallas race Joe Friday's car and carry a replica of his badge.

And now a book.

When we were first devising the radio show, from which the television program was derived, I shook hands with research for the first time. Many long hours were spent in squadrooms, squad cars, drinking the one a.m. cup of coffee with working detectives. I learned my first police rule: the solution of a crime is the work of many hands and many minds.

And so this book. It, too, represents the work of many. When you ask a huge, metropolitan police department to unbutton its vest, lean back, and sit there while you pore over its personal diary . . . how do you say *thanks?*

You don't try.

Instead, you set it all down . . . the victories . . . the defeats . . . the torments . . . the intimacies.

And you fervently hope that the end result brings a grin or a tear . . . not a blush.

JACK WEBB

North Hollywood, California

THE QUESTION

The way it is with so many women who live alone, life had held back on Karil Graham. She was likable and attractive, still a year on the sunny side of forty, sandy-haired, blue-eyed, trim-figured. But there was no husband – a marriage hadn't worked out – no children, no other man in her lonely life.

Karil bravely hid the hurt and filled the emptiness as best she could. Every day she went to work, on time, to her job as receptionist at a downtown Los Angeles art school. Nights, in her quiet apartment, she listened to music and dabbled in painting. She was just a dilettante, she knew resignedly, but records and easel were gracious cover-ups for emptiness.

Sometimes Karil counseled students who attended the art school. Often they were male students, and she took them to her heart in a mothering, protective way. She saw for them something more meaningful and zestful in life, the something that had somehow passed her by.

That year spring came very early, even for Los Angeles; in the third week of February, there was already a sparkle in the air, a premature stirring in all the backyard gardens around town. For women like Karil living alone, it was a bitter-sweet time. She decided to kill the loneliness, at least for a night, by inviting some of the art students to dinner at her new apartment in Westlake.

About ten minutes from downtown Los Angeles, awkwardly straddling a man-made lake, Westlake is the kind of neighborhood that attracts the Karils of the West Coast. Not proud, not shabby, once fashionable, now a little shiny at the elbows, the district includes older homes inhabited by retired couples, apartments, rooming houses.

The younger people who live there, mostly single or divorced, share the camaraderie of transience; and casual neighborliness abounds. They are gregarious, they like to party, and as a rule they are harmless. There isn't a soul in the house they don't trust. They live out of each other's coffee pots and share each other's lives. Sometimes, when they get home to their one room, they are high and careless, and the door is left unlocked.

Karil's apartment-warming went off beautifully. The dinner was good, the conversation about art stimulating, the night warm. About 10 p.m., Karil and a guest put on swim suits and went for a plunge in the big, new pool located in the patio. They splashed about noisily, and in fifteen minutes Eleanor Lipson, who managed the apartments with her husband, rather sharply reminded the new tenant that swimming wasn't allowed after 9 p.m.

Karil and her friend went back to the apartment and changed, and the party went on till about 12:30 a.m.

When her guests had left, Karil washed the dishes and tidied up her little place. She made up the studio couch for sleeping, and, though she usually didn't work Saturdays, set the alarm for 7 a.m. This Saturday, she had to be up early to help register a new class of students at the art school.

Then she slipped into a pink nightgown and went to her door and made sure that it was shut tight. The latch was broken, and she couldn't lock it. It really didn't matter much because the locksmith was coming up in a day or two to fix it.

*

Four hours later, most of Westlake was sleeping. The street lights were still on, and even the birds in MacArthur Park hadn't yet sensed the dawn. Occasionally, an auto streaked along Wilshire Boulevard, and the morning papers were being dropped at the street corners for the newsboys.

But one resident of Westlake, a blond young man with the body of a Greek discus thrower, was abroad. By day, he led the prosaic life of an eight-to-five laborer who mixed paint. Nights, he felt, he really lived; dangerously, excitingly, romantically, you might say. He was a burglar who preyed on women, the younger and the lonelier the better.

Once there had been trouble, bad trouble; and he knew it must not happen again. So he memorized the patchy streets of Westlake, the turnings of the halls in rooming houses and apartment buildings. He watched at the bars and eavesdropped along the lovers' paths in MacArthur Park, marking the women who were high or indiscreet. They often forgot to lock their doors, often were too sodden to hear him when he came calling.

In one hand, he carried a flashlight, and in the other, an iron bar. If the unexpected developed, he would rely first on his personal appeal to discourage an outcry. But he knew he wasn't irresistible, and so he carried the bar, too. What had happened before, the bad trouble, *mustn't* happen again.

So far, he hadn't needed to use the lead pipe.

As Karil slept out the last hour of her life, the burglar slipped silently into the backyard of one of the large, old houses not far away. From casing the neighborhood, he knew the back door should open. Confidently, he turned the knob. The door opened.

Inside, he moved quietly to the apartment where three pretty nurses were sleeping off the fun and excitement of

5

an earlier party. He found three purses containing $90. The nurses never stirred. He didn't have to swing the pipe. Outside, he dropped the emptied purses on the porch and drifted up the street to the new apartment building.

First, he checked the mailboxes, looking for the 'Miss' or 'Mrs.' that would identify the spinster, widow, or divorcée, the lonely woman he could charm or threaten if he had to. On the first floor, he tried two or three doors. All were locked. He tiptoed up to the second floor.

At his touch, the first door swung back. It was Karil's apartment.

Warily, he probed the darkness with his flashlight, then slipped in. Suddenly, the light picked out a woman's body on the couch. He could see that she was pretty, and he held the beam on her longer than was necessary. Pretty women made him feel warm and gentle.

Maybe it was the light or his heavy breathing. Karil stirred, and there was a click as he snapped off the flashlight. Then she awoke. For a moment, she listened. The room seemed black and empty. Then she must have heard the breathing. She gasped.

'*Who's there!*'

He froze, hand tightening around the pipe. Karil met the frightening silence boldly, too boldly. She snapped on the lamp beside her couch. Her drowsy blue eyes blinked, then widened, and her hand flew to her mouth. As she started to move, he moved faster.

Once before, five years ago, another woman in another apartment had called out, 'Who's there!' Then she had screamed, and he had run too late. Other tenants in the building had caught him, and he had lost four good, young years of life in San Quentin and Chino, first for burglary and later for escape.

Now he was on parole, and he wouldn't, couldn't go back! As he moved, he swung the iron bar. Not hard, just enough to scare her into silence. But she screamed, and at the sound, loud and eerie, panic seized him.

He swung again, harder. He brought the iron pipe down once more, and then again. At last, she was still and quiet.

He switched off the lamp, and stood trembling in the restful darkness for a few seconds. Then he walked out to the balcony and listened.

One flight above, though he didn't know it, a woman also was listening. Something had wakened her, but now all was quiet. She glanced at her clock, quarter past five, and went back to sleep.

The burglar returned to Karil's apartment. His flashlight picked up the bloodied form on the couch, and he didn't like to think that maybe it was watching him. He walked closer and wrapped Karil's nightgown around the crushed head, and the pink color deepened into a dirty maroon.

As he did so, her blood saturated the tip of his jacket.

Now his nerve came back, and methodically he ransacked the small apartment. From Karil's large straw purse lying on a chair, he extracted $25. Not much. There had to be more around someplace. He shoved the bills into his pocket and threw the purse on the floor. He poked through the bureau and the closet and even pried apart the pictures on the wall.

There had to be more! But there wasn't. He had killed for two sawbucks and a fin, and it hardly seemed worth it. He walked out, leaving a brief, blood-smudged trail from his soiled shoes and jacket.

At the art school that morning, they were tolerantly good-natured about it when Karil failed to show. Nobody called the apartment house. And there, Eleanor Lipson, the manager, prided herself on being the kind of apartment keeper who minds her own business and lets the tenants mind theirs.

7

During the afternoon, she brought a prospective tenant to the second floor to show an apartment. Passing Karil's room, she noticed the door was ajar; and, through the thin opening, she caught a glimpse of Karil's bare legs, warmly pink and glistening in a shaft of sunlight. Of course, a tenant should at least close the door while she takes a Saturday afternoon nap, but it was nothing to rouse her and make a scene about.

And so, because employer and house manager practiced the estimable virtue of tolerance, murder did not out till evening, and murderer picked up a lead of exactly thirteen hours and eighteen minutes over the police. In that time, he could have fled more than halfway across the country.

It was Mrs. Lipson's husband, James, who finally found the body. A breeze had come down out of the hills from the northwest, blowing Karil's door almost wide open. Lipson glanced in and, being a male nurse at the County Jail, knew exactly what to do. He picked up a phone and dialed Madison 4-5211.

Sergeant Jack McCreadie, working the night watch at the Homicide Division, handled the call. He entered it in the record at 6:33 p.m.

His viciousness spent, Karil's murderer had left her apartment in numbed despair, his gloved hand still clutching the piece of pipe. He got into his car parked in a nearby alley and drove to his hotel. He showered and changed into fresh clothes, from the skin out.

Then he made a tidy bundle of his bloodied clothes and shoes, the pipe and the flashlight. He couldn't sleep, and anyhow he didn't dare keep the evidence in his room. He went back to his car and drove – anywhere, everywhere – all day long. Toward sunset, he found himself in Santa Monica.

Parking near the beach, he waited for nightfall, the time

8

when he thought and operated best. The hour dragged, and the bundle on the seat beside him made him so nervous he was afraid he might panic again. He had to wait for full darkness.

Finally, the bundle under his arm, he moved onto a fun pier alive with Saturday night celebrants and quietly picked his way through the roisterers to the far end. With a quick, sidelong glance to make sure no one was watching, he hurled the bundle into the Pacific and turned back.

Midway down the pier, he suddenly felt hungry. He clambered onto a lunch counter stool and ordered a hamburger and coffee. He ate heartily. He had gotten rid of the only evidence that tied him to Karil. He was free! It was 9 p.m.

When Sergeant McCreadie alerted Homicide, everything rolled to Karil's deathbed. There were mobile units of investigators, criminalists, photographers and latent fingerprint specialists. Big brass rolled, too, because there was going to be hell to pay about this one.

In the past twelve weeks, there had been thirty burglaries in the Westlake area. Not one place had been forcibly entered – not a screen cut, a door forced, or a lock broken – and most of the victims had been lonely, defenseless women, whom the police are supposed to protect.

Now 'the open door burglar' had turned killer; and the newspapers were going to demand somebody's head – preferably, the burglar's, but if not that of the Los Angeles Police Department. Every LAPD man in the little apartment knew that and knew the odds, too.

Of some 27,000 burglaries yearly (not including those from autos), there are about 6,230 burglary arrests. So the odds on any given job were more than four to one against the cop. And the nearest thing to a witness, the woman on the floor above, told LAPD their man had a thirteen hour and eighteen minute lead on them.

Nevertheless, they ransacked the apartment more pains-takingly than the killer.

A full Crime Lab crew pored over the scene of violence, but all they came up with were worthless smudges and the bloodied trail that led no farther than the baseboards. Not a heelprint or footprint that could be recognized.

From kitchen to balcony, the print men dusted in vain. Graphite and aluminum – nothing showed through. Obviously, the killer had worn gloves.

The criminalists looked, despairingly, for any shred of physical evidence down to a thread, button, cigarette butt. There was nothing. All they could do was run tests of Karil's blood and record it so that *if* a suspect were bagged, matching tests could be made on his clothing.

Finally, the detectives, the scientists, the 'hard facts' men went away, knowing precisely what they had known before they rolled: A woman had been murdered.

Even LAPD's statistics unit with its long, electronic memory couldn't help this time. Here the modus operandi used by known criminals and that occurring frequently in unsolved crimes is separately filed and indexed. You just run thousands of perforated cards through the electronic sorting machine, and sometimes the machine, fishing through arrest and prison records, past crimes, addresses, associates, habits, and physical descriptions down to a limp, 'remembers' a priceless clue to the wanted man's identity.

Now they asked the brain, through cards, what it could remember about (a) a burglar (b) who preyed on women and (c) who used the open door as his modus operandi. The machine tried hard, but it proved no better than an ordinary human brain. It couldn't remember anything.

On Sunday, the day after Karil's body was found, while LAPD was counting its frustrations, the killer added to

10

their difficulties, though mercifully they didn't know it at the time. He quietly checked out of his hotel in Westlake and fled to South Pasadena.

At a sedate frame house there, he quickly won the heart of the kindly old lady who had advertised in the Sunday papers for a roomer. He was so young, only twenty-seven, and so handsome, blond, brown-eyed, a strapping 185 pounds, and almost six feet in height. And he seemed so lonely, too, needing a grandmother's care. Innocently, she took in the lodger.

'Just tell enough, not too much, and make it sound like there isn't any more,' the old cons had advised him in the prison yard at San Quentin. He told her truthfully that his name was Donald Keith Bashor. He touched her with the story of his broken home life as a child in Glendale and reassured her with his description of his sister and brother, nice, well-established people.

Donald, as she was immediately calling him, went out and got a $50-a-week job mixing paint. On most nights, he stayed home with her. When she found he was courting a girl on the other nights, she teased him about it. Yes, Donald said, he hoped to get married in the spring. Why wait, she asked, and Donald just smiled bashfully.

That was the part he didn't tell; about his burglary conviction and still live parole and his hideout from a murder rap. And, naturally, the old lady couldn't have a suspicion in the world about her adopted 'grandson.' Didn't he stay home weekends, helping her around the yard? Didn't he carry the shopping bundles home for her? Wasn't he as good a grandson as any lonely old woman could want?

Back in Los Angeles, the case stood still; the photographic glossies of the ugly crime, the records of interrogations and scientific tests just gathered dust. The

11

police knew only that the 'open door burglar' had escaped them; where he had gone, whether he would come back, they had no idea. He might be dead, in prison, or might even have gone straight.

For ten months, Bashor lived the quiet, irksome life of the good, and then, in the December following Karil's February killing, he struck again. At first, he concentrated his attentions in the San Gabriel Valley close to his room at the old lady's house. This is to the northeast of Los Angeles, and LAPD didn't know for several months that their man had come out of hibernation.

But one night in Alhambra, Bashor had a nasty turn. As he was shaking down an apartment, he found a police badge and a blunt-nosed, .38-calibre Detective's Special in its spring holster, both lying on a table. At first, like any cop-hating criminal, he was delighted at the opportunity to steal police equipment and make the sleeping officer look foolish.

But almost immediately afterwards, fondling the trophies in his car, he had a sobering second thought. Suppose the cop had awakened, as Karil had? He wouldn't have been a lead-pipe cinch like a woman. Suppose, in this strange territory, he blundered again into the wrong flat? He couldn't, wouldn't go back to prison!

The more he thought of it, the more Bashor decided the only safe place for him to operate was back in Westlake, his own backyard. He knew the locations of the streets and alleys; he knew the careless habits of many of its residents. Best of all, he knew he could take care of the unexpected – the occasional lone woman who might wake up. The next week, which was in the March following his December eruption, he was prowling the familiar rooming houses and small-apartment buildings.

By latter April, the complaints from Westlake filled an

12

embarrassingly bulgy folder in LAPD's Burglary Division. When Bashor worked, he hit two or three places in a night. As the reports multiplied, there could be no doubt about it. The 'open door burglar' had returned.

Quietly, a rolling stakeout was established. The number of police cars assigned to the area was doubled, and they were ordered to keep moving in a constant, criss-cross patrol which sieved Westlake. Even the innocent-looking panel truck used by LAPD for motion picture sleuthing roamed the neighborhood.

Each night, the truck was parked on a different street and from within two officers kept a weary watch through peepholes. But the prowler slipped through the rubber-tire net night after night; and by May, the continuing epidemic had Westlake terrorized.

Women demanded that the police 'do something,' and LAPD couldn't tell them how hard it was working without also taking the fugitive into their confidence.

From the new reports, another modus operandi check was run on the burglaries, and LAPD implored the electronic brain to *think*. *Think*. *THINK*. Yet Sergeant Joe Oakes of the Burglary Division, checking the results, could make only one unhappy deduction.

'We may have another murder on our hands if we don't get him,' he told fellow officers.

Yet all LAPD could do was to increase the patrol. Some four thousand police man hours had been pitted against the will-o'-the-wisp burglar, and they hadn't been enough. All LAPD could do was to spend more man hours – *and wait*.

Now it was a night in May, a pleasant night very much like the premature spring Karil Graham had enjoyed so briefly in February of the year before. Bashor was on the prowl again, this time in the western end of Westlake where it merges into the Wilshire district. A neat five-room bungalow, the kind a lone woman might occupy, caught his eye.

Inside, Mrs. Laura Lindsay, sixty-two, a brown-haired divorcée, was sleeping. Having for thirty years been a top-flight legal secretary in Los Angeles, Mrs. Lindsay was a prudent woman. Before going to bed, she had, she was sure, locked all the doors and windows; but anyone could have made the same mistake of oversight that she did. Only tonight, Bashor was quietly circling the darkened house, ready to profit by it.

Finding all the doors and windows secured, he was about to go away because he never could get up the nerve to force an entry. Then he spotted the outside woodbox which connected with the living room by an opening four feet wide and three feet high. Usually, the lid was locked, but this was Bashor's lucky night. He crawled through the opening and into the house.

Women, he knew, think in their peculiar way that it is safer to keep valuables nearby as they sleep. He made straight for the bedroom and hunted for Mrs. Lindsay's purse. Maybe he was clumsy in his over-confidence, or maybe in the fifteen months since Karil, it was just the law of averages working against him. Mrs. Lindsay awoke.

This time, for Bashor, there was no momentary freezing. As she started to rise, he was on her with a ball-peen hammer. It was a sickening, faster replay of Karil's murder. The woman fell back, and tried to rise. He smashed her head, savagely, again and again.

Then he stepped back, panting, and rested for a moment. For a second perhaps, Karil's younger death mask flashed before his eyes. He took a pillow case and Mrs. Lindsay's dressing gown and wrapped them around the head as he had shrouded Karil's head with her pink nightgown.

14

For some unaccountable reason, he picked up the body, carried it to a couch nearby and laid it there, the face down and hidden from his sight. He hurried from the house.

By sunup, Bashor had on a complete change of clothes and was in a restaurant, eating a substantial breakfast. Woman killing didn't bother him so much now. Beside him lay blood-stained clothing and shoes and a ball-peen hammer, all tied into a neat little package. But they could wait till dark, and meanwhile he would have another cup of coffee and then some rest.

When Irving Walker, a prominent Los Angeles attorney, stopped by to give his secretary a lift to the office, her body was still warm. This time, the killer had only a few hours' start on the police, but for all practical purposes, that didn't seem to make any difference.

The same frustrated, irritated group of specialists interrogated, pried, dusted, and popped flash bulbs, all in vain. LAPD's Scientific Investigation Division would have been a public laughing stock, except that the public was in no mood to laugh. This murder so like Karil's frightened the whole city. Westlake's terror was contagious; and neighborhoods Bashor had never even seen wanted twenty-four-hour protection.

Then Sergeant A. R. McLaughlin, LAPD's latent prints ace, found it. Inside and out, he had dusted the house, doors, jambs, locks, furniture, utensils, anything an intruder could conceivably have touched, and had come up with nothing. Finally, on the woodbox in the yard where a less painstaking man might easily have missed it, his dust brought up the fragmentary print of the heel of a palm. It was a rare discovery.

Carefully, the print was taken to the crime lab. An analysis proved futile, and it was filed away; but now the police had *something* if they ever laid hands on a suspect.

15

That night, Bashor followed form. Once again, he drove to Santa Monica and safely dropped his neat little bundle into the ocean off the far end of the pier. He decided that for the next week or so he would be wise to lay low.

During the breather that Bashor gave them, LAPD's men made Westlake into a giant booby trap. The rolling stakeout was again intensified. From other districts, plain-clothesmen were drawn in on emergency basis to question all suspicious men found on the streets. In alleys and hallways, on dark corners, teams of police spied on after-midnight activity.

In the hot panel truck, Officers D. C. Wesley and J. R. McCaslin were keeping a dull, uncomfortable peephole watch. This night, early in June, the truck was parked on a street of older apartment buildings, some of which were being torn down. There was no particular reason to think their man would walk down this street this night, but being good officers under orders, they watched, hour after hour, sourly meditating on a policeman's life.

An athletic-looking, blond young man passed the truck. He went into the vestibule of one of the apartment houses and carefully removed his shoes. Wesley and McCaslin still waited. Then they saw him train his flashlight on the names on the mailboxes.

Guns in hand, the two officers slipped out of the truck and advanced on their quarry. He saw them and fled out to the street in panic. Wesley and McCaslin yelled to him to stop. He kept on, turning into an alley between two buildings that were being demolished. They fired.

One shot caught their man in the left shoulder, and he stumbled. He recovered his balance and ran on, wildly looking for any escape route. Suddenly he veered into another narrow passageway between the buildings.

As he ran, his shoeless right foot came down heavily on a nail sticking out from a board. He went down with a scream, and Wesley and McCaslin were on top of him. It was Bashor. An ambulance surgeon sewed him up, and he went to jail.

When the detectives took over, they found they had a prisoner and that was about all. Bashor was mild enough, but he was too conwise to talk, or at least to tell the truth. *Just tell enough, not too much, and make it sound like there isn't any more.*

He had to talk some because the police gun stolen in Alhambra was found on him; and obviously he had broken his parole three ways from the middle by his suspicious actions, by carrying a gun, just by being out so late at night. Still, he tried to lie, reason, deny his way out of trouble.

First, he said he would talk only to Tom Donovan, the husky sergeant in the Burglary Division who had helped convict Bashor years before. That seemed plausible because criminals often want to deal with the policemen they know. But it soon became plain that he was trying to con Donovan into believing him innocent.

So the burglary sergeant got together with Sergeant Jack McCreadie, a homicide specialist for sixteen years. It was McCreadie who had taken the first phone call on Karil Graham's murder; and he felt a personal, burning passion to wipe that case off the books.

Bashor's palm print matched the fragmentary print that had been picked off Laura Lindsay's woodbox. If he had killed her, he had no doubt battered Karil Graham to death, too, since the murders fitted the same pattern of savagery. But if Bashor wouldn't admit the lesser crime of burglary, how could he be persuaded to confess two murders?

Between them, Donovan and McCreadie decided, they would give their suspect a real, razzle-dazzle interrogation.

First, Donovan would question him, and then McCreadie would suddenly take over. Always, the switch alarmed him.

'What are you questioning me for?' he asked McCreadie time and again. 'I'm here for burglary, not murder.'

Tantalizingly, McCreadie wouldn't quite come out and tell him. He didn't even tell him about the palm print. That was being held for a psychological break-through at the right moment.

For almost two days, the interrogation went on; and then the detectives got an unexpected assist from a civilian. From the showup, a woman singled him out as the intruder who had ransacked her apartment while she lay in bed, too terrified to scream.

With that as a lever, Donovan got Bashor to admit to sixty burglaries just in the Westlake area. Now was the time to put on the pressure. The second night he was in custody, it was McCreadie, not Donovan, who walked Bashor to the booking desk.

Bashor looked puzzled, but said nothing. McCreadie told the booking officer that the charge was a '187' in the California Penal Code.

'Is that burglary?' Bashor blurted.

McCreadie looked his prisoner full in the face. 'Murder,' he said evenly.

'Murder! I'm in for burglary. I told Donovan everything. You trying to *frame* me for murder?'

And then McCreadie played his trump with the delicate timing of a Culbertson. 'I didn't put your prints on that woodbox, kid,' he said softly.

This was the break-through, and quickly McCreadie brought the ashen Bashor into an interrogation room to follow up the advantage. The razzle-dazzle had kept him under constant pressure trying to outguess his questioners; and now he had run out of guesses and evasive answers.

Piecemeal, grudgingly, as though it hurt him, he began to talk about the two bludgeon deaths. Then the trickle of information became a raceway, and he talked fully and without remorse.

'They've got nothing more to worry about. . . . It was something I had to do. . . . Part of the job. . . . The calculated risk.' Almost pleadingly, he told McCreadie about his fear of being imprisoned again. 'I knew if I got caught, I'd have to go back. Finish my time, and then some. I didn't want that!'

Twenty minutes later, the stenographer reappeared with several sheets of closely typed onionskin paper.

McCreadie placed them in front of the suspect.

'Read it.'

Bashor complied.

'You've read the statement?'

'Yes, I have.'

'Initial each page. Both copies.'

Bashor did so.

'There's been no promise of immunity or reward made to you in obtaining this confession?'

'No.'

'Have you been threatened in any manner?'

'No.'

'I didn't hear you.'

'I said no.'

'This statement was made freely and voluntarily by you?'

Bashor answered in a firm, voice: 'Yes.'

And in an equally firm hand, he wrote the words: Donald Keith Bashor.

The Los Angeles County grand jury promptly indicted him on two counts of murder.

Now the bludgeoner of two women, the man who had preyed so coolly on dozens of other lonely women, lost the last bit of his nerve. He wanted to plead guilty, and get it over with as quickly as possible. When his attorney insisted on entering a not guilty plea, Bashor balked at a jury trial and put his fate in the hands of a judge.

He was convicted on both counts of first-degree murder and sent to Death Row in San Quentin, where he was executed in the gas chamber, October 11, 1957.

Donald Keith Bashor was young and handsome and often had other people's money to spend freely. In his twenty-eight years, he should have made friends who would grieve sincerely over his fate. Yet, in their investigation, the police found only one person who mourned. That was his little old landlady in Pasadena.

As he had taken from other lonely women their purses or their lives, he robbed her of an innocent, pathetic illusion. She lost her only grandson.

II

The pamphlet given visitors to Los Angeles says the City Hall stands just about at the geographical center of the city. On a clear day, if you ride the elevator some 450 feet to the observation tower, you see a mass of concrete, granite, timber and just plain rock – one of the strangest, most picturesque and complicated police beats in the world.

You look north fifteen miles to Mount Wilson in the Sierra Madres, west thirteen miles to Venice and the Pacific. To the northwest, Hollywood seems to huddle against the Santa Monica mountains, and twenty miles south lies the harbor, the biggest man-made port in the world. East and southeast stretch the city's major industrial areas.

Here is a sprawling, magnetic, fantastic city whose feet

rest on the sand at sea level and whose shoulders proudly rise to a mountain almost a mile high. Along coastline, mountain pass and desert flatland, you can ride its twisting perimeter for 312 miles. North to south, there are forty-four miles in which to hide a body. East to west, twenty-five miles in which to rob, plunder, attack.

And there are 454.749 square miles to break a cop's back – and, sometimes, his heart.

Once a sleepy pueblo, now crowding the top in U.S. population, Los Angeles has attracted all manner of men, vice, and crime. Among its 2,500,000 inhabitants, the daily collision of good and bad, hunter and victim, passes reckoning. While the homicide detective is investigating a rape near the beach, the robbery detective is busy with a supermarket stickup in the San Fernando Valley.

And in between, in the score of individual communities, in any of the one million dwellings, no one knows – no one can know – what other evil is being planned, or already taking place.

Once Los Angeles was the capital of glamour, and then the movie studios began to disperse and sometimes disappear. Then the aircraft plant, the rubber factory, and the automobile assembly line elbowed in. Once the Mexicans and Chinese flooded the city, but the pioneer from back East, today as well as one hundred years ago, has staked his claim here, too.

Since no influence vanishes entirely, there is a residue of elegant sin and two-bit robberies, fantan and poker, calculated crime and impetuous knifing. The Angeleno will travel half a day to spend thirty minutes admiring desert flowers or lunching in a native sycamore grove. In his unpredictable way, he also will step across the line and commit a crime that is as grotesque as anything that comes out of Place Pigalle.

Against the danger, the police in the largest

incorporated city in the United States have a dozen geographical enforcement divisions and dozens of specialists in every crime from bunco to murder. But unlike most federal police agencies, which are charged with enforcing specific laws, LAPD must be a housekeeper of all crime.

While the beach rape and the supermarket stickup are under investigation, traffic must flow freely during rush hour; and if a child strays from home, the patrolman on the beat takes time out to return him. Most of the work is far from spectacular, and often the spectacular is not successful.

For every individual, mostly Angelenos, who remembers LAPD's triumph in Karil Graham's murder, there are a thousand who remember another Los Angeles woman killing: The Black Dahlia murder. That is, so to speak, the other side of the shield.

III

She was a lazy girl and irresponsible; and, when she chose to work, she drifted obscurely from one menial job to another, in New England, south to Florida, westward to the Coast.

No matter how they die, most drifters leave nothing behind, and many of the 25,000 graves dug yearly in Los Angeles are marked by blank stones, for their occupants didn't even leave a name. Yet today, more than a decade after her strange and awful death, this girl remains hauntingly, pathetically alive to many persons.

To the sociologist, she is the typical, unfortunate depression child who matured too suddenly in her teens into the easy money, easy living, easy loving of wartime America. To the criminologist, though the case is almost

22

too melodramatic in its twists, her tortured, severed body is an eerie blend of Poe and Freud. To millions of plain Americans, fascinated by the combined savagery and cool intellect that went into her murder, she is 'The Black Dahlia.'

The other side of the shield.

Right from the first erroneous report to the police at 10:35 a.m. that gray mid-January day in 1947, the investigation was askew through no fault of the police. In the days, months, years of sleuthing that followed, it never quite got back into balance, again through no fault of the detectives. More than any other crime, murder is sometimes like that.

In the University section, along a dreary, weedy block without a house on either side, a housewife was walking to the store with her five-year-old daughter, scolding her a little because she wanted to play in the dew-wet lots.

Halfway up the block, the mother stopped in horror at something she saw in one of the lots. 'What's that?' the child asked. The mother didn't answer. Grabbing her hand, she ran with her to the nearest neighbor's house to call the police.

And the first, wrong alarm went out: 'Man down, 39th and Norton.'

Within ten minutes, about 10:45 a.m., the first patrol car had reached the scene. Quickly a team of detectives from Central Division, a full crew from the Crime Lab, newspaper legmen, and photographers followed. The street was blocked off to keep back the curious, and the investigation got underway.

Sergeant Finis Arthur Brown of the Homicide Division, who was going to live with this ugly thing for months and years, hadn't yet arrived.

At 9 a.m. that day, he had been in court to testify in another case. After that, he went to Sixth and Rampart

Streets to check out a dead-body report. An elderly man had died of natural causes, but Brown followed through with routine questioning of the rooming house operator.

Then there was a phone call for him. Captain Jack Donahoe told him to get over quick to the 3900 block on South Norton. 'Looks like we got a bad one, Brownie,' he warned.

At 11:05 a.m., just half an hour after the discovery of the body, Brown was there. He saw what he was up against, and, in another twenty-five minutes, additional manpower was at the scene. Nobody could say later that LAPD hadn't rolled hard and fast on this one.

Efficiently, detectives fanned out through the neighborhood. They wanted to find the woman who had made the first call. They hoped to locate some resident who had perhaps heard or seen something, *anything*, though the chances were one-hundred-to-one against them. The lot was a good hundred yards from the nearest house, and the body had probably been dumped at three or four o'clock in the morning.

They got nowhere. Neither did the 'hard facts' men who sifted patiently through the weeds, turning up broken glass, rusted cans and other rubbish; but not a clue. The only bit of physical evidence was a set of tire marks on the pavement; and, if they came from the killer's car, they were never to prove useful.

But there was the body.

Old homicide hand though he was, Sergeant Brown had to make a conscious effort to study it.

It was nude. It showed evidence of slow, deliberate torture. There were neat, deep slashes around the breasts and on them. Rope burns on the wrists and ankles indicated the victim had been spread-eagled to heighten her agony. Her mouth had been deeply gashed from ear to ear so that her face was fixed in a grotesque and leering

24

death smile. Finally, the body had been cleanly, surgically cut in two at the waist.

Brown was glad to turn away and check with Lee Jones of the Crime Lab. There were two interesting things to note. A sprinkling of bristles on the body indicated that it had been scrubbed. And, despite the lavish mutilation, there was only one drop of blood in the field.

Scientists, especially hard-bitten police scientists, usually don't give in to emotion. Lee Jones couldn't restrain himself. 'This is the worst crime upon a woman I've ever seen,' he blurted.

Sergeant Brown's pressing job was identification. But the body had been stripped, and there was only the long shot that maybe the girl had got into trouble and maybe her fingerprints were on file. Brown had copies of them rushed to the FBI in Washington by means of newspaper telephoto equipment.

Then he used the press another way, asking them to publish an artist's recreation of the girl's face (without the awful death smile). And, though not for publication, he had every inch of the weedy lot photographed, right down to three-dimensional shots of the severed corpse.

No one came forward to identify the victim, and though the forlorn files in Missing Persons were checked and re-checked, not a single description resembled the butchered remains at 39th and Norton.

But even before they knew whom they were looking for, LAPD launched the biggest crime hunt in modern Los Angeles history.

Every one of the city's dozen police divisions was sub-divided down to each radio car beat. House to house, door to door in the apartment buildings, more than 250 policemen rang bells and asked questions.

Did you hear any unusual noises or screams last night or yesterday or the night before?

Have you noticed anything unusual around the neighborhood? Anybody acting peculiarly? Anybody digging in a yard, maybe burying a pile of woman's clothing? Or burning anything?

Very possibly, one of the 250 officers talked to the killer that day, or to someone who had a terrible suspicion about his (or her) identity. Yet all 250 drew a blank. Where the girl had been murdered was as much a mystery as the why of it, and the who, for that matter.

Next day the FBI kick-back supplied the who. Her name: Elizabeth Short, age 22; height, five feet five inches; weight, 120 pounds; race, Caucasian; sex, female; description, black hair (dyed) and blue eyes.

The FBI had her because just once, four years earlier in Santa Barbara, Elizabeth had been picked up. She was a minor then, and a policewoman caught her drinking in a bar with a girl friend and two soldiers. In a sense, it was ironic. The wrong way of life that was to lead her to death at least had left behind a clue to her identity, and she would escape the drifter's nameless grave.

Now that Brown had something to go on, the pace of the investigation accelerated. Who was Elizabeth Short? Where did she come from? What did she do? Boy friends? Associates? Habits? When was she last seen alive?

For seventy-two hours, Brown and many of the original twenty detectives assigned to the mystery worked day and night without letup. In fact, during the next thirty days, Brown was to cram in an additional thirty-three days of overtime. During one three-day period, he never got around to changing his shirt.

At the end of the first, furious three days of investigation, Brown knew a great deal about Betty Short or 'The Black Dahlia,' as an imaginative police reporter had rechristened her for all time. Those seventy-two hours had yielded the secret of The Dahlia's past right down to the date of her disappearance. Another seventy-two hours of such detective work, at most a week, and by all the normal odds LAPD would be putting the collar on a suspect.

Four years later, Sergeant Brown was down in Texas, chasing still another lead that led nowhere.

The girl who was to bloom into a night flower was one of four sisters reared by their mother in Salem, Massachusetts. About the time the war broke out, when she was in her middle teens, Betty Short went to work. She ushered in theaters, she slung plates as a waitress. It was the kind of work where a girl too young and attractive would meet too many men.

For a time, her father reappeared in Salem, and then left again for northern California. Maybe there was something romantic about this man who came and went; maybe he told her stories about sunny California, so different from cold little Salem. At any rate, at eighteen, Betty went West and joined him briefly.

Then she struck out on her own for Los Angeles, the city of opportunity where many another waitress, poor but beautiful, had made it in the movies. She settled near the campus of the University of Southern California, and she may even have walked past the lot at 39th and Norton. It wasn't far away.

Los Angeles, like every other city, was at war. On a tip from a soldier, Betty went to Camp Cook, north of Los Angeles, and got a sales job in the PX.

Then the first ominous thing happened. Betty suddenly threw up the job. There were barracks room whispers that some soldier had beaten her up badly. Why? Nobody seemed to know.

Betty drifted on to Santa Barbara; and, after the police-woman caught her in the bar with the two soldiers, she returned to New England. For almost two years, she sort of settled down, working as a waitress and cashier in a Boston restaurant.

Restlessness seized her again, and she took a bus all the way to Miami, working there for a winter. Then she came back to Boston and got a job across the Charles River in Cambridge in a café near the Harvard University campus.

There was a brief romance with a Harvard undergrad. All spring they dated; they even exchanged photographs. But when the school year ended in June, he went home; and Betty was on the move again. For a time, she lived in Indianapolis, and then in Chicago in the bright and noisy hotels that cluster round the Loop.

Something happened there that never has been fully established. Apparently, she met a handsome young Air Force flier. Maybe she even married him. No one has been able to check it out definitely, one way or the other.

At any rate, she loved him enough to go halfway across the country when he pleaded with her by wire to join him in Long Beach, California. There he met her at the train and took her to a hotel room he had arranged. From there, they journeyed on to Hollywood.

And then one day he told her he had to fly East to be separated from the service. He was like her college student; she never saw him again.

The war was over, the men were going home. At twenty-one, when she should have been starting married life or maybe a modest career, she was already obsolescent.

For three months, The Dahlia moved in with a girl friend; then went to a small home for would-be actresses; moved again to a private home; then to a hotel for girls in Hollywood.

She had no job. She killed time hanging around the radio studios and attending the radio shows. She sponged off friends and even got money from her mother back home. She lost her clothes to the landlady in lieu of rent.

She mooched at the night spots and the bars where a pretty girl could easily cadge a drink. She was careless about the company she kept.

Two or three times, friends later remembered, Betty had hitched rides to the Sixth Street area when she was out of funds. After a day or so, she would reappear, mysteriously replenished. Where she got the money never was known.

Some six weeks before the end, The Dahlia met a salesman in Hollywood. The salesman rented a room for her in a hotel, but he signed the register 'Mr. and Mrs.' Later, he took her to a bus depot, bought her a ticket for San Diego and said good-bye.

In San Diego, aimless, drifting, The Dahlia happened into an all-night theater. She got into a conversation with the cashier. Little by little, The Dahlia let drop her affecting story of misfortune and unhappiness.

Generously, the cashier brought her home with her that night and then let her stay for the next month. But something seemed to be driving The Dahlia toward her fate. She met another young salesman and begged him to drive her to Los Angeles the following day.

Perhaps with romantic hopes in mind, he did so, but as soon as they arrived, The Dahlia skillfully avoided a dinner date with him. She had some other plan in mind. Her sister, she explained, was down from Berkeley and stopping at the Hotel Biltmore. Regretfully, the salesman waited while she checked her bag at the bus depot and then dropped her off at the hotel.

It was 7 p.m., January 10.

For three more hours, The Dahlia moved freely. Three hours in which chance, a friend happening by, or an attractive well-dressed stranger might have diverted her from her plan, whatever it was.

Dozens of men must have observed her, for she spent the time waiting near the phone booths and she was, in her black cardigan jacket and skirt, white blouse, red shoes, red purse, and beige sport coat, the kind of girl that men observe. Yet none offered a merciful, life-saving flirtation.

Once The Dahlia changed a dollar bill at the hotel cigar stand and made a phone call, maybe two. Then she waited, as though expecting a call back. When none came, she walked out the front door, smiling to the doorman as he tipped his cap. He observed her trim form swinging south on Olive Street toward Sixth, the slim legs striding easily, the red heels tapping purposefully on the sidewalk.

It was 10 p.m.

And thus Sergeant Brown traced The Dahlia back to childhood, forward to the brink of eternity. And there the investigation stood still. Five days, from the doorman's last salute to the living, up to the discovery of the mutilated thing, remained a blank.

Medical evidence could say what must have happened during part of that time, but not why or by whom, nor could it locate the abattoir.

The Dahlia had been roped and spread-eagled and then hour after hour, for possibly two or three days, slowly tortured with the little knife thrusts that hurt terribly but wouldn't kill. She had made the rope burns on her wrists and ankles as she writhed in agony.

Finally, in hot rage or *coup de grâce,* there had come the slash across the face from ear to ear, and The Dahlia choked to death on her own blood.

But the killer had not done with her body.

Afterwards, he (or she) drained the system of blood, scrubbed the body clean and even shampooed the hair. Then it was neatly cut in two and deposited at 39th and Norton.

Five days after the first report of 'man down,' the twenty

original investigators were increased to fifty. Now the newspapers were playing the case as no crime had ever been played in Los Angeles, and the publicity was both a blessing and a burden to LAPD.

Every hour seemed to turn up a new 'lead' that had to be checked out; and suddenly dozens of persons who had not recognized The Black Dahlia's sketch in the papers four days earlier volunteered bits and pieces of information about her life. Nothing, however trivial, could be ignored. Everything was run down, saved or discarded.

Some fifteen times, the Crime Lab and men from the Detective Bureau went over houses, from cellar to attic, where the slow torture killing might have been played out. They found nothing. Having been lost en route, The Dahlia's trunk at last arrived from Chicago. Again, nothing.

There had to be a touch of lunacy in a killing like that, and madness communicates with madness. Now the 'confessions' began pouring in to irritate and distract Finis Brown. One man telephoned that he was coming in to surrender, and he did – three or four times when the detectives wouldn't believe him the first time. 'Confessin' Tom,' they finally called the nuisance.

At Fort Dix, New Jersey, a soldier sobbed out the story of the murder he hadn't committed. Four times at his own expense, a man traveled west from Utah and sat, drenched with sweat in the interrogation room, while he begged detectives to believe his preposterous admission of the killing.

At times it seemed the case needed a division psychiatrist more than a Homicide man, but with remarkable restraint, LAPD booked only one of the confessers for insanity.

In all, thirty-eight confessions had to be double-checked, and the waste of time was deplorable. Scores more had to be at least listened to before detectives knew they weren't worth even a rundown. Now and then, fighting to unclutter his few hard facts from all the fancies being pressed on him, Finis Brown wondered if he wouldn't tip over himself.

But if a madman had killed The Dahlia, he might be among those psychos, and the loony bin had to be emptied, one poor deluded mind at a time, just to make sure.

Then there were the stacks of mail that came in daily, mostly abusive, obscene or plain crazy but now and then intelligently written notes that were even more annoying. These contained pompous advice from amateur detectives telling the police how to go about their business.

Everything had to be read because The Dahlia's butcher might just be the egocentric who would delight in needling the police. At first, Sergeant Brown kept a ledger to catalogue the mail, but the volume overwhelmed him. So names and addresses of the writers were filed on cards to be checked out gradually when there was time for it.

In ten days, the hysteria seemed to have run its course. For the first time, the newspapers took The Dahlia off page one, and LAPD enjoyed a moment of quiet. The quiet before the storm, as it turned out.

That very same evening, a mail truck emptied a box near the Hotel Biltmore, and among other pieces picked up a simple carton, wrapped in brown paper and addressed to the police. Next morning, when they unwrapped the package, Finis Brown and his detectives relieved themselves with words that would have made an old Army sergeant shake his head in envy.

Inside were The Black Dahlia's purse, her Social Security card, her birth certificate, a batch of miscellaneous cards and papers, scraps with numbers and names on them, even an address book. The killer was laughing at Homicide,

32

telling the detectives contemptuously to go ahead and make something of it.

But he (or she) had been careful to leave no traces. Postmark and printing, carton and brown paper, yielded no clues. There was a faint odor to the contents, and scientific tests confirmed the suspicions of the detectives. Everything had been carefully washed in gasoline to remove any trace of where it had been or who had touched it. Tantalizingly, about a hundred pages had been ripped out of the address book. Some two hundred names remained, and Finis Brown had each one checked out, in vain.

With this mocking gesture, the killer bowed out; and, though the papers hastily brought The Dahlia back to page one, though the humiliated detectives bird-dogged even harder, this was really the end of the line.

There is no statute of limitations on murder, and LAPD will not admit defeat.

Two years later, Finis Brown thought he had a lead on the mysterious soldier who had given Betty the bad beating at Camp Cook. The lead ran dry.

Three years later, he was able to make a complete check on the salesman who had signed the register 'Mr. and Mrs.' in Hollywood and then put her on the bus to San Diego.

Four years later, he was down in Austin and Dallas, Texas, and after that up in Boston interviewing the Harvard man who had dated her one spring.

Nothing, nothing, except to close out false scents and then try to get back to the right one.

Sometimes police know their man and yet cannot pin the evidence on him. Sometimes they sense with the hunter's intuition that they are close, very close, and lose him only because he has suddenly died or managed to flee into obscurity. Usually, almost always, they can reconstruct the motive and sex of the killer. Murder is their business, and these things are not surprising.

But with the monster who slowly, delectably tortured The Black Dahlia to death, they have never felt that they were anywhere near close. They have never known the motive, nor whether the slayer was man or woman, nor where the agony was perpetrated.

Was the killer The Dahlia's lover or husband who felt he had been betrayed? But what betrayal, even unfaithfulness or a mocking laugh, merited revenge like this?

Was it perhaps a woman who had taken The Dahlia as wife in lesbian marriage? Was that why the body had to be bisected, so that she could carry out the parts to her car?

Was the killer, man or woman, a sadist with a blood fetish who slashed for no comprehensible reason at all?

All LAPD can say is that its detectives have exonerated every man and woman whom they've talked to, including the scores who insist to this day that they are guilty.

Beyond that, you are free to speculate. But do him a favor – don't press your deductions on Finis Brown.

IV

Per capita, police protection costs you less than four cents a day in Los Angeles. Even for a year, the police bill of the average family is less than the gas bill for one month.

Is it worth it?

In sixteen months, LAPD managed to catch Donald Keith Bashor, who had killed Karil Graham and Laura Lindsay and terrorized the women of Westlake. In more than a decade, LAPD has, at enormous expense, made no progress in the Black Dahlia murder.

You've got to have policemen but are they worth $35

34

millions a year, twenty per cent of the whole Los Angeles budget?

Of course, if the gun is in *your* back, four cents, even $35 millions, is tragically insufficient. You don't count your life in those terms.

And if you're a cop, with better than any civilian's chance of catching a slug, you don't count your life in those terms, either. Something more than take-home pay is involved, and you don't like it when you're a hero today, a bum tomorrow.

With fewer policemen than it had only a few years ago, LAPD is making more arrests these days. A quarter of a million yearly, but just let the department blow a spectacular one and listen to the howls. 'Dumb cop,' 'flatfoot,' 'stupid.'

THE BADGE . . . how do you judge the men who wear it – LAPD, any department, your police force in your town?

Headlines don't tell the story and neither do statistics though they are part of the yardstick. The system and the way it operates is part of the yardstick, too. So are the scientific facilities and the physical equipment, right down to good, grooved rubber on the wheels of speeding patrol units.

It helps to have a bright, honest chief; and it's no drawback if the commissioners who backstop him and the whole department are dedicated men. In the complicated modern business of criminology, there are a dozen complicated reasons for the success or failure of a police department.

But, mostly, these reasons boil down to two: the man in uniform and the civilian in mufti. If the peace officer is good, if the public supports him *and he knows it*, you have an honest department with polish and morale.

Unfortunately, too many of us dismiss crime and cops as

35

an exotic something we read about in the newspapers. Maybe the kid's bike was stolen once, or there was a sneak theft of the milk money; but *real* crime, forgeries, sex offenses, beatings, poison pen letters, and especially murder, is what happens to somebody else. It is part of the price of modern living, *four cents a day*, and nothing to concern ourselves about seriously.

'The grave danger in such an attitude is in its possible spread to the police,' says Chief William H. Parker of LAPD. 'If the police philosophy of this country ever becomes permeated with a laissez faire attitude, we are in serious trouble.'

As a citizen, you owe it to yourself to know something about the police, their limitations as well as their triumphs. The easiest way to do it is to study LAPD in action, for LAPD, scaled down to size, might be *your* department.

After all, it is your life, your property that they protect.

THE POLICEMAN

You're a cop. You knew that when you signed on. Be a damned good one.

Everybody in the city knows him. He's the harness bull who shoulders through the street crowd watching a fight and growls paternally, 'All right! Break it up! Break it up!' He's the fellow leaning on the siren as he pushes his black and white radio cruiser through red lights. He's the motor-bike man in white crash helmet intent on making life miserable for some taxpayer speeding down the freeway.

He's the cop.

Los Angeles is the place where that comic libel on all police everywhere, the Keystone Kop, was invented. And like most cities, Los Angeles still feels a curious ambivalence toward the policeman. He gives protection, which is vaguely appreciated, but he also exercises authority which is resented if *you* receive the traffic ticket or court summons.

So every tour the LAPD Policeman – aged thirty-four, married, two children, paying for the house and car on time – has to prove himself anew. 'Policemen are soldiers who act alone,' somebody once said, and each day the LAPD man in his lonely way must demonstrate his brains, his heart, his guts.

Suddenly, on fancy Wilshire Boulevard, there are shouts and screams, and pedestrians scatter. 'What's the trouble?'

Policeman George Audet growls. They tell him. A mad dog is loose, and already five persons have felt its bite.

Now it's up to Audet, and a thousand pairs of eyes are on him. It takes guts, but he has to do it. He unlimbers his gun and follows the frothing, ninety-pound beast into a yard, cornering him so there can be no escape for either of them. The mad animal snarls, tenses; and then, as he leaps, Audet fires. He puts his slug coolly into the vital spot, and the animal drops dead.

Now the five victims must be rushed to a hospital, and traffic unsnarled. 'All right, everybody. Move along. It's all over.'

On a Wednesday early in June, Policemen William Morgan, driver, and Nelson L. Brownson, guard, are moving nineteen prisoners in the patrol wagon to the city jail. Suddenly, just as unexpectedly as a mad dog goes amok, a bus carrying seventy-five children to a parochial school near New Chinatown cuts off the wagon.

Then the bus runs a red light, jumps the curbing, almost hits a building and crazily weaves back into the street again.

Morgan and Brownson give chase, skillfully drawing close alongside the swerving vehicle. It takes guts; a man could fall or get crushed; but Brownson leaps into the bus, sprawling over the collapsed driver. He manages to push him aside and get the runaway under control.

An ambulance is called for the diabetic driver, who has gone into shock from an overdose of insulin.

'I don't think the youngsters knew what was going on until it was all over,' Brownson says. 'And they got to school on time, too.'

But always, you come back to crime.

For some reason, August and December are hot months

for burglary. It's August now, and Policemen Gerald L. Bryan and Alvin L. Porterfield are pushing Unit 3A91 through the University Division on routine patrol.

As they cruise past a market, its alarm is ringing. A '459,' radio code for burglary, is in progress. Guns in hand, they investigate.

Porterfield covers the front of the store. Bryan makes a quiet flanking approach to the back. Just as he is about to slip in the rear door, he hears someone trying to open it from inside. He backs across the darkened alley into the shadows along a concrete wall.

A perfect ambush. And then he freezes.

From alongside, on the other side of a wooden gate in the wall, he hears eleven low, cold words spat at him.

'Drop the gun, cop – or die with it in your hand.'

Bryan takes a chance and steals a fast look. Not ten feet away, a lookout is staring at him over the top of the gate, and the gun he holds is steady. The smart thing to do is to drop his own revolver.

Instead, Bryan suddenly wheels and pours three shots into the gate. The gunfire brings Porterfield to his aid; and the next moment they hear the crash of glass from the front of the store. Porterfield races back to the street, but the suspect has fled.

'Code 9,' he snaps into his radio mike in the cruiser car. That's a call for assistance.

Then he rejoins Bryan, and they find the lookout crumpled in a heap a few feet on the other side of the bullet-riddled gate. A loaded Walther P38 automatic is still in his hand, but he is too far gone to use it.

But before he dies, Bryan's quick questioning wins an admission of complicity and the identification of the accomplice who got away. When assistance arrives, there's not much to be done. See to it that a body is taken away and run down a name.

For the job, Bryan holds LAPD's Class A Commendation. That and twenty-five or thirty cents will buy a quart of milk at any store in town. He could have laid down his gun, avoided the awful risk, and his money would buy just as much milk today.

That isn't the point. In the squadrooms, they say, *'You're a cop. You knew that when you signed on. Be a damned good one.'*

Always the unexpected, and you play it hard and fast. Then the awkward thing, the change of pace, just as unexpected, but now you play it gently, compassionately.

The young mother is driving happily in the San Fernando Valley, her seven-months-old son alongside her. He is sucking on a slice of orange.

She glances down tenderly, screams and brakes to a halt. A nearby radio car pulls over to investigate.

'No!' she screams hysterically. 'You can't have my baby!'

All in a moment, he had choked to death on the orange. The cops quickly make sure the infant is dead. She grabs the lifeless form, hugs it, then drives off wildly with her dead baby.

Obediently, the radio car follows, mothering her along the highway till she gets home. They give her a few minutes to compose herself, and at last she realizes what has happened. Silently, she hands over the limp form. They quietly see to it that family and neighbors are summoned to comfort her and then go on their way.

II

Give or take a few, there are some 3,590 men and 110 women who draw pay for the rank of policeman with

42

LAPD. With their superior officers, they cover 6,000 miles of street in Los Angeles, operate 1,400 vehicles, and are outnumbered, five hundred to one, by the general populace. The odds don't seem quite fair, and the LAPD Policeman tries to make up the difference with brain and body power.

He stands five feet ten inches and weighs 165 to 170 pounds. He keeps in shape playing basketball or working out on the horizontal bars.

He is a combat veteran of either World War II or Korea. He still practices up on his shooting. He serves in the military reserve on his own time.

His IQ is close to 120 (compared with the nation's average of 100), and he is still going to college, on his own time. He is working toward a degree in Political Science or Public Administration.

On the average, this sedately married, thirty-four-year-old father of two has been plugging along like this for seven years on the force. Curiously, he originally came from out of state, and that is the only generalization you can make about his civilian background.

He may previously have been a truck driver, U.S. forester, clerk, lifeguard, plumber, salesman, or even have studied for the priesthood or ministry before going on the force. He may have been a math major at college (with a 140 IQ), who now rides a radio car in the Valley.

He might even be the brother of a Hollywood bookie; but he becomes an exemplary officer and lives as if there were no brother.

Whatever he was, LAPD has reshaped and hardened him in its $20,000 training mold, given him a metal badge and put him out on the street where the cop lives or dies.

'Be a damned good one,' the old-timers tell him in the squadroom.

*

Each tour, the unexpected.

Daytime, and Policeman Eugene R. Crammer Jr. is routinely directing afternoon rush-hour traffic at a downtown intersection. There is a cry for help, and Crammer, unlimbering his gun as he picks his way through the hurrying cars, makes for the scene.

In ten minutes, he has disarmed two gunmen and sent them off to Central booking for attempted robbery.

Nighttime, and Policemen C. J. Chapman and R. J. Brown are cruising on Hollywood Boulevard at 3:47 a.m. They are memorizing the latest addition to 'the hot sheet,' the license number of an almost-new sports car stolen from a street in Hollywood.

At Hollywood Boulevard and Cherokee Avenue, just twenty-five minutes after the report was made, they spot the fast, shiny bug. They give chase, and for three miles through the heart of Hollywood, they slue round corners at frightening speed.

In a way, it's ironic. There are 32,194 street intersections in LAPD's territory, and Chapman and Brown know them all, or most all. But at DeLongpre Avenue and Cahuenga Boulevard, just a loud yell from the Hollywood Division, there's a treacherous dip in the road.

Treacherous, anyhow, for a car thundering at their speed. They spin out of control, slam into two parked cars and escape, somehow, with just nasty cuts and bruises. They lose the bug, but their risk doesn't go in vain.

Thirty minutes later, while they are being sewed up at the hospital, other policemen find the sports car parked back exactly where it had been taken. But Chapman and Brown had given the thief such a scare that he accidentally dropped an identification card inside.

He is arrested and confesses. Chapman and Brown go home. Their wives wince at the sight of the bandages, and all they can say is, 'It was a little rough tonight, honey. But nothing serious. Nothing for you to worry about.'

Sometimes, in the smooth way of modern police, it's a triple play. During a tricky heart operation in a veterans' hospital, a crisis suddenly developed. The surgeon needed additional equipment, and he needed it fast, to keep the white-faced patient alive. The only place the equipment could be obtained was at Good Samaritan Hospital, and that involved a thirty-five mile trip.

In relays, Policemen L. S. Rasic, Charles Cunningham and Lawrence Berdlow got it and got it back to the veterans' hospital, passing it on from one to the other – all in 35 minutes. Risking *their* lives at better than mile-a-minute speed, they saved *another*.

Too often, just because of the miserable nature of the job, it's still the lonesome one-man operation it always was for an officer before the auto and radio were invented. They tell him where to go and get him there fast, and that's all they can do. He's alone with a dirty, dangerous one.

It's near the end of his long, hot day's tour, and though the July sun has slanted down in the west, the temperature still stands at 92. Patrolling all day in the western end of the San Fernando Valley, Policeman Paul Cleary has just about had it.

It's been the kind of day when the clayish soil of the West Valley gets as hard as asphalt and the asphalt softens to the consistency of clay. Cleary wants to get under a needle-cold shower, get a good cold drink.

'Code 3.'

The alarm – Emergency; red light and siren – shakes him out of his lethargy. He listens, and his name is tied to it.

'Debris on the railroad tracks one hundred yards west of Lindley. Train due at 5:20 p.m.'

Cleary glances at his watch. It is 5:15.

The radio sends him and the cruiser gets him there and now he's back on his own. It's 5:18 p.m.

Quickly he glances up and down the tracks. He sees nothing, and the pleasant words, 'Report unfounded,' come into his mind. He looks again and a good 400 yards off, west toward the hills that rim the Valley, he sees something.

He starts running in loose, easy strides, trying to pace himself. One hundred yards . . . two hundred yards. He's halfway home now, and he ought to make it.

Then he hears the train whistle.

Sweat pouring down his back, he runs at full speed now. He finds the obstruction, two lengths of pipe, two inches by five feet, and an old truck tire. They have been jammed on and between the rails.

The San Francisco Limited, highballing into Los Angeles from the coast, thunders into view. Desperately, Cleary claws at the pipe and tire as the train bears down on him. He pulls them clear, almost falling backward, and the train sweeps safely by.

Be a damned good one.

III

In LAPD, as in most big cities, the radio car patrol man is the departmental torpedo which can be fired from Headquarters, instantly and in any direction, in response to trouble. The men drive more than six million miles yearly. Every twelve seconds there is a new transmission over their car radio.

But a torpedo, or a submarine, is wasted unless it hits the target. Every LAPD radio man has to settle the emergency or at least wage a holding operation till his

46

Code 9 (Request for assistance) can be answered. And here, unlike many cities, the radio man operates alone, rather than in pairs, during the daytime patrol.

Actually, this calculated risk was forced on LAPD by a manpower shortage. By splitting up the two-man radio teams in all geographical divisions, the police doubled their daytime coverage. The move was made cautiously after field tests in tough and soft neighborhoods and drastic training revisions to teach the policemen how to fight a one-man fight. Then LAPD's bosses crossed their fingers and waited.

In the first year of solo operation, assaults against police officers dropped some 20 per cent (from 124 to 99), felony arrests increased slightly, and misdemeanor arrests were up by more than one-third. LAPD had won.

Curiously, nobody can say for sure *why* it has worked out. Some give the credit to the men themselves. They know they are on their mettle; and they know the fellow on the next beat is alone and on his mettle, too. By radio, they follow his activities, and when the going gets rough, they move in fast to cover him.

Hearteningly, the civilian has come through to help one beleaguered officer where he might not help a team. Police reports now list scores of incidents in which citizen assistance has reduced disorder and averted injury to the officer at the scene of a crime.

LAPD appreciates the neighborliness.

Behind all the street activity, disjointed though it may seem as the radio cars siren off in various directions, there is a directing voice.

Without talk, modern police departments just couldn't function, especially one like LAPD with such an enormous ground area to cover. Its voice, a massive electronic and wireless network of teletype and shortwave radio, covers not only Los Angeles but also can be projected throughout California.

In the Communications Division, the sixty-six sworn personnel are supplemented by eighty-five radio telephone operators, plus another fifteen in the teletype and message sections. A separate unit, the Radio Technical Division, keeps thirty-eight civilians busy, operating the main receivers and transmitters and maintaining the intricate equipment.

Through the combined efforts of dispatchers, operators, and technicians, LAPD's mighty voice can be heard in more than 800 two-way mobile units, some forty three-way mobile units which can talk car-to-car, more than twenty walkie-talkies and about fifty stationary receivers.

There is never a frog in its throat. That would be as disastrous, maybe more so, as a police department without a gun. Four main transmitters, spotted strategically throughout the city, are backstopped by two portable transmitters for emergencies and one completely mobile patrol station.

Additionally, LAPD maintains transmitters and receivers for inter-city and inter-state communications with police elsewhere. These handle radiograms for all Southern California law enforcement agencies, and a sixty-machine teletype system connects in with all county seats and major police agencies everywhere in California.

The good old days of outriding the posse to safety in the next county are gone forever!

Every minute of the twenty-four hours, the complaint switchboard is lighted with calls, and the policemen-operators must make their decisions on the spot. What does LAPD roll on? What is trivial and meaningless?

A complaint about a parked car blocking a driveway? Not unimportant if a physician is thereby prevented from making his rounds. The oh-so-familiar complaint about a barking dog? Not insignificant if perhaps the dog is barking because his master is dead. The decision must be made fast, the taxpayer gently treated.

'To every citizen, his call is important,' explains one operator. 'Sometimes all he wants is to talk to somebody, to cry on somebody's shoulder. We offer him the shoulder.'

At 4:17 p.m., the board suddenly receives a report about a store in the Wilshire District. There's no doubt that LAPD will roll on this one.

A little white form reporting Code 2 (Urgent; no red light, siren) goes on the conveyor to the dispatch room for instant transmission. A torpedo is fired.

4:20 p.m. The 'hot shot' phone, reserved for emergency calls, chimes beside the master control board. The radio car officer is already reporting back from the scene. It's a '211,' a robbery, and he needs help.

Code 2 becomes Code 3 (Emergency; red light, siren) and more torpedoes are launched.

Now Communications sweats it out. Will still more help be required? What extra units are available and how close are they?

4:29 p.m. The 'hot shot' phone rings again. Suspect apprehended, situation under control exactly twelve minutes after the first alert. All units return to normal patrol.

LAPD talks mostly in a clipped, number code not for purposes of secrecy but for quicker transmission and conservation of air time. With five to six calls going out every minute, each word is important, and 'Code 1' is considerably less longwinded than 'Acknowledge Your Call.'

There's a number for almost every contingency from 'Code 7,' Out to Eat, to the dreaded 'Code 13 Daniel,' which is a disaster calling in all off-duty officers, reserves, and auxiliaries. Plain numbers like '211' for robbery and '484' for theft indicate the specific crime involved by its section under the California Penal Code. (The full Radio Code is printed at the end of this chapter.)

The druggist on the phone with the complaint board is hysterical. He is begging LAPD to save a woman's life.

Two days earlier, he had made up a prescription calling for dilantin. Instead, by mistake, he had used a digitalis preparation. He has just discovered his mistake – a possibly fatal mistake, because if the woman follows the dosage prescribed on the bottle, she will die in about eight days.

From the sobbing man, the police obtain the prescription number; and in the next half hour, they accomplish this much:

The prescription is traced to General Hospital, where it had been issued three months earlier by a staff physician. The hospital gives a name and an address in East Los Angeles. The woman, it is found, had moved from there some two months previously. No forwarding address.

But detectives establish that she is of Mexican descent, thirty-four years old, five feet one inch, 115 pounds, red-haired. They find she has been known under three names and learn the whereabouts of her mother and other relatives.

Again, no luck. The mother explains that she seldom sees her daughter, and the other relatives can't help.

Now the only hope of saving a woman's life is a citywide search. Chief of Detectives Thad Brown immediately authorizes use of all LAPD's facilities.

Every patrol is alerted, all jails and hospitals notified, a teletype flashed throughout Los Angeles County. Under Captain Stanley H. Sheldon, the department's public relations unit appeals to newspapers, radio and TV to publicize the warning.

A Sigalert bulletin is drafted; and every quarter hour the city's radio stations, which between them reach into three states and Mexico, make this announcement:

ATTENTION: This is a Sigalert repeat. The Los Angeles Police Department states that anyone knowing Josephine Aguilar, also known as Josephine Sandez, also known as Josephine Sanchez, please advise her immediately that the prescription she had filled on February 16, between 6:30 p.m. and 7 p.m. at a drugstore in the southern part of Los Angeles, was improperly compounded. It contains a highly dangerous drug, which could cause her death. Anyone knowing this lady should report her whereabouts to 77th Street Detectives, Madison 4-5211, Extension 2618.

Lt. R. Selby

Lt. Lindsay Simmons
Ticket # 8-289

In just three quarters of an hour after the druggist's frantic call, the detectives' phones are hopelessly jammed with the public response. The flood of incoming messages must be partly diverted to the uniform unit and almost anyone with an extension, including Juvenile.

People who remember once having employed a Josephine Aguilar leave their homes at night and go back to the office to search old records for an address or phone number. Physicians and dentists who had treated patients of that name call in. Friends of the woman volunteer to help. Other Josephine Aguilars call to say they are all right and don't waste time looking for them. Just, please, find that poor woman before it is too late!

There is something heart-warming in the way the public responds so instantly to a call for help. Even hardened LAPD men are impressed, and yet with all the calls, nothing is accomplished. The woman is still missing.

During the night, the flood of incoming messages falls to a trickle, and then at 8 a.m., the switchboard lights up again. Everyone in the county, it seems, knows a Josephine Aguilar.

Finally, a little after nine, a woman's voice announces that she is *the* Josephine Aguilar.

Yes, she is the one who had the prescription filled. No, no, she is all right.

Right away, after getting them, she had noticed the capsules were the wrong size and color, not like the ones before. So she just hadn't taken any of them.

Where is she now? Calling from a phone booth near her mother's home.

When she got up this morning, she turned on her radio to a Spanish-language program. The announcer was talking about a big search for a woman with the same name. But she didn't realize it was she herself till her mother's name and address also were broadcast. She got dressed and went to mamma's to tell her she was all right.

Yes, she would meet the detectives in ten minutes and give them the bad bottle.

In less than ten minutes, detectives are at the door, and Josephine hands over the deadly capsules.

Be a damned good one.

IV

At the wheel, he is maybe a drunk or just a kid showing off for his girl. Whoever he is, he is threatening every living thing in his path as he roars past the parked motorcycle officer at ninety miles an hour. In the dark, it is difficult to see a license plate at sixty feet. At his speed, he is passing the officer at 135 feet a second.

With his right hand opening the throttle, his left

clutching the radio microphone, the officer takes after him.

'4 Mary 105 is in pursuit,' he says matter of factly to Communications. That means a speeder is being chased in the Hollenbeck police division.

Quickly Communications comes on the air.

'All frequencies stand by. Mary 105 is in pursuit.'

To avoid an air jumble, all broadcast ceases on the band. Other units wait for a pattern to develop so they can converge.

'Outbound Santa Ana Freeway,' Mary 105 now reports. 'Pursuit '58 Olds.'

Then silence.

Astride a 55-horsepower Harley Davidson, Mary 105 is now straining against the wind at one hundred miles an hour, trying to close the gap between him and the 265 horsepower Olds.

At that speed on a little bike, he is living, second to second, only by the grace of God. The blast of wind in his ears cuts off all other sound. He is at the mercy of the road, its curves, even a small stone. He couldn't stop suddenly, though his life might hang at the next turn on a quick stop.

He hasn't had time to slip on his glasses, and the wind rakes his eyeballs. He sees only space roaring toward him and a diminishing white line that slashes beneath his left foot.

Everything else, trees, houses, stone walls, are a meaningless blur. Light is shadow, and shadow is a black smear in the cobalt. Then a tail light ahead winks redder as the speeder brakes and finally stops.

The motor officer pulls alongside. For a few seconds, as he unwinds, he has a bad case of the shakes. He fights for self-control, then says evenly to the frightened teenager, 'All right, fella. Let's see the license and registration.'

A fast pursuit by motorcycle is one of the most hazardous

and draining of all police experiences. Quite accurately, LAPD calls its motorbike force the 'Ironhorsemen.'

Surprisingly, despite the ordeal, there are always scores of policemen on the waiting list hoping for a chance to join the Traffic Enforcement Division. Riding a bike can mean as much as $50 more per month, but that's the least part of it.

The standards for acceptance are challengingly high, the morale is superb, and TED is a flashy, spit-and-polish unit. Its twenty-five man motor corps drill team has won the national American Legion championships, and there's a proud jauntiness about TED that makes a man forget his own neck . . . some of the time.

Only policemen with at least one year's experience are eligible for the transfer. Those tentatively accepted then undergo a series of strenuous psycho-physical aptitude tests. After that, they must pass an oral examination before ranking TED officers, personnel, and patrol, which is double-checked by the Chief of Personnel and two inspectors.

And that isn't all.

There is a tough two-weeks' course in riding school and a training course in traffic enforcement and procedure, during which each novice is under constant observation.

Is he a throttle-snapper or a hot rodder? He washes out. TED wants wary courage, not recklessness, much the same standards set for our military airmen.

Finally, he must be a gentleman because he will ride out to sell something that nobody really wants – traffic enforcement.

The records and various spot checks disclose that TED *does* sell enforcement. Only one in a hundred drivers tries to give the 'Ironhorseman' an argument when he is ticketed. The other ninety-nine accept the paper graciously, or at least resignedly.

Before going on their individual watches, the 'Iron-horsemen' congregate at the Police Building for roll call. There they are posted on the daily orders and any changes in procedures, briefed on unusual overnight crime that may affect them.

Then, typical of their tight morale, they informally put heads together to hash over what they call 'f'rinstance cases,' theoretical situations which might just arise some-time and require special handling.

If the weather is rainy, they are given a reprieve from bike riding and temporarily assigned to Accident Investigation or Warrants. But if it is clear, they stand at attention by their bikes, suspiciously sniffing the air for signs of smog, then mount in unison and leave in smart, military formation.

With a loud, proud roar from his little 55-hp motor, each 'Ironhorseman' peels off in turn for his own beat, which has been determined for him on basis of seniority. There is no favoritism in TED, and at the end of any month, an officer without 'enough whiskers' can be bumped from his beat by an officer who outranks him and wants to change.

No officer can even guess what the day's patrol will bring before he signs off, '139, end of watch.'

Officer S. W. Combs was shocked and outraged one day to discover a nineteen-year-old North Hollywood youth driving one hand on the freeway – and he didn't have the other arm around a girl, either. He was shaving with an electric razor. Setting a new enforcement precedent, Combs cited him for reckless driving.

Responding to a Code 3 (Emergency; red light, siren), Officer Dale Phillips found that an unconventional bank robber had made his getaway in a taxi. Just as uncon-ventionally, Phillips on his bike, rather than a radio cruiser, captured the cab, prisoner, loot, weapons, and all.

Any time an 'Ironhorseman' overhauls a traffic violator, there is a quick, tense sizeup. The man behind the wheel may be just a careless driver and then again he might be a criminal.

Once, when Officer Fud Denny flagged down a car that had made a wrong lane turn, the driver convincingly flashed a bright new operator's license which indicated impressive past driving experience in Europe. Something smelled wrong to the officer.

Questioning the man more closely, Denny found that he didn't know the first thing about Los Angeles traffic laws. He detained him while Motor Vehicles ran a fast check.

The operator's license, DMV reported, had been fraudulently obtained, and a further check disclosed the motorist had illegally jumped a foreign ship then docked in Los Angeles. He was handed over to the immigration authorities.

Of course, drivers being drivers, some things are just bound to happen again and again, the 'Ironhorsemen' know resignedly. For instance, though they handle the wheel better, the men drivers are going to give the bike man more trouble than women drivers. Say what you will about that *woman* driver, it's the man who does the most speeding and commits the most deliberate violations. That's the truth.

The freeway is a more rugged watch than the 'surface streets'; that is, those off the freeway. Everything, anything can happen on the freeway, and the 'Ironhorseman' almost gets cross-eyed watching for speeders, creepers, tail riders and unsafe lane changers, not to mention truck and trailer violations and a few spilled loads here and there.

Whatever his beat, he is charged with enforcing all laws and ordinances regulating traffic. Since enforcement has to be selective because of the small size of TED, the motorbike man is deployed in the area where accidents are occurring. If inside passing has been causing the trouble, he tails traffic for a stretch, watching for the offenders. If it is speed, he parks on a side street till some Oldfield speeds by.

Rule o' thumb, the motorcycle police consider the 'normal flow of traffic' in judging speed. Depending on the street, time, and weather, this is an elastic rule which can be stretched from fifteen mph to fifty-five and even more.

Since a man couldn't possibly write all the traffic violations he spots during an eight-hour watch, general enforcement has to be discretionary, too. He picks out the best – or, rather, the worst – of them for tickets.

'There are no hard and fast rules,' says Fred McGrew. 'We just put ourselves in the driver's shoes.'

Officer Frederick J. McGrew, age 37, six feet one and a half inches tall, 195 pounds in weight, a veteran of the U.S. Armored Tank service, is one of TED's most imposing traffic-law salesmen. He draws more than average pay and has the privilege of riding his bike to and from work. (All LAPD motorcycle officers take their bikes home to assure the department a ready, mobile force, if needed.)

But he has extra costs, too. While the department kindly furnishes his white crash helmet, his uniform, including boots, costs more than $100, and his leather jacket stands him $55. His gun represents another $75 investment; and, in addition, at assorted prices to him, he totes a chain and whistle, Sam Browne belt, handcuffs, baton holder, ammunition case, gloves, flashlight, guide book, 'hot sheet' holder, baton, and pen. Also his badge and book of traffic citations. Fortunately, the latter two items don't represent much additional weight, and they come free, courtesy of the Los Angeles Police Department.

At the end of two weeks, McGrew's take-home pay is $156.55. But he is paying taxes and dues to the Police

Protective League and the American Legion. He is making payments on pension, insurance, and car. He is buying a house and bringing up two children. He rides a tight budget.

And like every other 'Ironhorseman,' he never knows what the next watch will bring. One night, McGrew and a partner were riding the night watch – 8 p.m.-to-4 a.m. – in a smart business-residential district. They rode that way by night in the motor corps, in tandem, one hand helping the other. It was a lazy night. The drunks were home, or hadn't yet left the bars, and the speeders weren't hitting this area.

At 12:30 a.m., as the officers were passing a commercial intersection, a man ran out of a large food store, waving frantically to them. He was the store manager, he explained, and he had returned a short while before to check the books. There had been strange noises – someone was in there right now!

Guns in hand, McGrew and his partner accompanied the manager inside. They turned on the lights and, in one office, found the safe door had been smashed open, apparently by a meat cleaver, which lay nearby. But the sizable weekend receipts had not been disturbed.

Obviously, they figured, the intruder had been scared off by the manager, but probably hadn't had the time to escape. Counter by counter, they searched the market, poked into comers and kicked the big food boxes stacked here and there.

McGrew kicked one box, and it didn't move. 'All right,' he snapped. 'Come out fast.' A head and then a hand clutching a .45 emerged slowly. McGrew sent the automatic spinning and collared his man.

The intruder, who was employed in another store of the same food chain, knew the weekend receipts would be heavy and knew the employer's routine. He had secreted himself in the store till everybody left about 10 p.m. and then had gone to work on the safe with his meat cleaver. Just as his industry had finally paid off two and a half hours later, the manager had returned.

It's not like that every watch, but even a comparatively quiet eight hours on the freeway leaves McGrew bushed. Even without trouble, he has ridden 200 miles, and he is delighted to radio his '139.'

McGrew then bikes home, does a little gardening, fools around with the kids for awhile and finally goes off into a room alone to work on his hobby. Nighttimes, McGrew draws cartoons and sells them to the magazines.

V

Always, you come back to crime.

You play it hard and fast and cagey. A policeman's salary won't cover a verdict for false arrest.

Early on a spring morning, Policemen Robert Coffman and Jack Carter are working the night watch out of Central Division. At 1:26 a.m., a 459 sends them to the apartment building at 251 Loma Drive, and the night's fun begins.

Returning from a show, a couple find their apartment has been thoroughly looted. Clothing, linen, books, and pictures are strewn about; closets and drawers have been emptied. About $1,700 worth of jewelry and clothing are missing.

To the police, the method of entry is obvious. The burglar placed a garbage can near the rear bedroom window, climbed atop it, then cut the screen, pried open the window, and entered.

But one thing bothers them. On the living room table, $70 in cash is lying in plain view. Why didn't he take it?

Either he didn't see it, which doesn't make much sense, considering his thoroughness, or the couple's return scared him off. In that case, he might still be around the neighborhood.

Carter remains in the apartment to get a description of the missing property, and Coffman scouts the neighborhood. On the parkway, near a parked car, he finds pieces of a broken piggy bank. He brings them back, and the victim's wife identifies them.

Now a DMV (Department of Motor Vehicles) license search discloses that the car is registered to a woman in Sherman Oaks, a good distance away. The car seems worth a stakeout. If the burglar used it, he should come back for it.

For an hour, then two, and finally three hours, Carter and Coffman watch the car. Just before dawn, they are ready to give up. But they've wasted three hours; and they may as well sit tight another half hour till it's good and light.

In a few more minutes, a man rounds the corner, passes the apartment house without a glance at it and heads toward the car. The officers hold back. Maybe he's a poker player coming home late or a guy just off the graveyard shift. Let's wait a minute.

Near the parked car, the man looks about cautiously, then walks up and quickly unlocks the door. From a hundred feet down the street, Coffman comes pounding toward him.

For a moment, the suspect seems about to take off, but Coffman is on him. He gives him a quick shake for a gun, then asks his name.

'Arthur John Stark.'

'You're up pretty late, aren't you?'

'I'm old enough. I guess forty-eight is old enough.'

Mr. Stark doesn't understand this routine at all. He has never been arrested in his life, and he doesn't like this kind of treatment. What does Coffman think he is, a *criminal* or something?

Coffman stalls a moment. The car, Mr. Stark?

Belongs to a friend, Mr. Stark explains easily, and he has just borrowed it for the night. Anything wrong about that?

Coffman chews it over. The answer is pat and yet somehow a bit evasive. Mr. Stark's good-citizen bluster seems a bit uneasy. But the move is up to the officer. If he takes him in and Mr. Stark is pure, there'll be hell to pay.

Coffman studies the car, looks into the back seat. It is covered with clothing.

'You'll have to come downtown, Mr. Stark,' he says quietly.

Stark is booked in Central Jail on suspicion of burglary, and Coffman sweats it out while the Burglary Division runs a make on Mr. Stark. He is far, far from pure.

Beginning at the age of nineteen, and that goes back to the Twenties, Mr. Stark has been in trouble. In Michigan, Oregon, Nevada, and California. He has done time in San Quentin and Folsom prisons.

A report comes in on the car he had 'borrowed' from a friend. It is stolen.

Stark was convicted of burglary on May 3, 1956, and sent to San Quentin as a two-time loser.

Be a damned good one.

VI

Sure, you'd had two or three beers, but that wasn't what caused it. The big, arrogant white Cadillac cut the corner sharp, forcing you to smack into a parked car. The Caddy keeps going, and when the radio cruiser shows up, there you are all alone, with a broken grille on your car.

Excitedly you tell the policemen what happened. Being

61

angry, you talk a little too loud, and perhaps you wave your arms. One of the officers wrinkles his nose. 'You been drinking, Mac?'

'Two or three beers,' you say belligerently. 'What the hell has that got to do with being cut off!'

The cops exchange glances. Never, in police history, has it been four or five beers. Never, never more than two or three beers.

'Think I'm drunk,' you say. 'Look!'

You touch your finger to your nose. One of the officers has gone back to make a radio call, and, drawing an imaginary line to the police car, you walk it straight toward him. Or almost straight, anyhow.

'Take it easy, Mac,' says his partner. 'AID will be right here.'

In no time, an Accident Investigation car swings up beside the cruiser. There's a little talk among the policemen, and then the AID man comes over to you, carrying a narrow, ten-inch-long cardboard cylinder.

He takes out a balloon and a couple of glass tubes which have some kind of chemicals inside. He hands you the balloon and says, 'Go ahead, blow into it.'

'What's this!'

'Go ahead, blow. We're taking a sample of your breath.'

You hesitate suspiciously. It's a trap.

'What are you afraid of? You only had two or three beers, didn't you?'

So you exhale into the balloon. He quickly turns a mouth valve to trap the breath inside, and then he runs the breath into one of the glass tubes. 'This is for the lab,' he says. 'Now blow again.'

The second time, he runs the breath into the other tube. It mixes with some chemicals, and there seems to be a faint discoloration. 'We'll have to check downtown, Mac,' he says.

Now you begin to sweat. You did have only two or three beers. The big Caddy did cut you off, but nobody saw it. Your whole case rests in two little glass tubes.

You go along with the officers, and you really sweat it out, waiting for the lab report. Finally, one of the radio men comes out of a back room at Headquarters.

'Take it easy, Mac,' he says. 'Like you said, it was only two or three beers. Now, are you sure you didn't get even part of the Caddy's license number?'

For the exoneration, which probably saved you from a '502' conviction as a drunken driver, you can thank a pretty young policewoman. Chestnut-haired, brown-eyed Geraldine Lambert, wife of an LAPD lieutenant, is one of the few policewoman forensic analysts in the country.

A graduate of the University of California at Los Angeles, Geraldine began her career as an analytical chemist with the Eastman Kodak Processing Laboratory. When she became a policewoman, she broke in the usual way with juvenile and jail assignments and a hitch in DAPs, or Deputy Auxiliary Police, the departmental youth group.

For almost a decade now, she has been in the Crime Lab, learning the fascinating intricacies of blood analysis under LAPD's chief chemist, Ray Pinker. She has been one of the two women chosen to serve on the Chemical Test Committee of the National Safety Council, and has been voted 'Policewoman of the Year' by the Exchange Club of Los Angeles.

At a cost of more than $12,000 for ingredients alone, Geraldine packs 4,000 chemical 'Intoximeter' kits a year. Not all return. Of the drunks that annually fill the balloons with telltale whiskied breaths, some 3,200 plead guilty and obviate the need of Intoximeter analysis.

But 800 a year dispute the drunk charge. Then the fine eye of science draws a bead on the facts. The Intoximeter tells the story.

Sometimes the accused is right. Sometimes he loses. The Intoximeter cost to the city, LAPD knows, is more than worth it, not only in nailing down some '502' convictions, but in clearing the innocent.

Often drivers in ill health like diabetics fail the field sobriety tests. Geraldine clears them. And sometimes defendants on other charges try to act drunk to mitigate their offenses. Geraldine's chemistry exposes the subterfuge. Whatever she finds, her testimony is almost always accepted by the courts.

The breath sample turned over to the Crime Lab is measured for the proportion of alcohol in the bloodstream. Magnesium perchlorate crystals in the Intoximeter tube have trapped the alcohol which is first steam-distilled and measured for quantity. By relating the quantity to the volume of breath taken as a sample, the proportion of alcohol in the bloodstream is ascertained. In turn, this can be translated into degrees of drunkenness.

Thus, your two or three beers might leave a trace of alcohol in the bloodstream. But so long as you run under .05 per cent on the test, you are chemically sober, and the courts will so agree.

From .05 to .10 per cent indicates that the subject has been drinking; .10 to .15 you are possibly under the influence of alcohol. From .15 to .25, you are under the influence of liquor and should not be driving. At .25 per cent you are obviously intoxicated; at .35 per cent you are a common drunk and probably unable to take care of yourself; and at .40 per cent, whether you are aware of it or not, you have passed out.

Beyond that, the percentages begin to indicate a grim prognosis. At .50 per cent, you have imbibed a lethal amount of good fellowship.

Sometimes, Geraldine's beakers and burners avert an improper booking. There was, for example, the known

San Pedro alcoholic, found one night slumped behind the wheel of his parked car. He was out cold.

It would have been the most obvious thing in the world to book him as a drunk. Instead, the officers awakened him and made him take the Intoximeter test.

Geraldine's report was an eye-opener. His blood alcohol level was only .02 per cent! Further investigation disclosed the alcoholic had gulped a vial of paraldehyde in an effort to avoid the DTs.

On another occasion, a husband beat his wife to death in their home in San Fernando Valley and then fled over the hill into Hollywood. Furnished with his description, detectives easily picked him up. Too easily, it seemed to them. He was found staggering through the streets, a half-empty wine bottle in his pocket, and, even if he hadn't been wanted for murder, he would have been bagged as a drunk.

The detectives promptly called for an AID car to give him the Intoximeter test. He proved out at .07 per cent, just possible tipsiness.

Later at his trial, the man tried to plead that he had been drunk and didn't know what he was doing when he killed his wife. The State then introduced the Intoximeter finding, and he was convicted.

More and more, police throughout the nation are using scientific chemical tests for intoxication, but LAPD is already testing another device which may prove to be both simpler and cheaper. While it uses chemicals, as does the Intoximeter, refills are only sixty cents against $2.50. The instrument can be used at the booking desk or even plugged into the cigarette lighter of a police car, and you don't need a chemist to read the results. The device feeds the breath past a photoelectric cell and snaps a picture of the breath content, which can be used in court.

In a way, there is an appropriate irony in the new, quiet

kind of detective work that Geraldine Lambert and Ray Pinker pursue far from the scene of a crime or drunken-driver accident. These offenders have not hesitated to spill blood, and by blood they are betrayed.

A .25 per cent reading in the bloodstream cannot be concealed; the blood-soaked handkerchief of a killer can be washed white, and yet, under Pinker's benzidine test, there will be a damning, blue-green chemical reaction. The guilty can dilute blood 300,000 times, and still Pinker will find it.

So far as science knows, blood is practically indestructible through age. It has been found in the marrow of Egyptian mummies several thousand years old. It is almost always there to point to a criminal.

Out, out, damned spot. But it will not out.

VII

Always, you come back to crime. And the street.

That is where the policeman lives, fights, sometimes dies.

In the Wilmington area down by the harbor, Policeman Dallas W. Walters, Harbor Division Warrants Detail, has just come out of a store. Three armed thugs surround him. It's a stickup, and the smart thing is to let them have his money, his gun, his badge.

Walters fights.

It's three-to-one, and he catches three slugs, one in each leg and the third in the shoulder. He goes down, but he's still shooting. He kills one bandit and critically wounds the second.

The odds are even now; so the third drags his wounded companion into a car and runs.

In no time, nine officers in four cars have reached the

scene, but everybody has gone except Walters lying in the street and his kill nearby. One radio car follows the ambulance that takes the badly wounded officer to the hospital, and there is a little reunion in Emergency. The wounded gunman had been dropped there by his pal. Later, the third man is found hiding in the trunk of the escape car.

Walters recovers, and only now and then, mostly in rainy weather, do the old wounds ache. He's satisfied.

As they say in the squadrooms, *'Be a damned good one.'*

Sometimes, because women and children are in the cross-fire, you play it soft, *pianissimo*, and just as dangerously.

'Al, this is Dee.'

'What!'

'Dee. Dee Lightner. The cop.'

The phone is suddenly silent.

'Al! I'm phoning from nearby.'

'Wait a minute . . .'

'The place is surrounded, Al. I want you to come out and surrender.'

'Gimme a chance! I gotta think.'

'You can take it the easy way. Or the hard way.'

'What do you want me to do?'

'I'm coming up after you, Up to the door. When I ring the bell, shove your gun through the door and you follow it. Hands behind your head.'

'Okay, okay.'

The phone goes silent again.

'Come on, Al. I mean it. I said it's a deal.'

'Okay. But don't let them shoot me. *Please!* Don't shoot me!

'You do it right, Al, and nobody will shoot you.'

The phone clicks dead.

Policeman DeWitt C. Lightner comes out of the booth.

'He said okay,' he tells the FBI agent waiting there. They look speculatively at each other. 'Let's hope he means it,' the G-man says.

Together, they drive a block to Firebird Avenue in Whittier, east of Los Angeles. They park across the street from the shabby little frame house where badman Albert J. Kostal is holed up.

Kostal is treacherous and quick on the trigger. He is wanted for robbery and perhaps two murders. Eleven days earlier, he had busted out of an eighth-floor detention pen of the Los Angeles Hall of Justice, taking two pals with him.

The pals were quickly caught, but Al had remained at large till an anonymous, early morning tip to the FBI had located his hideout. Now all police agencies in the Los Angeles area have blocked off the district. They are going to take Al the easy way or dig him out with shotgun, pistol, and triple-chaser.

But there are women, maybe children, in the little frame house, and Dee Lightner offers his plan. He knows Al pretty well, having returned him from Kansas City to Los Angeles just a few months before as an escapee from Folsom, the maximum-security prison.

Al was doing life, and now the state's bookkeepers are calculating how much more he owes for his two escapes. It's a lot to ask a man like that to hand out his gun, butt first. If he decides to play the long odds, he might shoot Dee and try a break. Or make him run interference as a shield. Or yank him inside as a hostage.

Five minutes after the phone call, Dee Lightner walks across the silent, deserted street, walks up the path and onto the porch, presses the doorbell. There is no answer.

Inside, Al hears him, all right, but he wants to try a last caper.

He runs to the back door, hoping he can reach his

getaway car stashed in the garage. He opens it, and four shotguns are raised against him. He hesitates in the doorway.

From behind the garage, a small child wanders uncertainly across the line of fire. Now, Al!

But a sheriff's officer jumps out, pushes the boy to safety and regains cover. That breaks Al. Slowly he walks back inside and goes to the front door.

He opens it, hands his gun to Dee Lightner. He comes out, hands behind his head.

Be a damned good one.

But always, you come back to crime. And the street. TED Officer Michael J. McAndrews was safe and off duty in his own home when it happened.

McAndrews was recuperating from a bout with the flu, and the doctor had warned him, 'Take it easy, boy. This thing is treacherous.'

'Sure,' Mike had said. 'Don't worry, Doc. I'll take it easy.'

And then it happened right outside his own window. A kid crashed a car, a stolen car, it developed later, and McAndrews saw him fleeing. Two deputy sheriffs were chasing him on foot.

It's always the cop's job to assist. McAndrews joined the chase and though it winded him badly, he caught the kid. He held him till the deputies took over. And then Officer Michael J. McAndrews dropped dead of a heart attack.

Yes, like they say, be a damned good one.

RADIO CODES

211	. . .	Robbery	484	. . . Theft
311	. . .	Indecent exposure	484PS	. . Purse snatching
390	. . .	Drunk (male)	502	. . . Drunk driver
390W	. .	Drunk (female)	586-586F	. Illegal parking
415	. . .	Disturbance	507	. . . Disturbance (minor)
459	. . .	Burglary	700	. . . Illegal burning

Code 1 – Acknowledge message

Code 2 – Urgent (no red light, siren)

Code 3 – Emergency (red light, siren)

Code 4 – No further help needed

Code 4 – Adam – Sufficient help at scene; suspect still in vicinity

Code 6 – Adam – Out for investigation; may need assistance

Code 7 – Out to eat

Code 8 – Fire alarm box pulled

Code 9 – Request for assistance

Code 20 – Notify news photographers

A.C. – Aircraft crash

F.B. – Fallen balloon

Roger – Message understood

Major Disaster

Code 12 – Disaster is believed present. Field units reconnoiter their beats and report evidence of damage. Off duty officers and reserves notified. Stand by for one hour for instructions.

Code 13 – Disaster has occurred. Field units reconnoiter their beats and report extent of damage. Off duty officers notified. Report as planned. Suffix will indicate area affected.

Code 13 FRED – Disaster has occurred. Field units reconnoiter their beats and report extent of damage. Off duty officers and reserves report as planned. Auxiliaries stand by.

Code 13 DANIEL – Disaster has occurred. Field units reconnoiter their beats and report extent of damage. Off duty officers, reserves *and* auxiliaries report as planned.

Code 14 – Recall Code 12 and/or Code 13 in its every form. All officers return to normal duties. Reserves and auxiliaries relieved of further duties.

NOTE: There are also a series of Civil Defense Codes, 1200, 1300, 1310, 1320, 1330, 1340 and 1400, directing police activity from the time enemy action is believed present through the recall. During disaster or civil defense, in answering requests for damage reports, units will use the following:

Code 16 – No enemy action or disaster damage on our beat.

Code 17 – Structural damage (damage of a major nature to streets, buildings, etc., rendering them useless) by enemy action or disaster on our beat.

During civil defense emergency, in answering request for 'Radef Report,' units will use the following:

Code 18 – No radioactive contamination present.

Code 19 – Radioactive contamination present.

NOTE: Beginning with 'Exec. No. 1' (the Mayor), 'Exec. No. 2' (Civil Defense Coordinator) and 'Staff No. 1' (Chief of Police), there also are a series of call numbers for the various department commanders and inspectors.

THE SERGEANT

They call him the workhorse, my boy –
Backbone of the Force, my boy.
He's the old three-striper –
Whose knowledge is riper.
He's the Sergeant, young man,
He's the Sergeant.

In LAPD, they call him 'sweetheart,' 'sucker,' or 'saint,' but never 'sir.' He's the harried three-striper who serves as aide to his boss, the lieutenant; and as supervisor, backstopper, and departmental chaperon to his own men, the Policemen. Often he is the very first officer at the scene of a crime and unless it's a real big one, he may be the only one out there in the mud and the rain.

Like the Army, a police department is run by its sergeants, and yet if you put all LAPD's three-stripers into the grand ballroom of the Beverly Hilton Hotel, they would hardly fill it. There are only 650 of them. Moreover, they wouldn't like it. Their beat is almost everything but ballrooms.

It is the birth in a taxicab, the death in a cave-in, the strangled nurse with a washcloth stuffed in her mouth, the bleeding boy left behind by youth gangs, the amnesic girl and the psychotic drunk, the half-dressed male corpse and what's left of a sedan at a grade crossing.

And it is triviality just as much as tragedy: the stolen purse, the property line feud, the broken window, the unnecessary-noise complaint, the sonic boom, the missing manhole cover, the dead dog in the sun and the unlicensed street peddler.

It is as varied as knocking at a door to break the news of a death or sitting with a father as he tells, haltingly, how the boy went bad. It's a catch-all job, really. It needs men like Sergeant Harry Donlon with his magpie recollection of little things about many people that sometimes trip them later. It needs men like Sergeant R. J. Long, LAPD's paper man extraordinary, the new kind of policeman who fights crime with statistics. And in these days of soaring delinquency, it demands lady sergeants like red-haired, blue-eyed Daisy Storms.

I

For seven years Sergeant Harry Donlon was one of the happiest officers in one of the toughest slices of Los Angeles. From First to Seventh Streets, he walked a beat on Hill Street that touched the fringe of Skid Row and covered Pershing Square, the park in the center of the city.

If you didn't know it, Harry's beat would have made the dreariest of impressions on you: cheap rooms, small stores, some big buildings, cheerless missions, bars, theaters, an occasional restaurant, parking lots, sidewalk hamburger joints, pawnshops, flophouses, and the square block of park with some trees, benches, and fountains.

Now parks are made for lovers, and Pershing Square would have impressed you drearily, too. On the benches sat the threadbare pensioner gabbing old yarns, the empty-eyed derelict, the furtive little man whispering conspiratorially in English or Spanish to his flashily dressed friend.

But Harry Donlon did know it, right down to the names and faces of those who lived or worked there, and he made it his business to know each new transient, too.

Hill Street, First to Seventh, was fascinating, really, when you applied Harry Donlon's street scholarship to it. Always, there were 7,000 to 8,000 persons in the district whom he could privately classify as suspect. He kept an eye on them. He shook them down discreetly, and went home each night to fill notebook after notebook with the scraps of information. Who had said what, when, where, in relation to what.

'I shook down everybody, whether they had any business to be suspect or not,' Harry says. 'You do it easy. You don't make them mad. Just a word, a greeting, and a question or two. They don't mind.'

If any one human brain can be encyclopedic, it was Harry Donlon's. Month after month, he averaged between forty-five and sixty-five felony arrests. He stalked Pershing Square and the entrances to bus and trolley terminals for the transients he would recognize in an instant. He picked up an average of fifteen fugitives monthly.

And he did it so gently that in all his years on the beat he drew his gun only once. He was in Pershing Square when a mountain of a man, six feet six and 275 pounds, suddenly went berserk.

'I'll show you!' he screamed. He advanced on Donlon, five feet ten and ninety pounds lighter. 'I killed a cop in New York with my bare hands. I'll kill you, too!'

Donlon aimed his gun to cool him down while he handcuffed the giant. Harry checked the office. Sure enough, There was a 'want' on him from New York for the murder of a policeman. 'That worked out fine,' Donlon says placidly.

There are a lot of brass in LAPD who joined the department at the same time as Donlon and have risen considerably higher. But, they acknowledge openly, almost with a touch of awe, he has a genius for the man-hunt that they could never, never equal.

'It's just a matter of being in the right place at the right time,' Sergeant Donlon explains modestly. 'And knowing who you are looking for. That adds up to luck.'

It was, he would have you believe, just luck, pure luck, that he put two and two together the day they called him in to work the Gamewell board. This is the telephonic instrument that receives calls from the men out on post, and it makes a cosy inside job. But Harry never did like the inside of a police station.

The morning dragged, and then about noon a 'want' was broadcast for a murder suspect, male, six feet two inches, 195 pounds, blond hair. He was believed to be somewhere around Hill Street.

'Lieutenant,' Donlon said hopefully to his supervising officer, 'a thought just crossed my mind.'

'What's that?'

'If I didn't have to work the Gamewell, Lieutenant, I think I could catch that murderer for you.'

The transparency of Donlon's little scheme, the pious look on his face amused the Lieutenant. 'That's fine, Harry!' he said enthusiastically. 'You just do that – as soon as you're through your watch here.'

'I know that guy,' Harry insisted. 'He wears his hair funny. It falls to the left side of his head.'

But he had to finish his tour at the Gamewell, and only afterwards, on his own time, could he scout the bars on Hill, between Second and Third Streets. That was where the fellow with the funny hair-do usually hung out.

Near one bar at Third and Hill, Harry encountered a couple of detectives on the same mission.

'Don't waste your time going in there,' they advised him.

'Thanks, fellows,' Donlon said politely.

And went in. It was dim and quiet.

At the rail, a girl was sitting with two sailors. There was a fellow near the door who looked familiar; but, after a moment's study, Donlon discarded him.

Down at the rear, a man and woman were sipping wine. Donlon took a step nearer to study him discreetly. He was big and husky like the wanted man, but his hair was black, not blond, and besides he had a mustache.

Something still bothered Donlon. He came a little closer to see better in the dull light. Of course! The way his hair was combed, it fell to the left side of the head.

Now he came up to the table. The man put down his wine glass, and Donlon didn't miss the fresh cuts on his fingers.

'What's your name, mister?'

'Otto Wilson. Why?' He turned resignedly to his companion, and she bristled at Donlon.

'How long you had those cuts on your fingers?' Donlon asked.

'These? A week, I guess.'

'They look pretty fresh for being a week old.'

'Well!' said the young lady. The one word made it pretty plain what she thought of nosy cops.

Then Donlon noticed dried blood on the man's mustache. 'How about that?' he asked.

Nervously the man brushed his lip. 'Must have cut myself shaving,' he said.

Even in the barroom half-light, Donlon saw that he wasn't freshly shaved.

'Stand up, mister,' Donlon said.

There was a moment's hesitation. Firmly, Donlon helped his man stand up, shook him down, hand-cuffed him, and walked him out of the barroom.

At the Gamewell box, as Donlon was calling in for transportation, Otto Wilson asked him to please reach inside his jacket for cigarettes and matches. Donlon did so. The matchbook, he noticed, carried the name of the hotel where a young woman had been found murdered.

Donlon got Homicide and told them he had their man. But Homicide was pretty busy at the moment working on another tip on the same death. If Donlon thought he had the man, he was brusquely instructed, then bring him in.

So Donlon asked for a radio car and brought in Otto Stephen Wilson, aged thirty-four, former Navy pharmacist's mate, now a café worker and woman hater.

En route, Donlon got his man to talk. Sure, he had strangled one woman and butchered another. 'I wanted to see how many of them I could get rid of,' he confided to Donlon. The young lady whom Donlon had just outraged by breaking up her date had been marked by Wilson as Victim No. Three.

Donlon presented his catch to Homicide, all neatly tied up. Otto Wilson subsequently went to the gas chamber.

Because of Harry Donlon's amazing knack for remembering facts and faces, Captain James Hamilton of Intelligence Division picked him as the ideal man to organize the airport detail for ID.

It was a sobering assignment. At an airport, speed and certainty are imperative in an identification. Single out the wrong man, hold him up to public humiliation, make him miss his flight, and maybe you will have a lawsuit on your hands.

From the beginning, Harry Donlon didn't like the responsibility and the carriage-trade suspects he was now dealing with. 'Police work is a funny thing,' he said worriedly. 'You *can* be wrong.'

But, like a good sergeant, he obeyed orders. He was given seven men, a fingerprint assistant, and a deadline of three months in which to get his squad functioning.

From all over the country, he ordered mug shots and background on known gangsters. He taught his fingerprint man to make preliminary classifications which could be telephoned in to Records and Identification for a 'make' in three or four minutes.

From airport officials, he wangled a room, telephones, and use of the airport public address system.

As part of his own preparation, he constantly carried fifty mug shots in his pocket, whipping them out every now and then to commit the scowling faces to memory. At the end of the three months, he had memorized another 1,500 faces.

But the man from the fringes of Skid Row wasn't happy with his new, plush job. In a way, he was like a small-town boy, lost and distrustful in the big city. As soon as he knew his detail was functioning smoothly, he asked downtown: Please, could he go back to Hill Street and Pershing Square?

Fortunately, Harry Donlon is something of a legend in LAPD, to the brass as well as to the rookies. His request was granted.

Now, instead of walking a beat, he supervises his Policemen from a radio car, noting how fast and capably they respond to their calls.

But habit and a memory like his are strong things. 'I ride the car on my patrol,' he explains, almost defensively, 'and I see things. If I can help out, I do.'

What that means is that rarely along Hill Street does he miss a suspicious transient or a bad native for whom a 'want' is out. As he always did, he puts the collar on, but with the courtesy of a good Sergeant, he turns over the suspect to the policeman on watch for the booking.

They call him the workhorse, my boy.

II

If Sergeant Harry Donlon, riding Hill Street, and Sergeant R. J. Long of the Analysis Section, Planning & Research Division – the street man supreme and the paper man extraordinary – were to swap jobs, they would probably survive, both being good officers. But they would be dread-fully unhappy, and LAPD would lose something, too.

Donlon personifies the old-time beat cop who walked like a shepherd among the people on his watch. Long is the remote, new kind of policeman who substitutes statistics for flesh and blood. Compared to Donlon, he is unspectacular; and, at first glance, his beat among LAPD's paper forms is prosaic. But even though you can't fairly compare these strikingly dissimilar sergeants, Long's work is every bit as important as Donlon's in the complicated modern police department.

Statistics on crime . . . statistics on budget . . . statistics of arrests and manpower. . . .

Sergeant Long had a degree in police administration from the University of Southern California when he joined LAPD. Nevertheless, he went through the break-in period, pounding a beat, riding an AID car and doing jail duty before he was assigned to Analysis.

Here, every day, crime is subjected to scholarly post-mortem. Rape becomes a mathematical problem, murder a pale study in costs and larceny just a question of logistics. Drained of blood and fright, the figures progress through slide rule, tabulating equipment and typewriter and come out at the end in the department's annual eighty-page *Statistical Digest*.

In a given year, how many reports of traffic property damage? 25,550. . . . How many sex offenses? 3,583. Suicide by gun (112) is the most popular form of self-destruction and jumping in front of a moving vehicle (one case) the least popular. . . . There are seven cases of sodomy; and 190 deaths from unknown causes are investigated. . . . In the Venice Division alone, 2,011 speeders are cited. It is the police-eye view of the community for that year imprisoned forever in the tables and data of crime, investigation, arrest.

Both policemen and civilians labor on the *Statistical Digest* on a year-round basis, but complete as it is, the result has not satisfied the 'corner pocket.' And that is where Sergeant Long comes in. He was handed the old form on which the 3,000 uniformed men make their daily field activity report, and was assigned to update it.

Chief Parker wanted the complicated, sprawling, unpredictable work of a policeman subjected to a true cost accounting system. How much does one police call to one house cost? Can the price of a robbery investigation be reduced? And what is that price, compared to, say, the apprehension of a pickpocket?

Many an old-timer, with a veteran's distrust of paper work, didn't like the idea at all, and many a competent outside observer agreed that law enforcement could not be sliced that thin into dollars and pennies. The old field activity report with its dozen or so questions was workable, they argued, and if a cop spent his time filling in blanks on a piece of paper, when would he be catching crooks?

But LAPD's administrative brass told Sergeant Long to go ahead. The old form had been workable, but it was not weighted by any basic rule of computation. In each of the department's dozen geographical divisions, the commanding officer himself completed the statistical picture, using rule o' thumb. And, division to division, thumbs weighed differently.

For weeks, Long struggled to encompass a policeman's day into some forty questions, a few repeated, but nevertheless thrice as productive in information as the old form. Then his draft was submitted to the supervisory level for final decision on which statistics were to be included and which discarded.

Today, LAPD Form 15.52 is a revolutionary piece of police paper. For the first time in the history of American police administration, the 'called for service' of any policeman is measured accurately down to the minute. At a glance, 15.52 tells every move he made during his watch.

Type of call, time received, time answered, time disposed of, all are there. At the end of each day, there is overall information instantly available which previously would have taken two dozen men two and a half months to tabulate.

The brass liked it. Form 15.52 meant surer, quicker command decisions: where to send men, what they must do there, how to get them there faster and more inexpensively. The taxpayer, staggering under a record property tax load, liked it, too. Now he could see how that $35 millions, twenty per cent of the whole budget, was being spent.

But the most important man in making 15.52 a success didn't like it at all.

Out on the watch, the policeman suspected darkly that it was a gimmick designed somehow to affect his job. Parts of it bewildered him, other sections seemed plain useless. What were they trying to do up in Planning & Research? Play quiz games?

So Sergeant Long carefully tucked his slide rule into an inside pocket where it wouldn't show and went out into the field to sell the men. Ten minutes at a time with an outraged policeman, he found, usually soothed him and won him over. After his missionary work, some 167 supervisors were called into the auditorium at the Police Administration Building. Down to the last decimal point on the card, 15.52 was explained and justified. This was the beginning of a long training process that brought about final departmental acceptance.

Any day now, a variation of 15.52 may be introduced in your own police department. The nation's police statisticians, meeting under the auspices of the International Association of Chiefs of Police, were tremendously impressed by the LAPD achievement. Thanks to the dirty work done by Sergeant Long, 15.52 can be painlessly adapted anywhere.

Without headlines, Long had accomplished a critically

important 'front office' job of police work – one reason why the International City Managers Association has called LAPD 'probably the most soundly organized large police department in the country.'

'Killings are cheap. They cost about $1.35 or $1.40 . . . It's like being on a quiz show . . . When you get to ten, you go for twenty . . . You always want more . . .

'When I was in Quentin, I borrowed books from the prison library. I was studying the operation of railroads. I planned to run a whole train off a bridge and watch them monkeys go swimming. I'd lie on the river bank and enjoy myself laughing at them.'

– STEPHEN NASH

How can you read any man's mind? Especially that of a gaunt, toothless, six-foot-three drifter who dreams such monstrous thoughts as these? How can you believe that in less than a year a man would perpetrate five senseless murders with knife and lead pipe (and perhaps half a dozen more)?

Sergeant Larry Scarborough was just a slow-talking rookie in the Homicide Division at the time. His background was the Narcotics detail where he had worked the previous five years. You couldn't reasonably expect that he yet would have developed that intuition, smell of blood, call-it-what-you-will, which sets the Homicide detective apart.

Yet the very first day he heard of Stephen Nash he knew instinctively that he was touching something evil. Something especially evil that would have to be stopped fast. At the time, Nash wasn't even wanted for murder, but

Scarborough suspected a little of the monstrous truth.

All that dull November day, from morning till late afternoon, two men, one a boyish twenty-four-year-old, the other an older sullen man, stood together on the Skid Row corner in the 'slave labor' belt, hoping for a job.

It was Friday, a bad day for the kind of jobs that are doled out on Skid Row, and they had no luck.

The younger man, Dennis Butler, had a few dollars. He offered to buy his new friend a beer or two, and they went to a nearby saloon. For an hour, the sullen, older, bitter man did the talking, and Butler did the buying.

The older man, it seemed, had a grievance against society that had begun in infancy and never had been assuaged. As a baby, he had been abandoned, and from that first, unfair stigma, life had continued to abuse him.

He was still talking when they left the bar and walked up Third Street toward a cafeteria where the food was cheap but good. He was talking louder and more bitterly, and waving his arms in rage, as they entered the Third Street tunnel. Butler began to feel uneasy about this new friend who hated anything, everything, with such a black, consuming hate.

Midway through the tunnel, the tall, gaunt man stopped and glared at Butler. Not a word was said, but the younger, smaller man tried desperately to back away.

It was too late. A hunting knife with a four-inch blade drove into his stomach.

Butler screamed, and his terror gave him the strength to run despite the burning wound. He fled out of the tunnel and into the lobby of a nearby hotel.

Knife upraised for the kill, his assailant followed him, trapping him in the lobby.

For some reason, perhaps because it would have been more merciful, he withheld the fatal thrust. Instead, deliberately, viciously, he stomped on his prostrate victim till he had broken Butler's collarbone. Then he fled.

Somehow, Butler survived the attack, and in the hospital he whispered to a radio car patrolman the name his assailant had given. It was Stephen Nash, all right, and the records down in R. and I. flashed out the story.

At the age of thirty-three, Nash had already done half a dozen years in San Quentin for strongarm robberies. He had brawled at a cannery where he was working, and done six months on a sheriff's honor farm at Santa Rita.

In the stupid, senseless way of some Skid Row characters, he was bad, but there was nothing to suggest that he was monstrous. Yet something clicked right then for Sergeant Scarborough. Wasn't it four or five weeks earlier in Sacramento that it had happened?

Scarborough checked the file of All Points Bulletins. Yes, here it was:

> Floyd Leroy Barnett, 27, cannery worker, body found in
> Sacramento River, bludgeon and knife wounds.

Scarborough wired the Sacramento police for full details. Standup mugs of Nash were printed up and distributed. All commands were briefed on his physical description, habits, and known haunts. To police in other cities, LAPD put out a 'want' on Nash for assault with a deadly weapon.

Privately, Scarborough knew the charge was an understatement.

Ten days later, the gaunt, toothless man is in Long Beach, twenty miles south of his Skid Row hangouts. He meets John William Berg, twenty-seven, and the young hairdresser invites him up to his apartment.

There is an argument, or is it one of Nash's tirades against society that can be satisfied only by blood and death? He fatally stabs the hairdresser. The next day, he has Berg's new clothes altered to fit him, sells his own shabby garments and disappears.

Back in LAPD Homicide, Sergeant Scarborough notes the modus operandi and adds a second murder to the case he is already building against Nash.

Now it is three days after the Berg killing, and ten-year-old Larry Rice is listlessly playing near the pier in the beach area at Venice. Now and then he glumly kicks a stone, but mostly he just stares out at the water, blinking occasionally.

Larry doesn't want to play with the other kids or go home to his empty house. He is just killing time in a lonely, inarticulate, small boy way till his father comes home from his job as an aircraft assembler. Larry is an only child; and, eight days ago, his mother died of cancer.

A gaunt man with a funny, toothless smile gets Larry to talking a little. They drift over to a foodstand, and he treats the boy to a hamburger and pop. Then they go under the pier and talk some more.

There's one nice thing ahead, Larry suddenly confides to his new friend. His face brightens in anticipation.

After it, well, happened – he blinks quickly and goes on – his daddy talked to him. Look, kid, these things happen, and it's better for her this way. Now, you be brave, and I'll tell you what I'm going to do. I'm saving the money, and we're going on *all* the rides in the amusement park. How's that! *All* the rides.

Larry likes that, he tells his friend under the pier. He likes his daddy. His daddy says there are going to be lots of more nice things, too.

He looks up smilingly at the gaunt man and wonders, in sudden panic, what did he say wrong? Larry tries to yell, but it comes out a small boy's squeak. He tries to run, but the gaunt man grabs him and slashes viciously with a knife.

When they find Larry a little later, there are twenty-eight knife wounds all over his body. He dies the same day.

*

It's *got* to be Nash, Sergeant Scarborough told himself. He added a third murder to his private 'want' on the killer. Next day, when Nash was bagged by the Santa Monica cops in a roundup of vagrants, Scarborough was on his way there.

In a showup of the suspects, several small boys recognized the gaunt, toothless man with his funny smile as the one they had seen with Larry Rice. An hour later, as Scarborough listened to his confession – a boastful, triumphant story the way Nash told it – the sergeant knew beyond all doubt that he had been right about this monster.

'He was a kid,' Nash said without a flicker of remorse. 'It was all there in front of him. His whole life . . . sex, fun, all of it! Why should he have it when I never did? I took it all away from him.'

Then toothlessly he smiled at the cops. 'Besides, I never killed a kid before. I wanted to see how it felt.'

Quietly Larry Scarborough snapped the handcuffs on Nash's thick, muscled wrists, noticing the cuffs clicked in the first notch and no more. He took him back to LAPD Headquarters for one of the most detailed, brilliant interrogations in LAPD history, one that was to win for him a special honor plaque from the California Association of Private Investigators.

Because he knew so much about his man even before laying eyes on him, Sergeant Scarborough had little trouble getting Nash to talk.

For two weeks, a tape recorder at his side, Scarborough listened and prompted as the killer bragged, whined, screamed, joked, wept, and ranted. Endlessly Nash reviled society and occasionally he laughed – when he described a murder or his hope to invent a new kind of murder by spiking whisky with iodine. Like the train wreck, he just hadn't had the opportunity to test it out, he added resentfully.

The story was even worse than Scarborough had suspected. He already knew about the killings of the cannery worker, the hairdresser, and the little boy, all in a six-weeks period stretching from mid-October to late November. Now Nash filled him in on two more.

Almost a year ago, the previous December, he had beaten William Clarence Burns to death with a lead pipe. Burns, an Oakland merchant seaman, had a good job, Nash thought, and that was reason enough to murder. The pipe and body had been thrown into San Francisco Bay near Richmond, just north of Oakland.

Then in August, two months before killing his fellow cannery worker, Barnett, he had murdered Robert Eche, a twenty-three-year-old draftsman for the Pacific Gas & Electric Company. This was the first time he used a knife, but the motive was the same as in all his wanton killings – an envious hate.

Afterwards, he told Sergeant Scarborough, he piled Eche's corpse into his car and rolled it down a cement ramp into the bay, off Pier 52, in San Francisco. The tide carried the car out to some oil docks where it got caught in the pilings.

Scarborough listened to a playback of the tape recording, and made some notes. The murders had occurred in December, August, October, and then two in November. Had this monster abstained during the long eight-months' period between December and August? Scarborough put it up to him, and Nash laughed teasingly.

Why, there were another half dozen killings he could talk about if he wanted to. But he wasn't going to. He was going to sell that information at $200 per body. Scarborough could believe it. The killer was miserly as well as bloody. He didn't even drink wine like most of his Skid Row associates because it cost too much, and he had saved up the prodigious sum of $450 from his cannery wages. But, as it turned out, though he repeated his $200 offer in court, he made no blood money. Neither the newspapers nor the authorities would give him the satisfaction.

When Scarborough took Nash into Los Angeles County Superior Court, the case was tight and tidy. Incredible as the quintuple-murder confession sounded, Scarborough had painstakingly corroborated it. On a weeklong tour through the state with Nash, he had revisited the scenes of the five slayings, and everything had checked out as the killer told it.

After listening to the tapes, there wasn't much for the jury to do except rule that Nash had been sane when he committed the killings. Since the death sentence was mandatory, there was even less for Judge Burton Noble to do. Sadly he called the New York foundling 'the most evil person who ever appeared in my court' and consigned him to death row at San Quentin.*

As Nash stepped into a station wagon for his last ride to San Quentin, he bragged to newspapermen:

'I'm the king of killers! I'll go to my death like any king should. I have nothing to die for because I had nothing to live for.'

A reporter asked if he wanted a Christian burial, and Nash laughed harshly. 'Who, me!' he exclaimed in derision.

Sergeant Scarborough had no statement. He was drained and sick at heart from his long, close association with evil. Neither did Larry Rice's father, who in ten days had lost his wife and only child to two equally monstrous forms of cancer.

Backbone of the Force, my boy.

---

*Nash was convicted of murder, and sentenced to death. At this writing an appeal is pending due to a question of 'due process' in connection with his sanity trial.

IV

You think the cop on a beat knows tragedy. Then you talk to Sergeant Daisy Storms. The tragedy the beat man knows is mostly a crystallization of inheritance, environment, circumstance. But whatever the cause, there is only one thing to do now, from the officer's point of view. Get the bum off the streets before he can hurt somebody else.

But what Daisy Storms sees is tragedy just beginning. The little punk trying desperately to become a big punk. The teen-age bully practicing strongarm tactics. The girl who has scarcely achieved puberty and knows what it's all about.

They are so young and malleable that somehow, you think, the right word, the right decision *now* will avert a misspent life. And sometimes, being a mother herself, Daisy Storms knows the kindly word that makes the suspicion of a tough, unloved kid dissolve into trust and friendship.

But there are always some whose blind hurt is so deep, their rage against the adult world so great, that nothing can be done. Those are the times that Daisy Storms says brightly, 'I could stand some lipstick.'

To the young, it never matters how they get to Hollywood, by boxcar, by thumb, or stowed away in planes, slow boats, and trailer trucks. They hit Los Angeles first and, being ravenous, make for the nearest hamburger joint. There is the delightful discovery of chili, tamale, taco, and burrito, and only after they are gorged do they realize that there isn't a movie queen in sight and Hollywood is still eight miles off toward the hills.

So they wander uncertainly past the store fronts, past the girlie joints that feature 'Russian Tease' and 'Naked Sin.' As they wander, they are innocently vulnerable to those who prey on the unsupervised juvenile. But if they are among the lucky ones, a team of plainclothes detectives on routine juvenile patrol will spot them first. Often the detectives are sergeants and sometimes, like Daisy Storms, the sergeant is a lady.

These runaways are the easy ones to handle. They are already scared and homesick and probably broke. A motherly hug, a notification wire home, then a seat on a departing bus, and case closed out.

But most of the time it isn't that easy, and there are so many of the young in trouble every day!

In Los Angeles there are 600,000 school-age kids, more than the total population of Cincinnati, Ohio. During a year, some 13,500 of them will get into brushes with the law; a few as many as twenty times during the twelve months. They come in for everything: murder, sex, larceny, robbery, burglary, auto theft. Eight hundred of them are picked up for using and selling dope.

Worst of all, where once a kid didn't normally foul up till he was seventeen, now it is the precocious children aged thirteen to fifteen who are the biggest group of offenders.

In line with California's juvenile court law, which is essentially rehabilitative, LAPD's Juvenile policemen wage a four-point program of counter-attack. They call it *discovery, investigation, treatment and referral,* and *protection.*

What it comes down to is this:

With the help of churches, schools, welfare agencies and parents, Juvenile patrol units smell out and try to anticipate child crime. Where delinquency is reported, they dig back into the home conditions, social attitudes, companions, habits, and aptitudes. On a broader scale, they work with civic betterment groups for removal of environmental hazards. When they must arrest a juvenile, they give him every possible break through the Probation Department, a social service agency or some other organization specializing in youth work.

*

But even for a lady cop, police work can't be just social service work.

In the living room of a shabby frame house in Central Division, Daisy Storms and a male Juvenile officer are surrounded by seven scowling teen-age thugs. They are looking for a fifteen-year-old girl who has been reported missing and the boy who seduced her.

There is a moment of tense silence. Then Daisy looks straight at the ringleader. 'We'd like to talk to Johnny,' she says.

'What do you want him for?'

'Just to talk. We're looking for a girl. Betty.'

Suspiciously Johnny steps forward, and Daisy asks him to please come out to the car. There is something she wants to check with him. Johnny hesitates, his friends sidle closer behind him. Daisy pretends she doesn't notice.

Then Johnny steps forward, and the tension is broken.

In the car outside, Daisy and her partner arrest Johnny for statutory rape and take him to the Georgia Street juvenile detention unit. She also makes a call to the Robbery Division.

A roving gang of young Mexican-Americans had been pulling a series of stickups through the city, and Daisy thought the boys in the old house answered the description. At the point of machine guns, the youths were arrested, and a small arsenal of weapons and ammunition confiscated.

The youths were charged with the holdups while Daisy Storms, checking through on her particular problem, located the missing Betty. A delinquency complaint was filed, and Betty was released under the supervision of a probation officer.

Who is responsible for the Johnnys and Bettys who go through the Juvenile mill by the thousands each year?

Daisy Storms' years of experience make her distrust glib

answers, and she comes back to the simple and obvious answer. It is the parent. The father who has fled his responsibilities, leaving a broken home behind. The mother who must work and cannot exercise a mother's supervision. The parent who wields too much or not enough authority, who just doesn't care.

Occasionally, too, you can blame a hurry-up civilization which demands too much too soon from its children and drives them into confusion. This is lofty-sounding talk, but there *are* the children to substantiate it.

Shortly before 8 a.m. on an April Wednesday, police of the Venice Division find four boys sleeping in a nine-year-old sedan. Two of them are thirteen, the third is fourteen, and the ringleader, who has taken his uncle's car, is all of fifteen. The police itemize the following fifteen pieces of property which they find in the car:

One machine gun.
Two shotguns and two rifles.
One .45-calibre automatic.
Two sticks of dynamite.
One bayonet.
Three hunting knives.
One black suitcase lined with ammunition.
Two copies of a curious document entitled *The Constitution of the House of San Miguel.*

At the office, Juvenile detectives interrogate the ringleader.

For a long time, he explains, the things going on in the world have been bothering him. He has had it on his mind that he would like to escape to the island of San Miguel, sixty miles due west of Los Angeles, and there create a new nation where boys could be happy.

The year before, he had begun stealing some things to prepare for his expedition. But, while driving a stolen truck containing his stolen supplies, he had collided with a tank truck. He was arrested and sent to a forestry camp.

After he got out, he sent a recruiting letter to certain reliable friends and enlisted five followers, including the three picked up with him. Their plan had been to cache their arsenal on the discipline grounds at Camp Cook until they could steal a boat for the expedition to San Miguel.

There, as the Constitution made very plain, the boys would farm, fish, hunt, and relax, and there would be no stealing, arguing, or other trouble like in the outside world. If there were, a fair trial and punishment were provided for by the Constitution.

A little sadly the Juvenile detectives ask him: Doesn't he know? The outside world and its troubles have already come to San Miguel. The island, owned by the United States Government, is used by the Marine Corps as a target for gunnery practice.

But there is nothing the detectives can do except charge all four with violation of the Juvenile Code under subsection 'M' dealing with illegal possession of explosives and a machine gun.

Is this how Tom Sawyer would feel if he wandered out of his lazy, happy 19th Century into today's world? It is at times like these that Daisy Storms says, 'I could stand some lipstick.'

V

The battleground is Hollywood. No other division in LAPD has had so many varied problems. There are the phonies still trying to storm the movie lots, though there are fewer lots than there used to be, and turning to crime

96

when they fail. There are the strongarm men prowling for furs and jewels. There is the nest of homosexuals, which lives under constant threat of murder, shakedown, and blackmail.

During the war years, the homos were victims of more than one thousand robberies and hundreds of other crimes – so many that the police appealed to the armed forces to keep their personnel out of the purple district.

When Captain Bert Jones commanded the Hollywood Division, he said the place reminded him of a crime recruiting office. 'We keep sending them to the penitentiary,' he explained, 'but the ranks keep filling up.'

In a place like that, where the crime scenarists just look out the window for fresh material, the strenuous sleuthing demands great detectives. Hollywood had three such: Sergeant Colin Forbes; Sergeant Arnold Hubka, his inseparable partner; and E. M. (Al) Goosen, who rounded out the triumvirate.

The detective is a counter-puncher. He waits for the first blow, and then hits back. Forbes, Hubka, and Goosen had to play it that way.

'We never played to the gallery,' Forbes says today, 'and we seldom got "screen credit." But we sure drew the people. Hollywood was a lodestone for the phonies, the connivers, and the bad eggs who thought the town was a pushover. That calls for work, if you're a policeman.'

Donald L. Rider was a guy, just a guy, it seemed, if you didn't know his FBI record which reached from Phoenix, Arizona, to Helena, Montana. By the age of nineteen, in just two exuberant years, he had worked at robbery, burglary, car theft, jail escape, and strongarm terrorism.

Now, with only seventeen shopping days till Christmas, he blew into Hollywood, extending the season's greetings at gunpoint to one and all. The first day, he stuck up a motel on Sunset Boulevard for $759. Haphazardly, he hit motels and restaurants and once paused on the street to relieve a passer-by of $150.

He wasn't very bright, and he didn't think big, but he was a busy mugg, and that kind causes just as much trouble to a detective. Forbes and Hubka were right behind, trying to make him a Christmas present for the division, as he ran up $5,168.15 in holdup loot. They missed their private goal by two days.

On December 27, Rider knocked over a loan company for $3,302, his biggest take, and casually lit a cigarette as he departed. That was at 2:50 p.m.; and, at 4:10, Forbes and Hubka collared him without a struggle in a hillside motel between Hollywood and San Fernando Valley.

'You guys are quick,' Rider observed professionally. 'How did you tumble so fast?'

Forbes asked simply, 'Who taught you to throw match folders on the floor of the place you rob?'

'Was that how you found this place?'

Hubka grinned. 'The folder had the address of this motel. Happy New Year.'

Rider drew a life sentence, and police recovered about half of his more than $5,000 loot. This was given back to the victims in proportion to the amount of their losses.

He's the old three-striper –

It was the kind of inside job that makes a detective talk to himself because it's so obvious and yet you can't put your finger on the culprit. The owner of one of Hollywood's smartest haberdasheries complained that money had been taken from the cash drawer of the open safe. Forbes questioned the employees, but didn't get anyplace.

About three days later, the owner called back to report the same thing had happened again; and thereafter, about every three days for the next four months, he was on the phone again with the same complaint and an increasing asperity of tone. *Were* the police going to do something?

Forbes was doing all a detective can do. He questioned and requestioned every employee. Without advance warning, he questioned some at their homes at night just to see if he could spot any expensive clothing, furniture, or jewelry.

He talked at length to the girl with the box office name, Nevada Skippy Murphy, a nineteen-year-old blonde, four feet seven, eighty-eight nicely curved pounds. Forbes didn't question what hope had brought her to Hollywood, and it was more polite not to ask. Skippy, right now, was cashier in the haberdashery.

Every three days or so, she told him, it was the same thing. She would go to the cash drawer, discover the money had been taken, and report it right away to her boss. A Hollywood detective has to know a good deal about women's clothing, and a quick rundown of Skippy told Forbes she was wearing what the average working girl would wear. She was obviously cooperating with him, and he crossed her off his list.

Then, by chance, on a routine cruise through Hollywood one night, Forbes saw a Cinderella. All decked out in an expensive gown and expensive jewelry, Skippy was just entering a smart night spot.

With his partner, Forbes followed and after a few questions, asked if she would object to having her apartment searched. 'Why no,' Skippy said calmly. 'I have nothing to hide.'

Why did she say it? The minute the detectives walked in, they spotted the new fur coat, the expensive wristwatch, the new pieces of furniture. 'Well?' said Forbes.

'I wanted to live nice,' Skippy said slowly. 'I wanted nice clothes. What girl doesn't! Especially here in Hollywood. But how many of us have the money? Well, I saw a way to get the money. I guess I was too weak to refuse it.'

But, Skippy made it very plain, she was *not* a thief. From a desk drawer, she took out a black ledger and handed it to Forbes. In it were dates and various sums of money which matched the dates and sums of the four months of thievery.

'Some day, when I got to be something in Hollywood,' Skippy said virtuously, 'I was going to pay it *all* back.'

She was sentenced to the Los Angeles County Jail for petty theft.

Whose knowledge is riper?

Sometimes a Hollywood detective plays it soft with the Skippys whose dreams betray them, and then sometimes hard when he's up against a killer. Once, Colin Forbes went on the trail of a shadowy character who had trussed, robbed, then killed a Vine Street tailor, leaving behind only the heelprint of a cowboy's boot on his victim's forehead. It took him two years, but he traced the boot to Texas and then found the murderer in an Army camp right in California.

Sometimes, you play it very rough. Forbes went up against Erwin (Machine Gun) Walker, the slayer of a California Highway Patrolman, and got a slug in the stomach himself. He still carries the bullet lodged against his spine.

When Count Rudeni arrived in town, the ladies were overwhelmed. He had the courtly manners of a count and, what counts don't always have, money, too, being by reputation a landed gentleman. There was also a dash of the virile about him; not one of those *decadent* counts, you know. He had been an FBI agent, he told them, and now he was in Hollywood as a technical adviser on an FBI picture. It was a complete mystery how so much feminine misinformation could have gotten around town unless perhaps it was spread by plain old Hymie Bernstein, which was the count's real name.

No sooner was Count Rudeni established in town than he fought a brief, losing battle with his worse half, Hymie Bernstein. He entertained a lady, drugged her, partially disrobed her and chastely plucked a purse containing $580 from her bra. There followed a four-year schizophrenic crime career in which the gallant count wangled the dates but in which Hymie did the dirty work, including the slugging of an eighty-year-old woman for her diamond ring and $1,200 cash.

In California, the statute of limitations on robbery is three years, and since they couldn't find the elusive count, Forbes and his partner obtained a secret indictment in the slugging case. Their foresight was justified.

From the license plate of a car which the count had been seen driving, they finally ran him down. It was two days after Hymie should have been safe because of the statute of limitations. But the secret indictment held, and he was tucked away in San Quentin for a period of five years up to life.

It was the same old malarky. But this one spelled it with a capital M. The name should have been plain warning, and certainly a less unblushing fraud would have changed it. James M-a-l-a-r-k-y. Malarky's business was selling people shiny new cars he didn't own, and he made a thriving thing out of it on one very simple gimmick. There was no particular shortage of cars the year Malarky operated, but nobody was selling them at *his* price – up to 40% off the list price.

So more than a hundred customers fought to make cash deposits or give Malarky their old cars in return for contracts which solemnly stated they would receive delivery of a car of their choice within the next month to three months Among them were buyers who most certainly should have known better. Teachers who might have speculated about this strange working of the economic laws; policemen who should have smelled the ripe, distinctive aroma of fraud. But even organizations like a teachers' association sent business Malarky's way, and the caper was overfed.

A high school principal paid him $3,300 cash for a new Cadillac, and after four months received one that didn't somehow seem brand-new. A month later he received a warning from a dealer in used Cadillacs that the car would be repossessed unless the payments were made on time.

Malarky, it then developed, had purchased the car, which already had had two owners, making the minimum down payment and the first two monthly instalments. Then he had turned it over to the school principal, and in Malarky's easy-come, easy-go way of doing business, that fulfilled his contract.

Another of the lambs traded a three-year-old Studebaker and $1,000 cash for a new Pontiac. The promise of a new Pontiac, that is. He waited several months, and then Malarky told him to pick up his car in Michigan – Pontiac, Michigan. Nobody there ever had heard of Malarky, with a capital M, that is.

The victim called Malarky long distance, and the dealer in imaginary cars was abjectly apologetic. The car had arrived in Los Angeles. But would the gentleman mind stopping off at Omaha on his way home and picking up a car, a year-old Chevrolet, at the airport parking lot? The keys would be in the airport office.

Dutifully the purchaser flew to Omaha, found the car which Malarky had described, and started west for Los Angeles. In Nebraska, the State Police stopped him for speeding, and it took considerable explaining on his part to assure them that he was in legal possession of the car.

Especially since he was pretty well bewildered himself by this time.

Twenty miles up the highway, he ran into a road block. The suspicious state police had double-checked his license number and found that it had been issued to a Caddy rather than the Chevvy he was driving. This time, he had to tell his peculiar story in court, and several phone calls were made for verification by the equally bewildered authorities.

Finally, they let him go – on payment of $15 court costs – and he staggered on westward toward home and the promised land of the new Pontiac. It isn't quite clear whether he ever laid hands on it.

But an Army colonel fared even worse at Malarky's game of city-city, what city's got the car. The colonel was directed first to a town in Louisiana. There was no car there, and by phone Malarky re-directed him to Kansas City. Again, no car, and he was told to try Pontiac. When that lead petered out, too, the colonel threw up his hands in disgust and went back to Louisiana. He bought a new Pontiac at a comparatively stiff price, but at least it was a car he could see.

At last Malarky's scheme of sedans-in-the-sky collapsed, and he knew he was bankrupt. He tried one more caper, arranging the 'burglary' of a $25,000 original Whistler painting which a friend had entrusted to him. He hoped to collect on insurance he had taken out, but Forbes took one fast look at the crime scene, and the hoax was uncovered. The chisel marks indicating forced entry were on the *inside* of the door.

Along with other investigators, Forbes worked twenty-five days to untangle the auto fraud. Scores of victims were personally interviewed, and their checks and bank slips scrutinized to prove that Malarky had actually received their money.

For two days, the victims crowded into the Hollywood Station to make their complaints. When the reckoning was completed, Malarky, spelled M-a-l-a-r-k-y, was shown to have stolen $80,000. He escaped with a sentence of nine months in the County Jail, plus three years of probation.

So you see, Barnum, though right, was wrong.

Of the thousand, two thousand emergency phone calls he received, Forbes will never forget the one that came without warning to his home one September noon. 'Forbes?' the man at Headquarters asked tonelessly. 'Yes.' Then Headquarters asked, rather than ordered, and Forbes said yes again, and hung up the receiver slowly.

From his pocket, where he had been carrying it for six years, he took out the photograph and studied it. He put it back inside, donned his coat and drove to southwest Los Angeles where his brother, Robert, operated a ceramics shop.

Other officers were already there, and they led him silently to a small room used for storing the pottery. Forbes looked down at the body of his sister-in-law, Despine, four bullet holes in her head, her face slashed and bloodied thirteen times from a pistol whipping. He braced himself and looked at the other body.

It was his brother, Robert, with four bullet holes in the head.

The officers looked at him, a question in their eyes, and he said softly, 'I want to handle this one.'

Efficiently, the investigation drove ahead. Who found the bodies? A bakery driver making deliveries shortly after 11 a.m. How long dead? More than an hour. Any physical evidence? One possible heelprint. Witnesses?

A service station operator half a block away told Forbes about the car that had parked daily across from his station, morning and afternoon, for more than two weeks.

Always, there had been a man in it, watching something. The service man had feared he was casing his station for a holdup. Apparently, he had been casing murder.

Other witnesses filled in bits and pieces. Robert Forbes had left the shop at 9:15 a.m. to get some breakfast for Despine and himself. The killer must have slipped in immediately afterwards through a door off an alley. He surprised Despine, pistol-whipped her, then put four .45-calibre slugs into her head from a gun equipped with a silencer.

Two bowls of breakfast food were standing on the table where Robert had placed them on his return to the shop. Before he even knew his wife had died, he got four slugs in the back of the head.

Sergeant Forbes again looked at the photograph that he had carried next to his heart for six years. It was that of James Merkouris, the epileptic son of a Greek priest and Despine's former husband. Forbes had feared this day ever since Robert married Despine and her ex-husband had harassed them with obscene letters.

Within an hour after discovery of the bodies, an All Points Bulletin was out for Merkouris and his car.

Very shortly, the first report was in from a Los Angeles County deputy sheriff. At 11:40 a.m. that day, he had sighted a car of the same description parked on a bluff overlooking the ocean near Malibu.

The spot was unusual, but because Malibu is good fishing territory, he thought a surf caster might be trying his luck below. After the APB, he quickly returned to the bluff, but the car had vanished. Next day police skin divers probed the ocean off Point Dune for the murder weapon, but it was never found.

The second report came from Pueblo, Colorado, where Merkouris' car was found overturned and wrecked. Forbes didn't entirely buy that. He had heard Despine say that Merkouris liked Hot Springs, Arkansas; and so the search was concentrated there. Merkouris was picked up and returned to Los Angeles.

Forbes had also traced him to a downtown hotel where he had been registered until the very day the murder watch of Robert and Despine had apparently gotten underway. But that day, Merkouris insisted, he had gone to Galveston, Texas, and hadn't returned. He denied any knowledge of the double killing. He was ordered to be held for sanity tests.

What the shock and the investigation drained out of Sergeant Colin Forbes, is impossible to know. Maybe there were other factors, too.

'For fifteen years I tried to make Colin sleep at least five hours a day,' says his wife, Vivian. 'If I wasn't doing that, I was nursing him through colds he received in rainy backyards waiting for hoodlums, or just worrying if he was all right when I didn't see him for three days at a time.'

'You can't work as hard as he did for twenty years and expect to keep your health,' says a fellow officer. 'I've seen him work twelve or fifteen hours a day for months to catch a murderer.

'And then he would work just as hard and long to see that the man's wife and kids had a place to sleep and plenty to eat.'

Then there were his close friends who were felled, too. Sergeant Hubka died of cancer. Al Goosen collapsed from diabetes, induced by stress.

Whatever the cause, Sergeant Colin Forbes has reached the end of the hunter's trail at the age of forty-six. He is a heart disease cripple, pensioned off at $300 a month.

> *He's the Sergeant, young man,*
> *He's the Sergeant.*

THE LIEUTENANT

At nightfall, the two tiny black leopard cubs nuzzled close to their mother for warmth and nourishment that cool spring night in Griffith Park Zoo. The next morning they had vanished as completely as though a hawk had scooped them up with his talons.

The gates and fences of the leopard cage were secure, the adjoining tiger cage seemed undisturbed. Except for the whining of the mother, there was nothing to indicate that the furry little mites had existed at all.

Quickly the zoo launched an investigation. A set of the rare cubs, one male, one female, would bring $1,500 and no questions asked. If they were hidden out a few months, it would then be impossible to identify them.

The regular attendant reported that he fed the leopards at the usual hour and all had been secure when he left. There was no reason to doubt him. But very probably, the zoo suspected, one of its new employees, a surly fellow with a hangdog look, had sneaked up to the cage afterward and stolen them. It would be simple to smuggle them out of the park in a small sack.

LAPD was called in, and detectives attacked the case with the solemnity of any missing persons report. What did the victims look like? When and where were they last seen? By whom? Any reason to suspect foul play?

To the police, the tigers next door looked like the

obvious suspects. Perhaps the cubs had strayed close to the dividing fence and the tigers had grabbed them.

Patiently the zoo officials explained that this would have been all but impossible. The openings in the fence were extremely small, even for tiny cubs, and besides they had already examined the tigers' run. There was no blood on the ground, no bones, no leopard hair.

First, the detectives said, just as routine, they would like to send a specimen of tiger dung to the Crime Lab for analysis. Resignedly the zoo agreed.

When the specimen arrived, the Crime Lab was having one of those days. An unidentified naked male body had been found in a remote canyon near the desert. The hands had been immersed in acid to erase the fingerprints, and the elements had done their work on the body. Now a Crime Lab technician would have to process the fingers with chemicals in order to restore the prints and then photograph them with appropriate side-lighting.

In addition, the day's work sheet at SID called for the processing of about a thousand sets of fingerprints, thirty photo enlargements, handwriting examination of some eight questioned documents, several Intoximeter tests of the breath of suspected drunken drivers, two gun identifications, nine analyses of narcotics to determine composition and identification for court purposes, one lie detector test.

During the day there would also be the usual two to three hundred phone calls, and in a dozen courtrooms technicians from SID would be waiting to offer evidence. When the detective explained his problem of the missing cubs, the Lab man, with great self-control, merely said, 'Who?'

However, this also being police work, the technician went over to a corner of the chemistry lab and compounded a special solution. He placed the liquid and the dung into a large pan which he slid into a glassed-in

110

cabinet. He told the detective he would know the results in mid-afternoon.

Then he moved on to more pressing problems: a ballistics test; the examination of toothmarks on a bar of candy bitten by a suspect; a detailed study of the pinch of dirt, the shred of clothing, and the broken headlight lens left behind in a hit-run accident.

When he got back to the dung, the chemical solution had prepared it sufficiently for probing. With tweezers, he put aside several patches of matted black hair. Just possibly this could be the tigers' own hair.

Next he found numerous tiny claws, but he was still dissatisfied. A thief might have wrapped the claws in some meat which he threw to the tigers, hoping to thus mislead the investigators. He examined the tiny claws more closely. Many were still in their sheaths.

In a way, the Lab man was relieved. It had taken considerable effort, but he had at least proved that tigers are no better than people. And all the rest of that day's work sheet was dedicated to proving that people, given the opportunity, are no better than tigers.

LAPD's Scientific Investigation Division is the finest police laboratory in the nation, differing from the superb FBI lab only in the volume of work. It is also the oldest, antedating the FBI's by seven years.

Back in 1923 when the night stick and billy still were the chief instruments of police work, the great August Vollmer strode onto the Los Angeles scene. The giant from Berkeley had come to reorganize the shaky LAPD.

If Vollmer knew anything, he knew the quick, short routes to solution of police problems. One of his pets was a bawling babe known as 'scientific investigation.' A lot of policemen had never heard of it. Most of the others scorned it.

But Vollmer, in one of the major changes he brought to LAPD as interim Police Chief, assigned young Rex Welsh to work as research chemist in the department.

He gave Welsh an antiquated microscope and a cubbyhole lab in a corner of a two-story building. A little later, a figurative handful of chemicals and a smattering of glassware were added.

With this, Welsh could but tug at the curtain concealing the mysteries of science from police eyes. He worked in the only way open to him, the painful and sometimes floundering method of trial-and-error.

But Rex Welsh was in business. And so was police scientific investigation in Los Angeles.

For the nation's handful of police crime scientists, there were then no books, no precedents, no courses in scientific investigation. Even fingerprinting was haphazard. The great FBI file had not yet been built up to its present eminence, and there was a tug-of-war between various lobby groups over control of a centralized identification of criminals.

A few private investigators – notably Arthur Waite, Edward B. Crossman, and Calvin Goddard – were doing some work in analyses of guns and ballistics, but for all practical purposes, this was an unknown science to the city policeman. Worse, popular skepticism about 'lab cops' was bolstered by the courtroom antics of pseudo criminal experts and unblushing quacks. A hod carrier, for example, received $50 a day as an 'expert' witness on physical evidence in a criminal trial.

Welsh, too, made mistakes. In an early Hollywood rape case, he predicted that he could identify the man by age from an examination of spermatozoa.

Since a prominent film figure was involved, the case had achieved wide publicity, and Welsh was sticking his neck out. He had no scientific precedent for his experiment, and less ebullient scientists cautioned him against going ahead with the test. But he persisted, the chemical analysis was futile, and both Welsh and his microscope blushed with failure.

In 1929, the Crime Lab received strong scientific buttressing with the addition of civilian Ray Pinker, a thoroughly trained technician. Pinker had studied chemical engineering for two years at the University of California at Los Angeles and had graduated from the University of Southern California with a bachelor of science degree in pharmacy.

Thereafter, Pinker took over the more technical work of sifting physical evidence in crime cases, while Welsh, until his tragic death by drowning in the early 1930's, concentrated chiefly on narcotics analyses.

To replace the pioneer, Lee Jones, an inquisitive young officer who had been dabbling in fingerprints, was assigned to the Scientific Investigation Division. He was of pioneer stuff himself: a grandmother of his had walked from Council Bluffs, Iowa, to Salt Lake City, Utah, in 1850; and a grandfather had ridden west with Brigham Young. Now he teamed up with Ray Pinker in a new, intellectual kind of pioneering, the completion of Welsh's work; and through the years, till Lieutenant Lee Jones' recent retirement at the age of sixty-one, Pinker and Jones were the most formidable pair of scientific policemen in America.

Against the stubborn skepticism of the old-time detectives, plus a few horse laughs at their creaky microscope and smelly chemicals, Pinker and Jones proved that *their* evidence – a speck of dirt or a tiny seed caught on shoe or trouser leg – would incriminate or eliminate a suspect.

It was hard for the policeman to understand, but they patiently demonstrated that no dirt is the same and every seed in the world is different. Hence, if a suspect carried scrapings which were similar to those found at the scene of the crime, he must have been there.

Nothing in this world, they taught, is found in exact duplication – not even two billiard balls. Why, if you could blow up a billiard ball to the size of the earth, there would be the same great peaks and valleys, mountains higher than Everest and depths greater than the seven-mile Marianas Trench in the Pacific Ocean. No indeed, no two objects are alike. Not even your own two front teeth.

The chances of fingerprint duplication, they preached, are one in a billion, and though there are more than two and a half billion persons on this earth, no one person has ever been found to duplicate another person in all physical characteristics. Or take two guns, the same calibre, the same shape, the same manufacturer, and yet the striations on the bullets will be distinguishable.

From being a dabbler in fingerprints, Lieutenant Jones made himself into one of the world's master criminalists. With a scientific third degree, he made the physical evidence talk and wrung confessions from blood, guns, narcotics, hair, fibers, metal slivers, tire marks, tool marks, bullets.

From the two-man team of Pinker and Jones, the Scientific Investigation Division grew into a sixty-seven technician operation. From a cubbyhole equipped with little more than a boy's chemistry set, it expanded into a million-dollar laboratory which occupies an entire floor in the new LAPD Administration Building. Here are ovens, furnaces, steam baths, balances, centrifuges, autoclaves, and electronic measuring devices.

As science has progressed, SID has kept pace, making new applications of new discoveries to its specialized field. In ballistics, it devised a better test mechanism, a water-filled steel tank, to improve the quality of the striations.

From simple photography at the scene of the crime, SID went on to use three-dimensional film and later motion picture photography for reenactments. The spectrograph was trained on the study of specimens of soil, glass, paints; and then SID delved deeper into the spectrum with the use of ultraviolet and infrared spectrophotometers for refined identification of organic substances.

But always you come back to crime – and conviction.

At 9 a.m. one day, the body of Jane Doe, head crushed by a blunt instrument, was deposited in the Los Angeles County morgue. The body had been found lying in blood-soaked grass near a tree in a lovers' lane, and the superficial evidence indicated that she had been taken to the lonely spot, possibly by force, then raped and bludgeoned. Almost the only hard evidence was a cardboard strip under the body on which a man's heelprint had been imprinted in blood.

That night, Paul Degley, a shipyard worker, reported that his wife, Charlene, was missing. At 7 a.m., he explained, she had driven him to the job, but when he got home, she was missing, and that just wasn't like Charlene. Police took him to the morgue, and he identified Jane Doe as his wife.

In the hopes of getting some lead on the killer, detectives sympathetically questioned the widower at the Degleys' little frame house. But as they talked, their eyes took in several things which made them feel considerably less sympathetic.

On the back door, they noticed, there were curtain rods but no curtains, and Lieutenant Jones had earlier removed a curtain strand from the dead woman's hair. On a radiator he spotted a wisp of female hair, and he noticed a large patch of floor near the back door which seemed to have been mopped recently. When it was tested for bloodstains, the reaction was positive. There was dried blood on the legs of a table, bloodstains in the kitchen sink, on a light switch, and on a towel which had apparently been used to mop up blood.

The woman obviously had been killed in her own home, but had her husband done it?

Next, Degley's car was examined, and the tread of one tire matched a track near the spot where the body had been found. Wild oats similar to those growing at the scene were caught in one of the car doors. Degley's car obviously had been used to transport the body, but had he been the driver?

The circumstantial evidence against him mounted. Neighbors told detectives of his quick temper. The night before, one of them said, she had heard screams about eleven o'clock and had looked out her bathroom window. She saw the lights go out suddenly in the Degley house.

When Degley's clothing was tested, one of his shoes gave a slight reaction indicating bloodstains. When the Coroner examined the body, he estimated the woman had been already dead for nine hours at the time it was found. Hence, she could not have driven him to the shipyard that morning, as he claimed.

But even though he was arrested for murder, Degley stubbornly denied any knowledge of his wife's death. Homicide detectives were certain that he had killed her in the house, taken her body to the lovers' lane in his car and there arranged it to indicate she had been raped. But they couldn't put him at the scene. All their evidence, hard and circumstantial, stopped just short of this convincer.

In court, Degley's lawyer conceded one important point. The heelprint on the piece of cardboard found under the victim's body had been left by the killer. He conceded that much, but he challenged the prosecution to prove that the print had been made by Degley's shoe.

It looked like a safe challenge. The heel had picked up only a little blood from the stained grass, and only part of the heel was imprinted on the cardboard. Besides, the cardboard had been creased, and this crease mark, too, would have to be matched into the print.

In the next three days, working against a courtroom deadline, Lieutenant Jones made many exemplars of the heels on Degley's shoes. Then he recreated everything: the amount of blood, the precise weight of the cardboard, even the pressure applied by the heel to the paper.

Under magnification, he spotted the damning bit of evidence. On the heel of Degley's shoe and on the cardboard print, there was one minute chip. He made a three-dimensional photograph of heel and print which was submitted as evidence in court. No other heel in the world could have stamped that particular mark on the cardboard, Jones testified.

The minute chip convicted Degley, and he was sentenced to life imprisonment for second degree murder.

When Jo-Jo met the flaming redhead in the green slacks, and he met her only once in his life, there was a touch of mocking predestination in the encounter. It seemed almost as if some irresponsible pagan god had deliberately thrown them together, saying to himself, 'Let's see what these poor human fools do now.'

In the first place, there was only that one night in the year when Jo-Jo could have met her. For ten years, Irene Beach had been happily married; and, by agreement with her husband, there was just one day, out of all 365 days, that she left home alone for fun and freedom.

But it wasn't quite what it sounded. At thirty, Irene was discreet, and she spent her twenty-four-hour holiday each year with the same girl friend. They drank a little, danced a lot, had some laughs and then went home.

Any other night, Jo-Jo would have looked in vain for a redhead in green slacks. As it was, he almost missed her. In his amiable, not very bright way, he was looking for a pickup and usually when he was on the petticoat prowl, he hit one downtown bar after another. This night, he stayed five minutes too long at one place, and then Irene came in.

Probably he amused her. Jo-Jo, listed on his Social Security card as Joseph Anthony Gowder, labored faithfully as a factory hand. What concentration his slow mind could muster was dedicated to the pursuit and capture of acquiescent girls, and he fancied himself as a bit of a poor man's boulevardier. He was dark, handsome, curly-haired and hard-muscled, a veteran of many cheap conquests – till he met Irene. She may have done the unforgivable. She may have laughed at him.

At any rate, as it was remembered later, they were together at the jukebox and later calling each other 'Irene' and 'Jo-Jo.' And that was all anybody could remember.

The next morning, a white collar worker hurrying to the office saw Irene Beach's body in her car parked down a side street in the industrial section of the city. She had been brutally beaten and then strangled sometime between midnight and two a.m.

Through the car ownership, she was quickly identified; and, when the story appeared in the newspapers, an informant telephoned police to give them the name of the bar she had visited. There, the owner remembered her having been with Jo-Jo and supplied his name.

On the blood-drenched front seat of the car, where the body was found, the Crime Lab technicians isolated Type A blood. On the back seat, so tiny they might have been missed, were several spots of Type B blood. Hence, the investigators deduced, Irene and her killer had first been in the rear seat, and there she had probably cut or scratched her molester. Then she had been dragged up

118

front where her blood, Type A, was so plentifully spilled.

Of all the principals in the mystery, only Jo-Jo proved to have Type B blood, and in addition his left arm was raked with deep and ragged teeth marks. He insisted he had received them a week previously at a beach party, but doctors judged they had been inflicted not more than forty-eight hours earlier.

In the face of Jo-Jo's dogged denials that he knew anything about Irene's murder, the strong circumstantial case didn't seem quite strong enough. Then Lieutenant Lee Jones' photographic crew photographed the bite marks on Jo-Jo's arm and the teeth of the dead woman. Blowups of the photographs disclosed that the teeth perfectly matched the wounds.

Jo-Jo was sentenced to life imprisonment for second degree murder.

The way tragedy strikes, it happened and was over in half a minute. The young waitress was late for a date that spring afternoon and hurried carelessly across the street. The motorist was in a hurry, too. When the girl saw the car bearing down on her, she leaned forward as though to ward off the blow. The car struck her and sped off, leaving her crumpled in agony in the gutter. She died that night.

Depending on which eyewitness they talked to, detectives established that the car was blue or green; a sedan or a coupe; traveling at either twenty or sixty miles an hour. No one had obtained the license number, and there was not a tire mark or headlamp splinter at the scene. The car had simply vanished.

Somewhere in Los Angeles, the detectives guessed, there must be a car with a dented fender. Undoubtedly thousands of them. But it was the only lead they had, so the AID cars in all districts distributed bulletins on the case to body and fender shops.

Late that same day, a garage in East Los Angeles reported back to Headquarters. A green sedan with a dented left fender had just come in. The owner was insistent on a quick repair job because, he said, he had to leave town the same night on business.

With the detectives, Lieutenant Lee Jones rolled immediately to the garage. He picked the sedan clean, then went over it a second time. There was nothing: no hair, no torn bit of clothing, no bloodstains. Then he studied the dented fender with microscopic care. Almost concealed in the dent itself was the perfect imprint of a woman's lip.

Jones called for a latent print expert, dispatched a second expert to the morgue – and set a criminological precedent. The lip impressions were taken both from the fender and from the body in the morgue, photographed, and blown up for comparison.

On the two sets, Jones found fourteen common, identifying marks in the form of creases, and the little waitress' pathetic kiss of death was sufficiently strong to support a felony manslaughter complaint against the hit-run driver. He was subsequently convicted and sentenced.

'It was the first time I had ever seen a lip print on a car in a hit-run case,' Jones says. 'And it was the first time we had ever tried to get a lip impression from a body. But each set of lips has its own characteristics, which are as identifiable as fingerprints.'

Since justice is a two-way street, SID is just as satisfied with the exoneration of the innocent as the conviction of the guilty.

On one occasion, a suspect was waiting trial for four wanton murders in a series of cocktail bar stickups. The case against him had been nailed tight by six eyewitnesses who had heard him speak and seen him shoot. In build and dress even to his hat, they swore, they knew this was the man.

Shortly before his trial, a lone holdup man knocked over a service station in south Los Angeles, shooting one employee and escaping with a batch of pay checks. A police alarm alerted all banks and check-cashing agencies.

Two days later, when a man presented one of the checks at a cashing establishment, the teller managed to stall him till the cops arrived. A quick search disclosed that he was toting a .38-calibre pistol in a paper bag, and the gun was turned over to the Crime Lab for routine analysis.

Sergeant Russ Camp fired several rounds into the Lab's water-filled ballistics tank, obtaining slugs with clear, strong striations.

Then the constant every-hour routine of check and crosscheck. He compared them under the microscope with the slugs taken from the bodies of the murder victims. He straightened up hurriedly and called Lee Jones on the intercom.

Jones studied the comparative specimens. 'It's a make,' he told Camp. 'All the bullets are from the same gun – the one that killed the bar victims.'

'I know that,' Camp protested. 'But we already have that guy!'

'Have we?' Jones asked quietly.

The new suspect denied any knowledge of the four murders. Why, he said, he had bought this gun legitimately in Temple City through a newspaper advertisement. Detectives located the seller, and he recalled the sale had been before the first murder. Thereafter, police proved, the buyer had kept possession of the gun, never lending it to anyone.

It was one of those flukes of mistaken identity which happen so rarely in real-life police work. Both suspects had the same builds and same facial features, the same

121

taste in clothing even to hats. But the second man was the killer, and the original suspect was freed.

Suppose *you* are in that nightmarish situation beloved by detective fiction writers. The net of circumstantial evidence has closed around you. Nobody believes your rather improbable story, so you demand the lie detector test. What happens then?

For twenty-four hours beforehand, almost as though you were being prepared for a major operation, you must get a normal amount of food and sleep. You should not be under the influence of alcohol, or suffering any physical pain. Severe respiratory trouble such as asthma or even a bad cold will disqualify you.

Once you pass your physical, you are placed in a chair and the measuring apparatus is fastened around your midsection and one arm and on the tips of two fingers. Thereafter, unless you are mentally deficient or extremely phlegmatic, the lie detector will record tell-tale changes in your blood pressure, the tempo of your heartbeat, your breathing and your skin resistance set up by sweat gland activity. These changes, which indicate your reaction to key questions, will be translated into squiggly lines on a chart by a moving recording pen.

You are accused of having pulled a holdup at a down-town Los Angeles jewelry store, and the detectives who have arrested you are standing silent near the polygraph, or lie-detector machine. Lieutenant George Puddy, an expert, is conducting the interrogation.

'Do you know if a .32-calibre gun was used?' he asks.

'No,' you say. There is no reaction on the polygraph chart.

'Do you know if a .38-calibre gun was used?'

'No.' Again there is no reaction.

'Do you know if a .45-calibre gun was used?'

'No.'

But this time the needle swerves sharply on the polygraph, and you have given yourself away. You *are* lying! After the holdup, the detectives had found a .45-calibre Colt outside the store. Despite all your denials, you must have guilty knowledge of the holdup.

No one ever is compelled to take the lie detector test. Though an experienced operator like Lieutenant Puddy will achieve remarkable accuracy in his findings, SID admits the polygraph has its limitations. In fact, a memo to departmental personnel on its use warns:

'Lie detector tests are not a substitute for a thorough preliminary investigation. Such examinations should be regarded as a supplement to a thorough and complete investigation.'

But, in confirming police hunches, in sometimes obtaining confessions which could be corroborated by independent evidence, in subjecting the guilty to a new mental hazard, the polygraph has been an invaluable tool. Sometimes, for clarification, victims and witnesses as well as suspects are subjected to the tests with their permission. These are always done with the knowledge of the Detective Bureau commander.

In LAPD, the lie detector was originally accepted with considerable scientific reserve. Its findings were not admissible as court evidence, and the Crime Lab admired its potentialities rather than its immediate prospects. Then at the end of World War II, Lieutenant Puddy returned to the department after making an outstanding record as an Air Force Combat Intelligence officer in the South Pacific. He had become an expert in the use of the lie detector and was immediately assigned to LAPD's polygraph detail.

In the years since, Puddy has refined the techniques for processing Polygraph subjects, improved the methods of interrogation and established more accurate standards for weighing the results. He has found that some individuals are not 'reactors,' that the best tests are made early during the police investigation, that prolonged questioning may exhaust or embitter the subject. Curiously, he has also discovered, the more intelligent the subject the less his chance of beating the machine.

Most curious of all, the guilty who are struggling with their consciences sometimes demand the test, subconsciously recognizing that this is a convenient preliminary toward facing up to confession. Perhaps that is why *you* insisted on the lie detector when you were being questioned about the jewelry store holdup.

Neighbors who heard the children crying discovered the murder. In the living room, the body of the young mother clad in a housecoat was slumped in an easy chair, a butcher knife through her chest. The three-year-old was trying to rouse her.

Obviously, someone who knew her must have taken her by surprise. There were no signs of a struggle, and the ash tray had not even been knocked off the arm of the chair in which the dead woman sat. But after four months of investigation, the sheriff's deputies of Kern County were at a standstill.

The victim's husband, an Air Force sergeant based near Sacramento, had been cleared through a lie detector test. Various neighbors in the little town of Oildale where the murder took place had been investigated without result.

Then the wife of Vinal Paul Carl reported to the authorities that in recent weeks he had been acting peculiarly. Carl had been among the neighbors who were interrogated and had produced a seemingly ironclad alibi. The authorities were skeptical of his wife's story, especially when she added that she had found a book of matches with the victim's name written inside.

'When did you find the matches?' a deputy asked.

'About a week after the murder,' she said.

'Why did you wait so long, almost four months?'

'It crossed my mind, but at first I didn't think much about it. I knew Paul knew where she lived. Then there was the investigation and, I guess, in the excitement I forgot. But lately he's been talking a lot about a lie detector test. He was wondering whether, if they found out he was lying, that could be used in a trial.'

The Kern County men picked up Carl and decided to give him what he apparently most dreaded – a polygraph examination. Lieutenant Puddy, who handled the interrogation for the sheriff's deputies, was convinced that the lie detector test showed Carl's guilt. But on Puddy's advice, the suspect was allowed to return home for the weekend on his agreement to return for additional tests the following Monday.

'You either know who caused the death, or you caused it yourself,' he was told bluntly as he departed. Puddy wanted the delay so Carl's fears would work on him. And, sure enough, first thing the next Monday, he blurted: 'I know who did it. My conscience has been bothering me terribly.'

It was his own father-in-law, he said. By chance, he had followed the older man on the night of the murder and seen him go into the victim's house. Puddy was dissatisfied. He got the father-in-law to consent to the polygraph test, and it was immediately obvious that he knew nothing of the slaying.

Carl was then re-tested, and the shaking polygraph needle made it clearer than ever that he was guilty. When police suggested a confrontation with the father-in-law, he broke and admitted the killing. But he was still lying. He tried to put the blame on the dead woman, saying that she had threatened to expose his infidelity, and that in

125

a struggle, she had been accidentally stabbed. A re-enactment showed that this story, too, was fiction. He finally admitted he had killed the housewife when she rejected his advances.*

Despite his many evasions, Lieutenant Puddy is convinced that Carl had wanted to be caught and had welcomed the lie detector tests. 'There is an inner writhing that must be quieted,' the lieutenant explains. 'We want to quiet it for them. At this stage, it's about all we can do to help them.'

There was one occasion when Puddy was rather worried about his beloved machine.

A Los Angeles jewelry firm had been robbed of $20,000; and, since entry had been made without tripping the burglar alarm, the owner was convinced it was an inside job.

One after another, Puddy patiently interrogated all forty employees without once making his needle jump. The only conclusion was that an outsider had beaten the alarm system, which seemed impossible, or that one of the forty had beaten the polygraph.

To Puddy, this also seemed impossible, but for two weeks the lie detector was under a cloud as far as everyone else in LAPD was concerned. And then in Arizona the thieves were seized with the loot. It turned out that one was a former employee of the firm and thus had known how to slip in through a skylight without setting off the alarm.

Although he hadn't cracked it, that case gave Lieutenant Puddy a great deal of satisfaction.

---

*Vinal Paul Carl pleaded guilty to first-degree murder, and was sentenced to life imprisonment without possibility of parole.

Charley Pellanda's great ambition in life was to qualify himself as a faith healer, and his mentor, Rachel (Butterfly) Uwanawich, assured him that his prospects were highly promising. But finally Charley came to the searching last test, which a less dedicated man could scarcely have passed.

As proof of his faith, Charley had to produce his life savings in the form of cash. The money was wrapped into a package and handed back to him.

'Take this out onto the sea,' the novice healer was instructed. 'Cast it into the sea. This way alone can you dedicate your inner self and join the sanctified and mystic order of the faith healer.'

Charley blinked but obeyed. Out in the open water between Los Angeles and Catalina Island, he yielded to a momentary nostalgia – because, after all, $21,500 is a lot of money – and peeked for a last time at the nest egg he was sacrificing.

It wasn't there. The package contained bundles of paper scissored to the size of greenbacks.

Immediately, Charley put about and returned to confront The Butterfly. More in sorrow at the loss of a promising disciple than resentment over his charges, she persuaded Charley that he needed rest in a hospital.

Charley agreed – till he found himself in the Camarillo State Hospital for the mentally ill near Los Angeles. Relatives sprung him, and he came to LAPD's seventeen-man Bunco Squad with his story of faith and disillusion.

The Bunco cops, recognizing an interesting professional variation on the old Mexican charity switch, promised to help Charley get back at least part of his money.*

*Rachel Uwanawich (Rose Wayne) was sentenced for grand theft.

Because so many retired persons cluster in southern California, Los Angeles is the national capital of the con man, and the marriage and religious bunks are almost a city industry. There are also 'doctors,' 'professors' and 'noblemen' who prey on hope, senility, and ignorance and those despicable practitioners of the 'fruit shake.' The latter, posing as policemen, threaten to 'arrest' homosexuals unless they are paid off.

To meet fraud with enforcement, the Bunco Squad is subdivided into teams of experts. One wars on the marriage bunks and social clubs, along with borrowing, short-change and auction rackets. Business bunks require a team of their own, while a third subsquad investigates false advertising, rental bunks and repair rackets.

In stores, streets, and theaters, another team quietly watches for touts, impersonators and similar phonies who dare to work openly. Finally, though you would think such grifts died with the Old West, Buncomen are still breaking up rigged coin games, three-card monte, and 'solid gold brick' sales.

Unlike most detective squads, the Bunco sleuths rarely use LAPD's elaborate IBM procedure to detect criminal M.O. Whether it's the Texas 'Atomotrone' (a $30 gadget supposedly efficacious in treatment of some 87 diseases) or the Denver 'tubeless radio' (a pocket-sized radio which would require a one-hundred-foot antenna), the squad keeps track of con games being pulled all over the country. Flimflam artists who have been run out of other states often relocate in Los Angeles; and the Bunco squad is ready and waiting with fat files on their M.O.s.

The game may be as petty as 'Dr.' John E. O'Malley's $5 street pitch, or as grandiose as H. C. Mills' $1,000,000 stock mining swindles. Bunco Division is impartial in enforcing the fraud laws.

The 'doctor,' who usually identified himself as a

Philippine physician, would approach the innocent on the street with a canning jar in his hand. 'I have a dangerous bug in this bottle,' he would say impressively. 'I *must* get to Stanford University at once in the interests of science! Can you lend me $5 for bus fare?' For $5, very few persons want to delay scientific progress, and the 'doctor' lived comfortably on his modest grift till the Bunco Squad checked his academic background. O'Malley was a graduate only of several state and federal prisons.*

Homer Cecil Mills, the sixty-seven-year-old gray flannel king of the mining stock swindlers, was a more formidable opponent. A disbarred lawyer who had done time for forgery, he knew every legal trick in the book and despite numerous actions by government agencies, he operated successfully for ten years.

Once, in fact, for thirty days, he singlehandedly stood off an entire battery of U.S. attorneys trying to pin a federal rap on him in the Chicago area. Afterward, he even sold his stock to some members of the jury which had acquitted him, according to the pained scuttlebutt which reached Los Angeles.

Bunco first heard of him through an anonymous tip that he had transferred his operations to a downtown Los Angeles hotel. He hooked his suckers through ads in the 'Business Opportunities' columns of leading papers in Los Angeles and a number of other large cities. He landed them in his hotel suite, a glittering sucker trap adorned with strange mining gadgets, specimens of uranium ore and sacks of gold dust. For the few doubting Thomases, he arranged personal inspections of his Nevada mine which was thoughtfully 'salted' in advance with specimens of high-yield ore.

Lieutenant W. C. Hull was LAPD's specialist on

*O'Malley was convicted and sentenced in February, 1956.

schemes involving corporate securities. He had been a detective for a dozen years, including five years in the crack Intelligence Division. But he knew that Mills was going to be the slipperiest challenge of his career. He began to amass his facts.

Mills was promoting the Blossom Mine, a supposedly rich uranium field at Searchlight, Nevada, which actually had once yielded a rich ore strike. But now, Hull determined, it was a washed-up hole, and furthermore Mills didn't have clear title or interest in the property. Posing as an investor in from Seattle, the detective phoned for an appointment, and the affable Mills granted him one the same day.

Thereafter, for almost three weeks, they met daily. As he lavishly entertained his new pigeon, Mills outlined a stock offer only a fool would turn down.

For $3,000, Hull could pick up 30,000 shares of Blossom at ten cents a share with the promise of ten per cent of all the revenue derived from the delivery of the uranium ore to a smelting company. Why, Mills indicated, he should double his money within a year!

Thus persuaded, Bunco Lieutenant Hull and his 'wife,' Madaleine Asdel, a civilian secretary in the division, visited Mills' hotel suite with a bank cashier's check for $3,000. Mills told him he had come just in time. A $4,000 ore shipment was then on its way to the smelter and a $10,000 shipment was scheduled to follow the next month. He showed him an assay report valuing the ore at $326.48 a ton.

While Hull scanned the report, Mills examined the cashier's check and accepted it. Almost as an afterthought, Hull said, 'Here's my business card.' He showed Mills his police identification and arrested him.

Search of Mills' files disclosed that more than two hundred persons, mostly pensioners and retired couples, as it turned out, had similarly invested and lost their life's savings. LAPD estimated that investors throughout the country had been taken for at least $1,000,000 since the Los Angeles victims alone contributed more than $600,000.

LAPD filed fourteen counts of conspiracy and theft against Mills, but the wily ex-lawyer got thirteen of them dismissed on the grounds that the police had illegally searched his hotel files and seized his mineral specimens, stock certificates, sucker lists and other documents. One charge, his stock sale to Lieutenant Hull, stuck. He was sentenced to a term of one to ten years in state prison.

Still he wasn't through. He appealed to the California State Supreme Court and after a turndown there, went to the United States Supreme Court, where his case is pending.

Nor did he for a moment lose the aplomb that had made him one of the master salesmen of his time. Frankly, he advised Bunco Captain Harry Didion, the police would have been smarter to invest rather than arrest. Didion and Hull passed.

Once his testimony had been given, Lieutenant Hull plunged immediately into another case; for the war against the bunks is unending, and a stiff note on the Squad Room bulletin board reminds the detectives:

'All officers work mornings and nights when necessary and are subject to call from Detective Headquarters, and must give the case at issue immediate and proper attention.'

III

A thoughtful, scholarly cop, an authority on labor problems, an expert on the intricacies of leftwing politics throughout the country, Lieutenant (now Captain) Joseph E. Stephens holds down an improbable assignment in LAPD. He commands the expendables, the commando cops, the suicide squad of seventy policemen, two lieutenants and eight sergeants known officially as the Metropolitan Division.

A Policeman in the Harbor Division may never see duty in San Fernando Valley, some forty miles to the north, and a Robbery detective sensibly leaves murders to the Homicide Squad. A Bunco man cares nothing about traffic problems.

But Metro, the small, tough, mobile force of super-specialists, is all over the place, geographically and procedurally. On loan-out assignments, they work a month in each division, communications, forgery, vice, scientific investigation; and there isn't a phase of police know-how in which they do not excel.

Shotgun handling . . . Stakeouts . . . Picket line duty . . . Traffic control . . . Riot work . . . Walkie-talkie . . . Chemical agents . . . When to shoot. . . .

Metro is the rolling force that is thrown in for the kill after routine procedures have failed. Once, in considerable annoyance, a Metro squad spent 200 man-days disguised as women to find one rapist. They got him.

Another time, four Metromen staked out an alley for seven nights to catch 'The Eel,' who had successfully made eleven raids on a garment shop located five stories up in the loft of a building. Finally, they spotted a five-foot, one hundred-pound wisp of a man sneaking into the alley with a long rope.

They challenged him, and he fired. They fired back. They got him.

Every crime report in LAPD bears a number assigned by the Division of Records, but it is Metro's DR numbers that make some of the best reading. On holdup stakeouts, they

132

shoot it out with trigger-happy stickup men. On night watch, they sometimes double as firemen till the apparatus arrives, evacuating the young, the aged, the frightened. And sometimes, but not too often, because courage is expected of them anyhow, there is the award of the precious round medal which says, 'Los Angeles Police Department – For VALOR.'

For months a daylight burglar had been making life miserable for the Central Division. Little by little, as he pulled seventy-five jobs, detectives put together a composite picture from what witnesses could tell them.

Dapper, personable, about thirty-five to forty-five years old, he carried a briefcase and walked and talked like a successful salesman. He stole only cash and small valuables which could be stuffed into the briefcase. In a few minutes, he was in and out of an apartment building and then lost on the street among dozens of other prosperous-looking salesmen.

In fact, the police knew practically everything about him, except who he was and where he would strike next. And that was when Metro was called in.

First, Metro detectives analyzed a map of the section where he operated. From his pattern they picked out the area of a few blocks which he probably would visit that same day. Then Lieutenant Stephens blanketed the pocket of less than a square mile with ten two-man teams.

From cars and doorways, on street corners and in front of stores, the stakeout waited patiently, unobtrusively hour after hour. Then late in the afternoon, an affluent-seeming gentleman with a briefcase stepped briskly from an apartment building on a small side street. Two Metro men jumped him before he could fight or run. It was a nice, clean take.

LAPD hit him with seventy-five burglary charges, and

then San Francisco, Portland and Seattle police said they'd like whacks at him, too, for a total of more than three hundred burglaries in their cities.

To Metro, it had been a real pro job. The street on which he was grabbed was so narrow you might miss it at a fast walk, but it was just about dead center of the area which the Metro detectives had marked off on the map with their prophetic slide rules.

When Joe Stephens took command of Metro in 1950, he had a double mess on his hands. Morale and work output were low, and the division was the unwanted orphan of LAPD. By wangling better equipment and assignments for his men, by delivering pep talks and dressings down with equal fervor, by selling departmental brass on the theory that Metro could do anything any time anywhere, he lifted his division by its bootstraps. Today, there is a waiting list of almost two hundred policemen who want to transfer to Metro.

But that was only half of his problem in 1950. A major assignment of the division is the policing of labor disputes; and labor hated the cop. To the union card carrier, he was just the boss' bully boy who broke up picket lines with a night stick.

For sixty years, Los Angeles had suffered stormy and often bloody labor relations. A typographers' strike against the Los Angeles *Times* in 1890 left a twenty-year legacy of walkouts and lockouts in various business fields which finally exploded in tragedy.

In 1910 the Los Angeles City Council made labor history with an ordinance which barred labor picketing. Within a few weeks, almost five hundred union members were arrested; and then, at 1 a.m. that October 1, the Los Angeles *Times* was dynamited. Twenty employees were killed in the blast and fire, and the building was leveled.

The two McNamara brothers, Jimmy, a member of the Typographers' Union, and Joe, secretary of the Structural Iron Workers, were named as the brains in a nationwide bombing conspiracy. For fourteen months, Clarence Darrow conducted a skillful defense and then, in a maneuver to save their lives, had them switch to guilty pleas. Jimmy got life and Joe was sentenced to fifteen years.

For years afterward, the bombing outrage poisoned labor relations in Los Angeles, and LAPD was aligned always with the anti-labor faction, the unionists felt. Before and after World War II, as the area increasingly industrialized with aircraft and auto assembly lines, rubber and oil, labor's hostility to the cop deepened. They said he wasn't much more than the boss' private guard in a public uniform, and since Metro handled labor details, it was Metro that labor particularly hated.

Joe Stephens was probably the only man in LAPD who could have straightened out this dangerous division between the working man and the policeman.

All during the war he had worked on the subversive detail and afterwards he helped southern California labor leaders eliminate communism from their ranks. In public and private, he moved with the Left, and in addition to pinkos, phonies and deep Reds, he met many sincere labor leaders. He learned to talk their language and he became sensitive to their problems. They trusted him as a sympathetic outsider.

When interim Police Chief William A. Worton assigned him to Metro, Stephens promptly called together the top labor men of Los Angeles. The Division would continue to police disputes, but he promised a one-word slogan for his men – *impartiality*. They would side neither with management nor with labor. He told them of his own abhorrence of stick-swinging on picket lines, and pleaded for their support in restraining their own men. Trusting him, they gave it.

Today, as the third largest industrial area in the nation, Los Angeles has almost 800,000 union members. Yet, a Metro survey showed, during one recent year only six of thirty-five strikes in the city itself necessitated uniformed police patrols. These cost the city 202 man-days, an all-time low.

Impartiality has been paying off.

Under Lieutenant Stephens, Metro's labor specialists watch vigilantly for any indication of labor racketeering. They record all attempts to organize factories and businesses and analyze inter-union strife. Though they maintain a hands-off policy on purely union affairs, they know what is going on so they can step in quickly if the union itself doesn't keep a clean house.

On one occasion, Metro was deeply concerned with the organization of coinbox operators through a local of the International Brotherhood of Electrical Workers. Practically all factories in Los Angeles have coin-operated coffee and cigarette machines for the convenience of their workers. Since the president of the IBEW local was an important man in the factories' labor relations, he would be in a strategic position to force acceptance of his coinbox operators and exclusion of non-members. While LAPD was investigating, IBEW's international union quietly lifted the charter of the local, and the coinbox scheme collapsed.

But rarely is the solution that simple. Joe Stephens devoted two years of his life to another investigation which paid off with only a single indictment. And yet the probe gave the taxpayers a two-year respite which saved them from a small but nasty racket.

The first tipoff came from a woman, one of the

thousand independent rubbish collectors in Los Angeles, who operated a little one-truck business in San Fernando Valley. Almost apologetically, she wrote to the City Council that she was being 'pushed around' because she wouldn't buy protection from a collection association, and shouldn't City Hall know about this?

Together, Joe Stephens of Metro and Captain Hamilton of Intelligence dug into her complaint. They visited the offices of various rubbish collectors' associations, checked on a local of the Teamsters Union and talked to the frightened small operators.

By the simple device of grabbing control of the city dumps, the detectives found, association men were putting the squeeze on the little fellows. If they couldn't find a place to unload their trash, they were simply out of business.

From William L. Crowder, an independent, who collected rubbish from 1,250 homes in San Fernando Valley, Stephens got names and places. Crowder had been barred from his customary dump because he wasn't a union member. He visited the Teamster local involved, paid a $25 fee and then was referred to one of the rubbish associations to 'get squared away with them.'

Here he was told that he would have to pay an initiation fee, which usually ran into hundreds of dollars, and additionally give up half his clients to other members of the association. When he refused, he said, his trucks were blackballed at all the dozen dumps in the city.

Another little man, Daniel A. Rosati, said he had been subjected to intimidation and sabotage when he tried to resist 'organization.' Finally, in return for his personal safety, he said, he was forced to 'sell' his $8,000 worth of assets for $1,300. He was ordered to pay a $250 initiation, $500 to the rubbish men's lobby fund at the state capital, and waive his thriving collection area in favor of a marginal zone. ' "I am at your mercy," I told them,' he later related to the police. ' "I concede defeat." '

The Stephens-Hamilton combine was particularly concerned because the Los Angeles County Board of Supervisors had set a deadline to end all rubbish burning in backyard incinerators. The praiseworthy purpose was smog elimination, but the practical result would have been deliverance of the city taxpayers to the 'organized' rubbish collectors.

When the Board of Supervisors persisted in its plan, Mayor Norris Poulson appealed to the public. He charged that not only was there a monopoly in rubbish pickups but also that crimes were being committed to perpetuate that monopoly. When a grand jury investigated, Lieutenant Stephens and Captain Hamilton gave detailed substantiation to the charges.

Dissatisfied with the pace of the grand jury investigation, Mayor Poulson launched his own probe under a rarely invoked section of the City Charter. Again LAPD came through, producing a taped telephone conversation in which one of the rubbish syndicate leaders had bragged:

'. . . We'll break the Mayor if he gets in our way. . . . If he tries to legislate us out of business, we'll put him out of office!'

After that, the State Legislature had to dispatch its own investigating committee to Los Angeles. The legislators found the situation was exactly as LAPD had pictured it. Of those questioned, the only casualty was a Teamsters' official later convicted of perjury, and he promptly appealed.

Offhand, this might not seem productive police work after two years of investigation. But LAPD had fought a delaying action for the backyard incinerators and given its Mayor time to establish a municipal rubbish pickup system.

THE CAPTAIN

At Los Angeles International Airport, the swarthy man with the expensive luggage shoulders ahead of his fellow passengers who have just arrived from Chicago. He nods brusquely to a waiting character who takes his bags. A man in plainclothes joins them.

'Eddie Vance?'

'So?'

'Police officer.'

The swarthy airport *arrivé* scowls. But the plainclothes-man persists.

'There's a plane taking off for Chicago in an hour. Be on it, Eddie.'

'What for? I'm clean, copper.'

'That's not what our files say, Eddie.'

'Files! Listen, you, I'm a businessman. I got nothing to be afraid of.'

'You're a celebrity, Eddie, not a businessman. You got a big name. The kind the newspapers might like to get hold of – in Chicago as well as Los Angeles. Now whadda ya' say?'

The swarthy gent winces.

'Okay, pal. You win.'

He crosses the waiting room to the ticket counter.

Ordinarily, hoodlums aren't thin-skinned, but beginning in the early 1950's, LAPD detected a major shift in nationwide underworld activity. The rackets bosses had decided to go respectable. Some openly, some through stooges, they invested heavily in manufacturing, oil, and a variety of wholesale and retail businesses. Publicity could be ruinous, and Intelligence decided that mere exposure in newspaper headlines might keep the out-of-town racketeers out of town. The policy has succeeded handsomely.

In the decade before Intelligence was organized, there had been some eight gang bumpoffs, Chicago style, and LAPD feared that organized crime was getting a foothold in Los Angeles.

In every case, promising suspects were seized, but all had air-tight alibis. Against the underworld clam-ups, detectives were powerless.

Then, with the organization of the Intelligence Division, LAPD went over to the attack. Instead of the futile, 'pinch-'em-and-sweat-'em' tactics of the past, its thirty-seven men were charged with collecting every scrap of information about the workings of organized crime. The approach, based on the military G-2 system, meant that investigations would get underway *before* the violence erupted.

Offhand, Jim Hamilton, the new commander, was no gangbuster. He came from rural stock. His father had been born on a wagon train fourteen days out of Salt Lake City, and his mother lived all her life in the little San Joaquin Valley town of Lathrop. Jim's first job was as an accountant in the State Controller's office. He transferred to LAPD in the mid-1930's because policemen got $170 monthly compared to an accountant's $132.

But Hamilton had three special qualifications for the job. He kept busy, planning and moving all the time. He knew how to pick men of close-mouthed integrity because in Intelligence the security of the entire operation would rest on each one of his thirty-seven detectives. And he had the vision to see the almost frightening scope of his new assignment and draft the only possible counter-attack:

'There is a criminal army in the United States, well-organized, disciplined, with its own laws, courts, and executioners. It is nationwide in operation and control. It is a government within a government, levying a sometimes hidden but heavy tax upon all citizens.

'The carefully selected and trained members of this inner circle operate in the twilight zone of quasi-legality. They plan, direct and reap the profits from crime but seldom perform violent criminal acts themselves.

'Effective action against the disciplined regulars of organized crime requires specialized methods. As with any subversive element, it can be combatted best by highly trained intelligence agents who operate through information, infiltration, and surveillance.'

The first thing Intelligence did was to assemble, from dozens of sources, its own *Who's Who of U.S. Crime*. Detailed case histories running into thousands spelled out the hoodlums' backgrounds and connections, their daily associations with other hoods, their hangouts, their businesses, the brand of toothpaste they used. From other LAPD units, from newspapers and from out-of-state law enforcement agencies, each dossier was fleshed out periodically with notations of current activities.

This growing, changing file which the underworld would gladly buy for $1,000,000 is secured in a ceiling-to-floor safe made of heavy steel and always under guard of Intelligence detectives.

In other ways, too, LAPD's Intelligence men continued the drive toward the prevention of big, organized crime. They saw to it that word got out to other cities that Los Angeles was a 'hot town' for alien hoods. And locally, they followed the individual, rather than the crime.

At the first false step, Intelligence tipped off Robbery or

Homicide, and the pinch was made. For the underworld, it was aggravation all the time.

Finally, the word went out, 'L.A. is closed,' and the locals, musclemen and gang leaders, vice overlords and major gamblers, went into obscurity. There was still crime everywhere, as there always is in a big city, but LAPD felt confident that organized crime had been purged.

But before that happy day arrived, Intelligence along with other LAPD units had to perform two pieces of major surgery.

Tony Brancato and Tony Trombino were out of Kansas City. They hadn't quite made the big time, but they were ambitious and they had a record of serious accomplishment behind them.

At the moment, Brancato was out on bond while fighting extradition to Las Vegas. He was wanted there for questioning in a $35,000 stickup at the Flamingo casino. In Los Angeles, he was suspected of having taken part in four murders, and he had won national honors by being named on the FBI's list of 'Ten Most Wanted' criminals.

Trombino had a record of narcotics violations and muscle jobs. Only two months previously, he had beaten a Los Angeles rap for receiving stolen property.

Tonight, the two Tonys enjoyed a spaghetti dinner prepared by Trombino's wife, Mary, and then went riding in Trombino's car. Sometime after eight p.m., they picked up a friend. At least, they thought he was a friend because they let him sit in the back seat behind them. On a fashionable residential street not far from the Sunset Strip in Hollywood, they parked and talked.

Probably about money. They had pressing bail and legal fees. Trombino puffed on a cigar, and jingled forty cents, which was all he had. Brancato had the same amount, a quarter, a dime and a nickel, plus a $10 bill folded in his pants pocket. So they probably talked it all over with their friend.

But, sadly, he wasn't their friend. In the dark he quietly drew a .38-calibre pistol and put two slugs into the back of Trombino's head, a third into his shoulder. Brancato, too stunned by the roar of the gun to move, got it next, and a piece of brain tissue splattered the back seat. The killer fled.

Within an hour, Chief Parker was personally directing one hundred detectives on an all-night search for the murderer. As men wearied, new ones were thrown into the investigation; and for the next ten days the Los Angeles underworld was shaken out from top to bottom. Witnesses by the dozen – party girls, businessmen, loafers, movie bit players, musclemen and grifters – were questioned and re-questioned. Five hoodlums and gamblers were booked on suspicion.

Day and night, Hamilton's Intelligence teams were rounding up friends and suspected business associates of the late Tonys', checking out whispered leads, scouring every dive in town. When an eyeball witness said he had seen a man running across the street after the shots were fired, the police hauled four of the suspects back to the scene. Then, while the witness watched from a hidden vantage point, the detectives made them run across the street. He couldn't positively identify any of them.

With all its sources, Hamilton's division ran into silence every time a lead seemed promising. And with all its powers, the Los Angeles County Grand Jury encountered the same frightened wall when it called twenty-two witnesses in an independent probe. The reason was inadvertently blurted by slim, red-haired Mary Trombino, now left with an eleven-months-old son to support.

Mary was a pathetic figure as she wept and trembled on

the witness stand. Gently a grand juror asked if she was afraid to tell the truth.

'Oh, no sir,' Mary sobbed. 'As far as I'm concerned, life ended for me when my husband was shot. But something might happen to my baby.'

To Hamilton, it was clear enough, though he couldn't prove it. The two Tonys had been killed by the Mafia, and under the ancient code of this Sicilian thuggee band, not even relatives of its victims could accept help from the law. *Il morte solo non ritorna,* the Mafia warned all, good and evil alike. *Il dimenticato ritornará.*

Only the dead do not return; he who has forgotten will return.

Intelligence came close enough to the central mystery to believe that a Mafia court in the Midwest had handed down the double death decree. As in any uncivilized court, the defendant does not appear before the Mafia or enjoy the right of either counsel or appeal. Once the Tonys were thus sentenced in absentia, a Mafia representative was summoned from Los Angeles and told what had to be done. He was responsible for seeing that Mafia 'justice' was carried out.

One of the principal suspects in the 'Two Tonys' murders was Jimmy ('The Weasel') Fratianno, who has been dubbed by many as the Mafia enforcer in Los Angeles.

Shortly before the two Tonys' sudden deaths, The Weasel had held several mysterious meetings with them. His alibi was suspiciously thin under police grilling, and he gave a sketchy time sequence of his movements that night. Intelligence couldn't nail him for the murders, but thereafter he was never out of their sight.

Two years later The Weasel tried to move in on an oil field developer, threatening him with death if he didn't receive part of the businessman's royalties. But Intelligence moved faster, and with the victim's consent made a tape recording of The Weasel's conversation.

In wild and obscene language, Fratianno made his demands and warned of 'the power of those people' who were backing him up. Their influence, he said, reached to the highest places and could command almost any result. Unfortunately for The Weasel, 'those people' couldn't influence LAPD or the courts, and he was tucked away in San Quentin for extortion.

Jimmy (Squeaky) Utley was an old-time carnival hustler who had come to Los Angeles in the mid-1920's; and, through years of subservience to the rackets bosses, had gradually risen to success. He joined up with the ousted police chief of a desert community to run a bingo and gambling club. He had been a partner in the notorious gambling ship *Lux* which had operated briefly off the coast of Los Angeles. He had a hand on the abortion and narcotics rackets, and sometimes on behalf of the under-world he tried to dabble in city politics. He was powerful and dangerous and knew it. He referred respectfully to himself as 'the little giant.'

So long as Squeaky remained at large, drugs, vice, and gambling would have a common directing overlord. Almost worse, Squeaky represented the local underworld as liaison man with the big mobsters. He had never lost his old-time carny respect for the rich and powerful. Whenever an outsider sought a friend or a foothold in Los Angeles, Squeaky obligingly held open house for him.

Adding it all up, Captain Hamilton decided that Squeaky should be put on ice. But how? Despite numerous arrests, the slippery 'little giant' had been convicted only once, on a charge of possessing and selling dope. Maybe that was it. In highly unorthodox police fashion, Hamilton went to work.

Through his own mysterious channels, the captain made contact with a suave French soldier-of-fortune who sometimes hired out to big-city police as a professional decoy. Hamilton put it up to him. Though Intelligence men would always remain as close as possible, he was to work strictly on his own, and gain Squeaky's confidence. Then, with Intelligence definitely on hand, he would make the kill – a narcotics buy from Squeaky.

Slowly, over a period of months, the Frenchman won his way into the good graces of Squeaky. They met more than thirty times and began moving together socially. The Frenchman was deferential toward 'the little giant,' and Squeaky warmed to the treatment.

Through electronic devices, Intelligence eavesdropped on almost all their conversations. The Frenchman's car was mined with tape-recording equipment and often one of Hamilton's G-2 detectives was hidden in the trunk compartment.

It was slow, unproductive going. Squeaky never went to a meeting without backtracking to make sure that he wasn't being followed. He never entered his apartment without double-checking whether it had been wired in his absence. Even to his new friend, he was reserved on dangerous subjects like dope and rackets.

Finally, the Frenchman told him he had a problem. He *had* to lay hands on a heroin supply. A lot of it and fast. Squeaky backed off. Heroin is TNT, he told his friend. The men who handled it were very touchy. But, he promised, he would ask around.

Alone, Squeaky set up a meeting with Jack Dragna, alias Antonio Rizzoti, the .45-calibre rackets king of the area. The California Crime Commission had called him 'the Capone of Los Angeles,' and the Kefauver crime probers tabbed him as the California boss of the Mafia. Dragna's nod could put the Frenchman in possession of heroin – and Intelligence in possession of Squeaky.

But Dragna was too wily. He took a ride in Squeaky's Cadillac and asked a few questions. Who was this Frenchman? Where did he come from? And then he rasped the question Squeaky should have asked himself: *Who knows him?*

Squeaky's answers didn't convince Dragna, and 'the little giant' had to admit to his French friend that he wasn't such a giant after all. He just couldn't put him in touch with the right people. He couldn't sell him anything personally.

Chagrined, the Frenchman reported back to Captain Hamilton that their long campaign to trap Squeaky had failed. Then he disappeared from Los Angeles.

A few months later, the Frenchman returned. His professional pride had been bruised by the fiasco, and now he wanted another go at Squeaky. At his own time and expense, too, he added with Gallic spirit.

On a day's notice, the Frenchman moved into a luxurious house in San Fernando Valley, fast-talking the landlady into waiting for her rent. Impatiently he stood by while Hamilton's men wired the house and set up listening posts nearby. Then he dialed Squeaky's private number and exclaimed, '*Mon ami!* I return!'

Once again, Squeaky, the Frenchman and the Intelligence agents went into their minuet. It was a re-play of the earlier campaign. Squeaky was charmed, Squeaky wanted to be helpful – but he never stepped over the line. With their earphones and tape-recording equipment, G-2's eavesdroppers amassed great quantities of conversation, but not one incriminating fact.

This time, humiliated beyond expression, the Frenchman left Los Angeles, never to return.

It had been almost two years now since Hamilton pushed the button on Squeaky. His men were still following him, day and night, noting several suspicious addresses and questionable meetings but coming up with nothing criminal.

One night, when he was about ready to admit defeat, Hamilton got a jubilant phone call. An Intelligence team had shadowed Squeaky to an address in Long Beach. It was one of the suspect places. Homicide was notified, and Lieutenant Herman Zander of that division joined up.

Outside, the detectives waited an hour, two hours, then three hours. Squeaky didn't emerge. So they walked in as a customer walked out. The house was an abortion mill, and Squeaky was standing in the middle of it.

Jimmy (The Little Giant) Utley went to state prison for the term prescribed by law.

II

Unlike most officers, they are chosen partly for their looks. Almost to a man, they seem so young and innocent. And they dress the part. The day shift (ten a.m. to six p.m.) goes uniformed in blue jeans, checked shirts, straw hats, and boots. The night swing (seven p.m. to three a.m.) wears blue slacks, sports shirts, loafers; no hats.

To cover the city's 454 square miles, there are only a handful of them: thirty-three policemen, one police-woman, four sergeants, one lieutenant, two civilians and Captain Charles Stanley. They enjoy the status of a division which is responsible only to the Chief of the Bureau of Administration and Chief Parker himself. They hit anywhere in the city and they outrank any division men on their specialty.

They are the officers of the Administrative Vice Squad which oversees all police vice enforcement and steps in whenever a division lets sex or gambling get out of hand.

'The public thinks we stink,' says one baby-faced Ad Vice man. 'Some of our colleagues agree. The public doesn't think we're sporting. Some police officers don't think we're even cops.'

Captain Stanley agrees that his men carry a scarlet V on their foreheads. 'Vice men have a bad public reputation,' he says unhappily. 'The work we do is scorned. The public thinks we are just a bunch of bulls sneaking around to break up somebody's friendly Friday night poker game.'

In a locality as traditionally, determinedly tolerant as a big city, the sidewalk bookie and the street corner floozie neither shock nor outrage the taxpayer. Even the courts often seem to express the tacit opinion that the police should be worrying about more important criminality. Girl and gambler are given toss-off fines of $10 to $25 and virtuous admonitions to go forth and sin no more. Dope pushers who peddled marihuana and 'benny' pills to high school students have been jailed for months rather than for years.

When there is a big vice crackdown, the public knowingly speculates about the other pinches that might have been made at the same time. Maybe, just maybe, money passed hands. And when for a while there are no pinches at all, it's not because the Ad Vice men can't get the evidence. Money *did* pass hands.

In every metropolitan city, the vice cop is scorned and suspect. But you have to know something of Los Angeles' lingering, purple past to understand his particular plight in what is sometimes called the City of the Angels.

The rambunctious tradition was planted at the dawn of the century when the crude flicker industry arrived in town. Colonel William N. Selig's cinema cowboys fired their blanks up and down Hollywood boulevard, the shooting crews caused traffic jams and confusion, and the good people hung out signs, *No Dogs or Actors Allowed.*

From the beginning, the police couldn't quite cope with the eccentricities and excesses of Hollywood. As the movies became the major industry, the situation only worsened. Wild Hollywood parties, wild drinking, wild dope orgies became commonplace, and the police couldn't have stopped them if they had tried.

But they didn't particularly try, so they were marked by the public as either stupid, Keystone or grafting cops.

When to most of America dope was a remotely awful thing, the California State Board of Pharmacy listed five hundred movie people as addicts. In the crazy Twenties, dope was smart in Hollywood. Before a party in his mansion, one film luminary emptied the big sugar bowl and refilled it with cocaine as a practical joke. Another needled his ace leading man into the morphine habit when his natural stamina ebbed.

Occasionally, there was a scandal and a temporary cover-up. For three years the idol who had made fifty-two box office hits in seven years suffered from morphine addiction and simultaneous blackmail. Courageously, he went 'cold turkey' for two months and then one day collapsed on the lot in the middle of shooting a scene.

'One moment he had been the smiling and upright hero on the set,' an eyewitness later reported. 'Then, in the bat of an eye, he began to drool and stagger.'

He was taken to a remote mountain cabin while his studio announced he was suffering from 'Klieg-eyes.' A month later, he died and the scandal could not be suppressed. In the United States Senate, a debate on the League of Nations was interrupted as Senators warned Hollywood to clean up or face federal action. For a while discretion ruled, but not for long.

During a two-year period, a director and a director's

mistress died violently, the idol succumbed to his brave withdrawal attempt, and a one-time Ziegfeld beauty now a cocaine addict killed herself in Paris. On Broadway, they put out all the lights for the night between 46th Street and Columbus Circle in her memory, and again Hollywood sobered momentarily.

But the reform was transitory. Hollywood remained the place where you ordered sex, dope, and Prohibition whisky by telephone, where bookies were protected on the movie lots (so that shooting schedules would not be interrupted by frequent phone calls to the horse parlors). Unlike many other sections of the country, Los Angeles had no long-standing social traditions of its own. Thus, for thirty years, what the stars did was accepted as the local mores.

And the police stood by.

Occasionally an honest cop revolted. During the 1930's, Captain Carey M. Buxton, then a rookie, was ordered to check on a complaint in the tenderloin district. The place was a house rather than a home, and the madam brusquely told the young officer to get out. She was paying her weekly protection money 'downtown,' she said, and if Buxton didn't go, maybe he would be transferred.

The officer went, but only as far as his police car. He sat parked in front of the house all day, thus discouraging a number of potential visitors. The following day he was put on another beat.

Even more recently, in the 1940's, Jim Fisk, now an inspector in LAPD's Traffic Bureau, blew his stack over the 'Guarantee Finance Company,' a pseudo loan agency, which fronted for a $6,000,000 bookmaking ring. Guarantee operated in territory policed by Los Angeles County, which was snugly beyond Fisk's jurisdiction.

One day, in a burst of righteous anger, Fisk stepped over the line, crashed through a skylight into the bookies' huge telephone room. He knew he couldn't make any arrests, so he did the next best thing. He tore up all the betting slips and wrecked the equipment.

For Fisk, there were no reprisals, and his spectacular raid put the heat on 'Guarantee.' When the California Crime Commission seized its books, 'juice' payoffs of $108,000 for protection were disclosed. The joint was padlocked.

But for the most part, even sincere police action was frustrated. Information was sought through paid informants, and the gamblers and bawds retaliated by hiring lookouts to flash early warnings. The raiders' battering-ram was met by the barricaded iron door, and the bookies devised counter-security measures to beat the newfangled wiretap.

The crusher came when Mayor Fletcher Bowron's reform administration took over City Hall just before the war. At last, it seemed, graft and incompetence in vice enforcement were gradually being licked – and then came the scandal of Brenda Allen and her 114 pleasure girls.

Redhaired Brenda Allen worked indefatigably to keep her 114 girls regularly employed and her blue-chip clientele happy. She subscribed to a telephone answering service used by physicians and lawyers, occasionally inserted chaste ads in actors' directories and distributed her phone number to cabbies, bartenders, bellhops.

However, she accepted only the wealthiest applicants, and some officers believe she was the first madam to run a Dun & Bradstreet check on her customers. Similarly, her girls were analyzed as to their more intimate characteristics, all jotted down on a card file. It was always Brenda's hope to bring about meetings of the wealthiest men and the most versatile girls.

As Brenda posted her sex ledgers, which often showed

daily takes of $1,200 on the traditional 50-50 split between madam and girl, vice teams investigated in vain.

Months were wasted in surveillance of Brenda's home because for the most part her girls kept outside trysts with the men in Hollywood or Beverly Hills. Decoys, undercover men, wiretaps were futile. Almost twenty times, the police bagged her, and every time she was released the next morning.

Finally, they made one arrest stick, and like the woman scorned, Brenda began to talk before the Los Angeles County Grand Jury. Among other things, she charged that she had been the mistress of a Los Angeles vice detective. The investigation snowballed, and though nothing much was proved, the vice enforcers of Los Angeles were thoroughly smeared.

By report, one team of Hollywood vice detectives were shaking down prostitutes, dope addicts, and homosexuals, exchanging immunity for payoffs . . . Other V cops were padding their expense accounts to bet on the horses . . . Still others were harassing certain bars to soften them up for sale to an outside purchasing syndicate.

In the end, the scandal simmered down to a handful of resignations and dismissals from the department. But to LAPD, the Brenda Allen case is an administrative landmark. Out of it came today's technique for handling both the oldest profession and the oldest police problem, the Administrative Vice Squad.

Though he suffers unfairly from the sins of the past, the young Ad Vice man is an entirely different kind of officer. Instead of closing his eyes to trouble, he goes out looking for it, and no device is too farfetched for him if it means a conviction.

On one occasion, a ring of prostitutes in Skid Row had Ad Vice completely stymied. They had gone to great pains

155

to memorize the description of every V detective, and there was no way to close in on them.

Then, in somewhat embarrassed fashion, one of the young detectives offered a suggestion to Captain Stanley. 'You may think I've been going to too many movies, Captain,' he said. 'But how about working in a disguise?' Stanley gave the okay.

The detective turned himself over to the makeup men at Republic Studios. After long conferences, the experts decided to transform him into a latter-day Lon Chaney.

Shortly afterwards, a deformed stranger with hunched back and scarred face moved into Skid Row. Slowly he got to know the prosties, their habits and their customers. It was an unpleasant way to live, and the job went on for weeks. But he got the evidence that smashed the ring.

To Ad Vice, the heartbreaking thing is that often months of preparation are washed out not by clever criminals but by their non-cooperative victims. Ashamed to face publicity, they refuse to press the complaints which are necessary to prosecution. In no other form of police activity do the 'good' citizens so often protect the underworld.

All night, for weeks, V operatives 'lived with' a Hollywood Hills mansion, one-time home of a silent screen star, where they knew a rigged dice game was operating. A raid would result merely in misdemeanor charges for gambling. What they wanted was evidence that the game was crooked. Then they could hit the operators with felony charges of grand theft.

Finally, a wealthy lumberman in town from the Northwest was steered into the game, and in two hours dropped $30,000 to the loaded cubes. He complained loudly to the police, demanding to know why LAPD didn't protect out-of-towners. There was the implication that maybe the police were letting the game operate for reasons of their own.

This was what Ad Vice had been waiting for, and joyfully they took the lumberman back to the house for a confrontation with the crooks. The dice men professed distress that there had been any 'misunderstanding.' To prove their good sportsmanship, they were herewith returning the victim's 30 Gs, they said, and under Ad Vice's noses they counted out the long green.

When the victim was returned to Headquarters, he balked at signing a written complaint. 'Don't see any point in making a fuss about this,' he said. 'After all, I didn't *lose* anything.' But Ad Vice did. The long stakeout had been wasted, and they were back where they had started. All they could make stick were the misdemeanor charges.

From an eighth-floor office at Headquarters, Captain Charles Stanley administers his little Ad Vice Squad and worries. Worries about the long hours his men work and the risks they take. And particularly about the public's lethargic, tolerant attitude.

'Vice is small most of the time,' he says, 'but it could be big. And vice has broken more city administrations than any other single thing. Look at vice enforcement this way. To the degree of vice you have, you have that degree of corruption. This we try to combat.'

Charlie Stanley worries that Ad Vice is undermanned for the job, but he carries on because all his life he has had to fight against the odds. When he was only twelve, his father was killed in an accident, and yet he went on to UCLA. He was a star linesman on the '26 team. In LAPD, he rose to probationary sergeant and then a week before his tryout ended he was adjudged 'unfit to be a supervisor' and busted in rank along with seven other sergeants and four lieutenants. Eighteen months later, he was No. 1 on the new sergeants' list.

Small as it is, Ad Vice has purged Los Angeles of its red

light houses, and call girls can operate only sporadically by means of elaborate phone setups. An Angeleno has difficulty locating a bookie, and a stranger finds it practically impossible to lay a bet.

'We are an undermanned army,' says Charlie Stanley with a touch of pride in his voice. 'But we are a vigorous army. We're doing what we think helps the community most. We're *cops*. Vice in Los Angeles has mostly been driven underground.'

III

It is a crowded, colorless room. A bent, withered man sits with his back to the crowd.

The man faces a California State Senate committee on narcotics, in hearing at Los Angeles. For the record, he is 'Mr. X.' But life knows him otherwise; as the father of eight grown children. His story is familiar to the men of Captain William H. Madden's narcotics detail. It has been retold a thousand times.

'I don't know where it went wrong,' the old man says in a soft, troubled voice. 'We have a good family, the rest of them. Seven of the kids are wonderful. All married. All have families and make good livings. They're all wonderful . . . except *her*.'

Even she, his second youngest, had been wonderful till she was sixteen. The family lived in the suburbs then, and one night she wanted to go to a party. He thought she was a little young, but when he visited the house of her girl friend, the latter's mother reassured him that she would chaperone the affair.

'The next thing I heard of the party was when a deputy sheriff called. Our girl was in custody. It had been a marihuana party. My wife and I tried to explain to her

158

what this meant. That marihuana was the bait, and dope addiction the trap.

'We thought she understood. She seemed so repentant . . .'

To get her away from the bad crowd, they sent her to school in the East and, when she didn't like it, to another school away from home.

'Whatever she had, she had it bad . . . In the new school, she took her first shot of heroin. Just for kicks. She was hooked . . . My little girl . . . at sixteen. . . .

'She was never really bad, not ever. But she had this craze. She used to say, "Daddy, I've gotta have it." She meant the heroin. "That or alcohol." She had to have it; when she didn't, she drank alcohol like water.'

After that, there had been an interracial marriage, a child, a breakup of the marriage.

'Yet, even now, she is lovable, sweet, sympathetic, kind . . . one of the kindest people I know. I am her father and I love her.'

Gently one of the Senators asks a question. The old man looks up, then drops his eyes. 'Why, I guess, she paid for the stuff by prostitution . . .

'I love her. You can't help loving your child, no matter what. But I'd rather see her in her casket than the way she is today . . . I tell you this – all of it – in the hope that you gentlemen can find some solution to this problem of drugs among our babies . . .'

Ask any man on the 'hop squad' – he'll tell you. Vicious as Hollywood's narcotics kick was, it was concentrated in a small, wealthy group. And they were adults. Today, dope is being peddled to the teen-ager who progresses from 'goof-balls' to the weedy pseudo-ecstasies of marihuana and finally to 'H,' the deadly heroin.

The lingering public apathy to the narcotics problem bothers men like Bill Madden of LAPD. But they keep at it

159

in the daily grind – and sometimes in a rather spectacular manner.

With the cooperation of Los Angeles Police Academy officials, an entire class of twenty-five cadets was placed under secret around-the-clock surveillance. In class, on the training field, at meals, in the locker rooms and even off-duty, they were 'staked out' just as though they were criminals. Each man's appearance, behavior, class work and characteristics were noted and compared. Finally, the twenty-five were winnowed down to nine prospects, and they were called in for briefing.

A multi-million-dollar dope ring was operating throughout the city. Because they were known to the higherups, the regular 'narco' men could not get close to them. New and unfamiliar faces were needed.

'This is strictly volunteer,' the nine were assured. 'Your standing in the Academy will not be influenced by your decision.

'Your life will be in constant danger. During the operation you will forget about your normal associations at home and elsewhere. You will be living somebody else's life. This is top secret.

'You will not receive extra pay for this. You will not have fixed hours. You will probably not like what has to be done.'

The nine listened with painfully fixed wooden expressions. Maybe they were only cadets, but they were going to accept this like pros.

And then came the clincher:

'Above all, you must make the decisions and suffer the consequences, whatever they may be. You cannot rely on LAPD protection.

'We will offer you the best training known for the job to be done. After that, you are on your own.'

There were three more words, and they came like pistol shots. 'That's it, gentlemen.'

Not one of the cadets backed out.

In the next few weeks, the nine moved into the dirty gray world of the pusher and addict. They learned a new language, the lingo of the dope trade, and the kind of 'stuff' that was being pushed. Not only 'grass' and 'H' but also the whole modern family of barbiturates known as 'yellow jackets,' 'green dragons' and 'red devils.' They were taught how to distinguish the 'drugstore stuff' from the milk or sugar.

There is a proper way to approach a pusher and make contact for the buy. They were shown how to accomplish it without arousing suspicion. They learned how to 'split' from a 'buy' and how to stash their evidence. And, all through, they were warned to follow the cardinal rule of undercover work: *Never become part of the crime itself.*

Now they were almost ready. As the last touch, they grew goatees and sideburns and practiced the insolent walk and talk of the sidewalk punk. They swapped their trim Academy khaki for loud sports shirts, striped trousers and gone jackets and disappeared into the dark corners of Los Angeles. They were on their own, and if they got into trouble, LAPD couldn't help them.

Cadet Leighton L. Sleigh was twenty-three, and he had a pretty young wife whom he hadn't seen in weeks. Instead, he was play-acting a 'hype' to gain a pusher's confidence. One misstep and he might never see her again.

He won over the pusher, bought his 'fix' – and now trouble. The pusher wanted to share it with him, and as they rode around aimlessly in Sleigh's car, he kept remembering the warning. *Never become part of the crime itself.*

He stalled, complaining about the price of the 'fix,' and the pusher was becoming suspicious. Sleigh had an inspiration.

'I'll give you nothing!' he shouted in simulated rage. 'How do I know who you *really* are? You might be working with the cops!'

He pulled over to the curb. 'Get out!' he yelled at the protesting pusher. He shoved him into the street and drove off – with his evidence.

Cadet Bill Anderson, thirty and single, had seen Intelligence duty with the Air Force in World War II and in Korea. But with all his undercover know-how and specialized Academy training, two weeks passed before he made a contact.

Now he was standing near his car with a pusher when a radio unit drove up. The policemen didn't like the looks of the two characters and started questioning them. Anderson was sweating. A pickup on suspicion would kill the contact he had been working on so long.

'You guys are a drag,' he growled at the officers.

'Yeah?'

'Yeah. I've gone this route before.' He glanced wearily at his narcotics friend. 'Next thing they'll want to do is shake my car.'

'That's what we want to do,' one of the officers snapped. And that was just what Bill Anderson had hoped for.

As one of the officers searched the car, he pulled up the floor mat and in the beam of his flashlight spotted Bill's identification card. Quickly he slapped the mat back into place, and glanced covertly at Bill.

'It's clean,' the officer said to his partner. They warned Bill and his friend to move along, and then drove off. 'Lousy cops,' the pusher said sympathetically to Bill.

At last the nine cadets had the evidence, and on a full-moon night in spring more than one hundred LAPD officers launched the biggest mass crackdown on dope peddlers in the department's history. Working round the clock for two days, they seized 160 pushers and broke the back of the huge ring.

So many other narcotics characters fled town that adjacent cities sent urgent requests for LAPD files and photos on known peddlers. In their stampede out of Los Angeles, they had invaded the surrounding areas by the dozens.

LAPD's first wholesale narcotics raid was followed by sharp plunges in crime indices, with burglaries and other types of theft leading. A slump in the crime rate, while pleasing, is hard to explain by police. But it is their accolade at the end of a long stretch of planning and labor.

Still the work load runs on, increasing by the hour. 'Since World War II the narcotics problem has grown steadily, without letup,' says Bill Madden. To meet the tide, LAPD puts fifty-four men and a woman in the field around the clock. They range through the city in the battle that never ends.

And the forty-two-year-old commander of LAPD's Narcotics Division expects no truce. 'They keep growing in numbers,' Madden says of the narcotics crowd. 'The youngsters just get older, and the older ones never quit.'

IV

'. . . Men with honor and brains and guts. . . . You tore down every best part of 'em. The people who read it in the papers, they're gonna overlook the fact that *we* got you . . . that we washed our own laundry and we cleared this thing up. They're gonna overlook all the good . . . they'll overlook every last good cop in the country. But they'll remember *you*. Because you're a bad cop. *You're a bad cop.*'

The hurt and indignation a good cop feels about a bad cop were expressed by Sergeant Joe Friday in a DRAGNET program. It was based on the true story of an officer who had gone sour in Los Angeles. But they might just as easily be the words of Captain John W. Powers, Internal Affairs Division.

Johnny Powers weighs 185 pounds and stands six foot two, and all cop. Before him, his father was a policeman in Poughkeepsie, New York, for thirty-six years and one of the ace fingerprint men in the East. Before that, his grandfather was a policeman in Newburgh, also in New York state.

To Johnny, there just couldn't be any life but a policeman's life, and he worked and waited six years to make LAPD. For four years, he was on the private police force at Warner Brothers Studio while he hoped for an opening. Just about the time it was due, a police scandal froze the lists, and he waited another two years. In 1940, when he finally entered the Police Academy, he was twenty-seven years old.

Immediately he began making up for the lost time. When he was graduated from the Academy in mid-December, he was sent to Parking and Intersection Control to help with the Christmas shopping rush, but within three weeks he moved on to the Metropolitan Squad, LAPD's commandos. And three weeks later he was almost killed in a close-range gunfight.

With his partner, Charlie Hart, Policeman Powers ran into two young hoodlums from the East who had just pulled a $25 cigar-store stickup in downtown Los Angeles. They were trigger-happy, and as the officers approached, they began blazing away. Powers and Hart fired back.

In ten seconds, twenty-eight shots were fired, one hood was fatally wounded, and his companion was lying jack-knifed against a building, both lungs punctured.

The officers had got it, too. Charlie Hart was sprawled in the gutter with slugs in the thigh and jaw. Johnny Powers, stretched out on the sidewalk, was bleeding profusely from the right hip.

Sometimes, and you can't blame him, a man gets gunshy after an ordeal like that, but not Johnny Powers! A year to the day later, almost to the hour, he was shooting it out again.

For two weeks, a gang of purse snatchers operating from stolen cars had been terrorizing women on the street. One night, they suddenly stepped up the pace of their operations, and in less than two hours seven snatchings were reported. All the police knew was that the gang was using a stolen tan sedan.

Officer Powers was working with the Gangster Squad of the Robbery Division which patrolled beer joints, pool rooms, and other gathering places of punks and petty criminals. His job this night was to hold down the office, but studying the reported movements of the tan sedan, he spotted a pattern and had a hunch. And Johnny always rolled on 'these feelings,' as he calls them.

A short time later, he was parked alone near an intersection in southwest Los Angeles. Five minutes later, the tan sedan appeared, then roared off when the driver spotted Johnny's police car. Johnny called the radio board and set out after it. Unexpectedly, the sedan braked, and four men piled out to blaze away at Johnny. He kept firing back, but by the time radio cars came to his assistance, he had been wounded again. Anyhow, Johnny says, the suspects were taken.

To a good cop like that who has spilled his own blood, a bad one deserves no breaks, and Johnny's 'IA' Division is respected in the roll call room of every police building in Los Angeles.

In LAPD not only the public life but also the private life

of a policeman is closely regulated. Instead of enjoying special privileges, as the public often thinks, he signs away his rights as a private citizen when he takes the oath and the badge. But he continues to pay taxes.

He can't have any bad debts. He can't get drunk in public view. He can't break any unwritten laws or the accepted code of morality. On duty, off duty, he always acts in the tight, disciplined manner of LAPD or he hears from IA.

As a minority group who are often subjected to public hostility, the police instinctively try to cover for one another. In the past, this 'country club code' quashed many a police scandal before the public heard a whisper of it, but Chief Parker has done his best to stamp this out of LAPD.

Thus, though IA handles almost two complaints daily against Los Angeles officers, Chief Parker insists that the facts and the trial board hearings be open to the public. Sometimes, this proves embarrassing to LAPD, but the Chief and his disciplinary boss, Captain Powers, are agreed on the basic philosophy.

'A good police administrator backs up his men when they are right, although they are accused of wrong,' explains Captain Powers. 'But when there's scandal in the department, he does something about it. And quick. If he does nothing about it, this is what can kick a chief out of office. And quick.'

In a typical year, there will be almost two hundred complaints against policemen of conduct unbecoming an officer and more than one hundred each charging use of excessive force and neglect of duty. Some will be accused of dishonesty, others of violating civil rights, a few of sex offenses. IA doesn't pull its punches in the follow-up investigations and about one-third will be convicted after hearings.

In its administrative peculiarities, three of the toughest and most critical jobs in LAPD are handled at the level of captain. Intelligence for Jim Hamilton and vice control for Charley Stanley are more than man-sized assignments. But, in many ways, Johnny Powers holds down the hottest desk. A rogue cop, a crook masquerading in the uniform, who knows the inside workings of the department, is an almost frightening figure.

From the beginning, there was something suspicious about the outbreak of burglaries in the West Los Angeles Division. They were scattered over a large area, but they always occurred on the morning watch between two and four a.m. and they were confined to business places which sold gardening equipment, sporting goods, and hardware.

After each outbreak, police stakeouts were posted through the division, and the burglaries immediately stopped. The stakeouts would then be lifted, and there would be fresh complaints from the businessmen. There was, at least, a leak in the department. Reluctantly the divisional commander, a captain, suspected something worse. And, sure enough, shortly afterwards he picked up an anonymous tip that one of the policemen on the morning watch had, suddenly and suspiciously, come into possession of a power lawn mower. But which officer the informant didn't say.

Four detectives were assigned to the investigation, and then another four. They listed all the men assigned to the division and then slowly eliminated those who lived in apartments, those who didn't own their own homes, those whose time could be completely accounted for. There was still a sizable number of names, and the touchiest part of the job was ahead.

Somehow, without arousing suspicion or stepping over the tight legal restrictions on illegal search-and-seizure,

167

they had to get into the suspects' homes. So the plain-clothesmen got cover jobs with private firms which gave them entree. After sixty days of undercover sleuthing, they had turned up one power mower – which belonged to a gardener.

And then, when they were pretty well convinced the original tip had been phony, they found a brand-new mower in the Valley home of a policeman. Further, he had once before been the subject of a personnel investigation.

On the pretext that a personnel complaint had been lodged against him, the suspect was brought in for inter-rogation. During routine preliminary questioning, before the detectives had even gotten around to the lawn mower, he suddenly blurted out that he had stolen property in his possession.

He admitted having stolen the mower himself, and involved fellow policemen. Detectives rounded up fifty other officers for grilling and searched their homes. After checking out every bit of hardware, clothing, and tool supply that seemed suspicious, they narrowed the field down to a handful of men – seven officers who had been on the force anywhere from seven to fifteen years. They were family men and several had excellent records.

What went wrong?

All residents of San Fernando Valley, they had formed a car pool to make the winding trip across the mountains to their division headquarters. Little by little, grousing about a cop's low pay and the high cost of keeping a home, they formed their scheme.

Somehow, they rationalized that taking only what they *really* needed wouldn't quite be stealing. They made their plans two weeks ahead when some of the gang would be on the morning watch. Then two of them jimmied open the skylight of a seed store while two others waited outside with a truck.

The original plan had been to pick up a few lawn mowers, some garden tools, a few sacks of fertilizer. Now, seeing so much unprotected merchandise there for the taking, they piled the truck high with thousands of dollars' worth of loot.

After that, the stealing came easier. They hit a camera shop, a store specializing in skin diving gear and a hardware store. They even raided a boxcar loaded with furniture which had been left on a siding. From modest larceny, they turned to professional burglary, and several sold off their loot to fatten their bank accounts.

When they were caught, they received a trial before a Police Board of Rights under Section 202 of the city charter. Five of them turned in their badges during the trial, and the other two were dismissed from the department. Subsequently all seven were brought to trial in a public court and convicted of theft.

Six were sentenced to the Los Angeles County Jail camp for a year, and one fought his conviction through an appeal, the decision on which has not yet been handed down.

Of all the disciplinary crises weathered by Chief Parker and Captain Powers, the worst was the 'Bloody Christmas' scandal in Central. The heat on LAPD was so intense that the wiseacres were predicting Parker's imminent stepdown to status of deputy chief. But Parker acted so decisively and IA investigated so thoroughly (making a report of 204 single-spaced typewritten pages) that LAPD survived its ordeal by headlines and politics.

Ironically, it all began with Christmas cheer, both in Central where about one hundred policemen were enjoying a party and in a small bar in a rough part of town.

Two policemen, rolling on a 'trouble' call to the bar, tried to eject two holiday celebrants. A brawl broke out, and the outnumbered officers were beaten up, one so badly that he had to be hospitalized.

Reserves hustled seven of the merrymakers off to Central, booked them and put them in a waiting room. So far, routine, for Christmas Day.

Then, among the police celebrants, the story spread that the more seriously injured officer was going to lose an eye. Immediately, the enraged policemen began taking turns to work over the seven prisoners. Before they were through, the floor was blood-covered, the walls were spattered red.

At least, that was the story, though precisely what did happen has never been fully established. Parker and LAPD were subjected to attacks which continued for months. Six of the young celebrants were freed by a judge who denounced 'lawless law enforcement.' 'Police Brutality' became almost a standing headline. The grand jury launched an investigation.

In his biggest departmental shakeup, Parker shifted fifty-four men, including two deputy chiefs, two inspectors and four captains. But he refused to acknowledge the action was disciplinary, and he went on TV to warn that the underworld was taking advantage of the furore to discredit LAPD.

Subsequently the grand jury indicted eight policemen for felonious assault. But Parker was not to be outdone. On the basis of IA's monumental investigation of some 400 policemen and officers, he suspended thirty-three.

At last, he was able to get across his point to the public, and the agitation subsided. Not only should LAPD discipline LAPD abuses, but the department most certainly *would* do so.

In truth, Captain Johnny Powers is unexpectedly sympathetic to the officer in trouble. IA runs close herd on him, could even bust him out of the department, but Powers knows many a civilian has been an accessory and should be standing before the same Police Board of Rights.

'Policemen are subject to more temptations than workers in any other type of occupation,' Powers says.

'Bar owners are happy to give an officer a bottle of liquor, hoping that this will sometime influence his official actions. For the same reason, women offer themselves readily at times to a policeman.

'There is always ready money for the policeman who will forget he is a cop. Policemen are put to great stress living on their "just-get-by" salaries.

'They have trying work schedules, bad hours that make it tough on home life. They are subject to a rigid promotional setup which, mathematically, makes it impossible for everybody to advance.

'We're all human, we policemen. We have the same emotions as other men, the same tensions, the same drives.'

But, to a good cop, these things just can't matter. Johnny Powers' voice bristles with pride. 'When a man takes the Badge, he must learn to control these things inside him. If he doesn't want to control them, he won't stay on this police force.'

THE INSPECTOR

Thursday: 11:35 p.m.

Tom Reddin, junior inspector in LAPD's Detective Bureau, had gone to bed fifteen minutes earlier and was just comfortably drowsing off when the phone rang. From years of training, he was instantly alert and already unbuttoning his pajama top as he scooped up the receiver.

'Inspector!' The voice from Headquarters crackled with unprofessional excitement.

'A bomb was thrown into a café near Normandie and 59th Street. We know two people are dead.'

'On my way.'

Like a fireman, Reddin kept his pants hung so that he could slide into them in a couple of minutes. He was still buttoning his shirt as he hurried out the back door to his car. From his home in the Westchester section, he had a long drive through town. He jammed down the gas pedal and the car leaped forward.

Bomb?

A few weeks earlier, shortly before dawn, a café in the Wilshire district had been bombed by a crude explosive.

'Maybe some guy we threw out got mad,' the bar owner had told Reddin. 'Maybe a nut did it. When you run a bar, you can expect things like this.'

Now this one. Reddin wondered.

11:50 p.m.

When Reddin reached the scene, the little Mecca Bar was still burning. Ambulance sirens whined, and fire apparatus cluttered the neighborhood. Already, dozens of patrol and traffic policemen were blockading off the streets and pushing back the curious. Arson investigators were at work, and divisional detectives had reported on a standby basis.

As the inspector in charge, Reddin first had to get a fast rundown on the tragedy, then tie together the police, fire, and emergency efforts. All kinds of help, almost too much, had rolled on the first flash, 'Bomb!' and he had to coordinate the dozens of men into one team.

It was worse than he had feared. Probably half a dozen people had been killed, another dozen or so badly burned. There might be still more bodies in the smoking building. Quickly he gave the orders.

One team of detectives went to the morgue to begin identification of the dead. Other teams were dispatched to the various hospitals for interviews with the injured. More men circulated through the crowds, rounding up witnesses and a few survivors who had not been badly hurt.

Reddin set up his headquarters in the 77th Street Station and began the investigation that was to carry him through forty hours without sleep.

What had happened in the Mecca? From the hysterical, often conflicting stories of survivors and passers-by, he put together the story and made decisions. Outside, forty newsmen and photographers were clamoring for attention. Yes, let the cameramen go to work, Reddin ordered. Tell the reporters I'll be right with them.

The Mecca Bar was a cosy, neighborhood tavern and the quiet, Thursday night crowd of twenty patrons almost filled it. It wasn't the kind of place where brawls start, but tonight four strangers were making nuisances of themselves. They were loud and foul-mouthed, and one began pestering a pretty brunette to dance with him. Some of the regular patrons defended her.

A fight started, and the four were thrown out. The Mecca settled back into its Thursday night calm. The juke-box played, and people laughed. 'Just happy people, having a good time,' Larry Fenton, the bartender, later told Inspector Reddin.

At 11:30 p.m., Fenton happened to glance toward the doorway. Howard Marriott, who was sitting on a bar stool near the door, saw Fenton's glance and turned to look over his shoulder.

A man was pouring liquid from a container onto the barroom floor. Marriott thought it must be a gag. Then he smelled gasoline.

A moment later, a shorter, second man suddenly appeared. He seemed to be holding a ball of fire which he hurled into the puddle. The two men fled, and for just a split second nothing happened.

And then holocaust.

When a pool of gasoline is ignited, a small column of flame fans up into a fiery umbrella, which first consumes the fumes lying heavily in the air. Then the fire eats back to the pool itself, de-oxygenating the air and exploding.

'A sudden flash and the café turned into a hell on earth,' said Larry Fenton.

They ran.

Clothes and hair aflame, they ran forward through the flames into the street. They ran out the back into an alley. They tried to hide from the blasts of flame in the rooms marked *Girls* and *Boys*.

Mrs. Robert Hartner of Gardena happened to be driving past with her husband as the Mecca suddenly vomited flames and screaming, burning human beings. Some were stumbling, others were crawling on their hands and knees.

177

Mrs. Hartner whipped off her skirt and jacket and tried to help a girl who seemed to be on fire from head to foot.

'She was hysterical and hard to help,' Mrs. Hartner told Inspector Reddin afterwards. 'As I pounded out the flames, she kept screaming, "I'm burning! I'm burning!" Then she fainted. And when she came around, she moaned, "Why did they do it?" "What about my children?"'

These were the lucky ones.

One patron remained riveted to his bar stool in paralyzing fear, and his charred body, stripped of its clothes, was found by firemen still crouched on the blackened, twisted stool. Another who was trapped in a booth screamed, then collapsed forward on the table as acrid smoke filled his lungs.

In all, six persons never got out.

Thursday: 2:36 a.m.

In three hours and six minutes, Inspector Reddin established that the Mecca outrage must have been a grudge bombing unconnected with any form of racketeering. He held his promised press conference and frankly told the reporters the whole story, asking only that they hold back a few details which might possibly help the perpetrators. The newspapermen agreed.

With his detectives and watch commanders, Reddin plotted the job ahead:

On the assumption that the arsonists were two of the men who had been thrown out of the Mecca, the police were looking for a quartet of drunken, irresponsible characters, possibly drifters. Unless pure chance had directed them to the neighborhood-type bar, maybe at least one of the four lived somewhere nearby on the Southside. Reddin directed that some 1,200 homes and apartment houses in the area be canvassed.

Unless they had drained the gasoline out of a car, they must have purchased it at a gas station. They had needed some kind of a container for it, too, and probably they had thrown it away right afterward. The inspector ordered more than fifty gas stations double-checked and called for a foot-by-foot search of a mile-square area near the Mecca. In all, hundreds of cans of all descriptions were found and discarded by the searchers and another two hundred were brought into the 77th Street headquarters for scientific tests before being discarded. From as far away as San Bernardino, one hundred miles distant, calls later came from persons who thought they had found the container.

Eyewitness leads? No good. An aircraft mechanic reported having fired three shots at the fleeing car. He thought he had hit one of the fugitives, but hospitals and physicians had no records of a gunshot patient. Somebody else thought he had gotten a fast look at the license plate. It didn't check out with D.M.V.

Reddin ordered that every survivor, every street witness be questioned again. The four must have addressed each other by their first names or nicknames, names that might be listed in LAPD's huge 'moniker' file.

Suspects? Too many. But not the right ones. Every drunk on the streets, every criminal with an arson record was checked out. More than one hundred were questioned and eliminated in the field. Another twenty suspects were grilled and cleared.

2:36 a.m. and all Reddin could be sure of was that Los Angeles had just sustained the biggest mass bombing in its history since the Los Angeles *Times* outrage almost half a century earlier.

Then came a break. Or was it a break? The survivors were still so shaken that you couldn't be sure about their

179

stories. But suddenly a woman patron remembered something.

'One of those four guys who caused the fire said he was a brother-in-law of Bob and Lyle Jacobson,' she said. 'And he said his name was Oscar. I'd never seen this Oscar before, but I think the Jacobson brothers live around 25th and Vermont.'

'You *sure*?' a detective pressed her.

'I'm positive. I know he said his name was Oscar. You just find the Jacobsons. Then you'll find Oscar.'

The upside-down book was checked – the telephone directory, which lists subscribers by street addresses. One Robert Jacobson lived at 1321 West 29th Street. Reddin ordered Felony Car Officers C. F. Call and R. R. Irwin to run it down.

3 a.m.

Drowsy, a little frightened, the Jacobson brothers answered the door. Sure, they would do anything to help the police. They'd heard the news flash earlier on the radio. It was awful.

But, the only thing was, they just didn't have relatives or in-laws named Oscar. Officers Call and Irwin told them, 'Think about it. Maybe you know an Oscar.'

That might be it, the brothers said. They did have a brother-in-law named Clyde Bates, and he worked with some fellow named Oscar. But they didn't know Oscar's last name or where he lived.

Didn't even know Clyde's address, come to think of it, though they could find the house. 'Get your clothes on and come with us,' the officers told them.

Through the deserted, early morning streets, the police car raced a mile to a frame house on a quiet old street about in mid-city. The house was dark, and there was no answer when Call and Irwin pounded heavily on the door. They looked at the Jacobson brothers. 'This is the place, all right,' they said. 'We're positive.'

Circling through the big yard, the two officers spotted a beat-up old blue sedan parked off in a corner. Inside, two men were snoring heavily. There was the stale smell of whisky.

Roughly Call and Irwin shook the bleary-eyed pair into consciousness. 'That's Clyde,' the Jacobsons said, pointing to the man in the front seat. 'Who are you?' the officers demanded of the other, who was in the back.

'Brenhaug. Oscar Brenhaug. What the hell's going on here?'

5:30 a.m.

The Jacobson brothers went home with the hearty thanks of LAPD.

At 77th Street, Officers Call and Irwin reported to Inspector Reddin. He ordered the suspects booked on suspicion of murder and asked for a quick fingerprint check.

Both had previous records in Los Angeles, and Bates had also been arrested on various charges in Ohio, Alabama, Pennsylvania, and Tennessee. He had done twenty-one months for taking a stolen car across state lines, and his accomplice had been arrested about a year previously by LAPD for drunkenness. Both worked for the same company.

Against this possibility, Reddin had detained all the uninjured witnesses through the night. Now he arranged an immediate show up of the prisoners. Larry Fenton, the Mecca bartender, singled out Bates as the man who had poured the gasoline on the barroom floor. Other witnesses were escorted outside to look at Bates' blue sedan. They agreed that it was the getaway car.

Inspector Reddin knew that neither of the prisoners was yet aware how many lives had been taken. Maybe, if he gave them the shock treatment, they would blurt out a confession. Then he decided against tackling the conwise Bates who had admitted having been in the bar earlier. Bates had denied any connection with the fire itself, and from his long experience with the police he knew enough to stick to his story as long as there was any chance of its being believed.

Instead, Reddin had Brenhaug brought from his cell to an interrogation room. Silently the inspector stared at him. The prisoner's eyes shifted nervously, and he bit his lip. Reddin suddenly tossed a morning *Times* into Brenhaug's lap, and the banner headline, SIX KILLED IN BAR BLAST, screamed up at him. He withered.

'Not very nice, is it, Brenhaug? Tell us about it.'

Brenhaug gestured aimlessly. 'It's hard to remember. You know? I had a few. And, well, things are a little hazy.' He bit his lip again.

'That's all right, Brenhaug. We've got the time.' Reddin held him with a cold stare.

Fitfully Brenhaug's memory returned. Not fully, not enough to make *him* look very bad, just enough to keep the detectives from pressing him too hard.

Bates and he had decided early Thursday night to go out for a few drinks . . . They ran into a couple of young fellows . . . Bates knew who they were . . . Personally he couldn't remember . . . There was some bar-hopping . . . They wound up in the Mecca . . . Then a fight . . . They were thrown out. . . .

'A couple of the boys got real mad. They said, "We'll show them! They can't throw us out!" We went to another bar and had a couple of quick rounds. I think they were trying to get an alibi.'

And that was all. Brenhaug's mind went conveniently blank on everything that had happened thereafter. When they returned to the car from the second tavern, he had passed out. He couldn't very well be expected to remember any more, could he? Was he responsible for what somebody else did?

7 a.m.

Two hot reports, one from the Crime Lab, the other information which had been volunteered by a citizen, needed Inspector Reddin's immediate attention.

Not only on Bates' car but also on the suspect's clothing, the Crime Lab had detected traces of gasoline. He assigned Detectives E. E. Cummins and R. M. Sluder to locate Bates' wife and dig out everything possible about the man and his associates.

The citizen's information was less specific. Maybe, he thought, one of the quartet was a fellow known as 'Machete' or 'Chavette.' The 'moniker' file at Headquarters pulled a blank on both nicknames.

Good so far, but not good enough. After seven hours and ten minutes of investigation, Reddin had one solid suspect who wouldn't talk and one who said he couldn't remember. He had nothing on the other two except that they were young.

During the afternoon, Detectives Cummins and Sluder located Clyde Bates' wife. She wanted to help, but she just didn't know much about Clyde's friends.

'Tell us what you can,' they said.

She thought some more. 'I don't know if this means anything,' she said doubtfully. 'But I remember him saying sometimes he went with a fellow named Manuel Chavez. Yes, Chavez; that was the name.'

'Do you know where he lives, Mrs. Bates?'

'No, I'm not sure. Something like 25th Street. Yes, I think West 25th Street. That sounds like it.'

Friday: 6 p.m.

Detectives Sluder and Cummins ring the doorbell at a house on West 25th Street, and a young man answers.

'Does Manuel Chavez live here?' Sluder asks.

'Come in,' says the young man. 'I've been expecting you.'

8 p.m.

Chavez was booked on the same charge of suspicion of murder. He denied any connection with the torch job and insisted he could not name the fourth man since he didn't know anything about the crime. Reddin sent detectives to talk to Chavez' young wife.

Saturday: 3 a.m.

On information supplied by Mrs. Chavez, a five-man team from Felony drives to the home of one Manuel Hernandez, aged eighteen. He is arrested as the fourth and last suspect.

On through the night and past Saturday noon, Inspector Reddin drove himself to wrap up the case. Now he could parcel out responsibility for the cleanup, and he chose two good homicide men, Sergeants J. A. Tidyman and V. V. Little, who were attached to 77th Street Detectives.

To Tidyman and Little went the long, dull chore of re-interviewing all the witnesses, reconciling any conflicting stories and whipping the mass of evidence into shape for presentation to the grand jury.

Saturday: 3:15 p.m.

After forty sleepless hours, as Inspector Reddin buttoned his pajama top, his last conscious thoughts were: *Who sold them the gasoline? Where is that damned container? That's all we need now.*

On Sunday morning, Sam Campbell Ledgerwood, who slept days and worked nights, rarely saw a newspaper and didn't bother much with radio or TV, strolled casually into 77th Street. Sam did like the *Examiner* on Sunday, and this morning he had at last got around to reading about the events of Thursday night.

'About these four fellows,' Sam drawled to the desk sergeant. 'The four fellows mixed up in that bar fire, you know. I might have some information.'

'What kind of information?' asked the sergeant. For two days people had been volunteering information, and the sergeant was skeptical.

'I sold them the gasoline, I think,' Sam said.

In about two seconds, the sergeant was talking on the phone to the Detective Bureau, and a patrolman was escorting Sam to their office. 'Say, maybe I should have dropped around sooner,' Sam said.

Late Thursday night, Sam recalled, two men had come to the gas station where he was night attendant and asked him to fill up an old five-gallon paint bucket. Sam remembered because the bucket was pretty dirty inside, encrusted with dried paint and little chunks of gravel.

It didn't seem quite legal to put gasoline in that kind of container, and Sam had asked whether they didn't want him to scour it out. No, they said shortly. Just fill it up. So he had pumped $1.45 worth of gasoline into their dirty old bucket, and they went away.

Of the four in custody, Sam singled out Bates and Hernandez, the teen-ager, as the pair who had made the

185

purchase. From his description of the bucket, detectives finally located it, and Sam identified it.

Now, after the police had worked a total of 477 hours overtime, the case was cleaned up,* and a LAPD commendation report cited the teamwork Inspector Reddin had masterminded and the skill of his men.

As soon as Tom Reddin woke up . . . he'd be interested in that.

II

In Los Angeles almost half the population is non-Caucasian. This is far more complicated than the collision of white and Negro which has touched off so many race riots in metropolitan cities. It is a dozen collisions, the Oriental, the Mexican, the Indian, the Southerner (both Negro and white), the Easterner and the Westerner; intra-racial as well as one skin pitted against another of a different color.

From different countries and sections of our country, newcomers bring old prejudices, old teachings, old social barriers. Confusingly, some of them bring new and different philosophies, alien to those of their own race. The Negro who migrates to Los Angeles from New York or Chicago is entirely different from the one who has come up from the South. In just one section of the city, the police find three sharply distinct social groupings among the Negro population.

To LAPD race war is a latent but ever-present threat which could bring only tragedy and shame to the city and

* Brenhaug turned state's evidence. Bates and Chavez were found guilty of murder, and sentenced to death. Their automatic appeal has not yet been returned. Hernandez was sentenced to life imprisonment, and is now doing time.

recriminations to the police who are charged with keeping the peace. Yet the problem cannot be tucked into one powder keg marked 'Race Relations – Sit on This.' It is a multi-faceted problem which involves parts of neighborhoods as well as whole areas, public places where the races meet, youth gangs, and sudden, ugly rumor.

The police aren't supposed to be social do-gooders, but in LAPD's philosophy they aren't supposed to stand by till the reserves and National Guard have to be called out. So there is a Community Problems unit charged with preventing racial frictions from boiling over into street riots.

Once a disturbance is reported, or even the threat of one, Community Problems rolls. What is the dispute about? Who are the principals behind it, and where do they hang out? Who are their associates? What kind of cars do they drive?

Attached to the unit are both white and Negro officers. They work with community groups and church organizations as well as LAPD's Gang Squad. They listen for trouble and then call for help. Only if more gentle persuasions fail does LAPD lean. And then, having been briefed all along by CP, it leans hard and fast to stop trouble in its tracks.

Wrigley Field is located in a largely Negro district, and the attendance at its baseball games was always racially mixed. Angelenos are passionate ball fans, especially when the Los Angeles and Hollywood nines were playing their intra-city series, and usually umpire-booing has a warming, inter-racial unanimity to it.

This time there was trouble. Several Negro players were involved in a contested decision, some white fans charged onto the field, and fist fights started sporadically. A '415,' designating a disturbance, flashed over the police radio to all units.

As seat cushions flew toward the infield, police reinforcements poured into the stadium. Systematically, the officers broke up the fights between fans and players. When the rhubarb was over, a few players and spectators were removed, and the game went on. But CP sniffed trouble.

To call off the series between the Angels and the Stars would have been a municipal calamity, possibly riot-provoking in itself. To continue it was to risk a race war unless the police could somehow reason with or overawe the fans.

Inspector Noel McQuown decided to try it both ways. For the rest of the week, as the series went on, he sat in a box at the ball park with the best view of the field, but he didn't see a minute of a game. By special arrangement, the field announcer was posted beside him. If trouble erupted, McQuown had the loudest voice on the field to reason with the crowd.

To nip trouble in the bud, he conspicuously sprinkled uniformed men all through the grandstand. They were under special instructions: Keep pacing all the time; make sure every fan sees you.

Gradually the tension slackened. When the boos came, they were the outraged complaints of the man in the stand who always seems to see better than the near-sighted, not very bright official behind the plate. White fans booed when Negro players were called out, and Negroes groaned in sympathy as a white batter passed up three obvious balls and the umpire called them strikes. McQuown relaxed and began to pay attention to the game.

Sometimes, though, preventive policing can't move fast enough to avert unnecessary bloodshed. From the harbor district at the city's most southerly limits to San Fernando in the north, no section is free of the juvenile gang. There are the Negro gangs, the white gangs, the Japanese gangs,

188

the Mexican gangs, and sometimes combinations.

They are classified by age as the 'babies,' 'midgets,' 'gangs' and 'seniors,' the latter of whom have graduated from pack society into marriage or possibly the penitentiary. They fight with knives, guns, clubs, lengths of pipe; and they fight over anything from dope and girls to social status and racial issues.

One night McQuown was making a late check of Patrol Area Number One when his police radio picked up an 'ADW' call, assault with a deadly weapon. As he turned toward the scene, there was a second call: 'Several wounded and all not found.'

On a quiet neighborhood street in the East End, he found a dozen wounded youths lying on the sidewalk, one of them with fifty stab wounds.

McQuown dispatched radio car men through the area and they found half a dozen more casualties who had crawled into yards and under porches. It was the biggest youth gang bloodletting in LAPD history, and the inspector wanted to know why it had happened. He radioed Communications that he needed the Gang Detail assigned to Homicide.

As ambulances carried away the victims, Gang men briefed McQuown on the habits, sizes and peculiarities of the two warring gangs. The immediate spark had been jealousy by one gang because the other was reorganizing its strength. And eighteen youths paid for their animosity with broken heads, broken arms, bullet wounds and disfiguring knife slashes.

As a seven-year-old back home in Streator, Illinois, Noel McQuown used to sit on the curb at dusk and watch the town patrol wagon as it clanged bravely toward the lockup with the nightly roundup of drunks. He decided that someday he would be a policeman, and at the age of twenty-three he made LAPD.

But then his career took an unpredictable turn – as all police work has taken an unpredictable turn between the early 1920's and the 1950's – and McQuown today is LAPD's authority on minorities and race relations. No longer is this a problem that can be driven back at the point of a night stick. The modern policeman must be something of a sociologist and very much a tolerant, understanding human being.

McQuown learned race relations the hard way as a Lieutenant in the Newton Street Division where some 80,000 residents, overwhelmingly Negro, are jammed into an area of less than seven square miles.

The crusaders for better race relations usually protest the breakdown of crime statistics by race, pointing out logically that poverty, ignorance, and vice are common to all colors of skin. But to the cop pounding a beat in New York's Harlem, off the Loop in Chicago, or in LAPD's Newton Street Division, the argument holds little consolation. Whatever the cause, crime runs high in Negro areas.

McQuown found himself assigned to the division with the highest rate of murder, rape, and aggravated assault in all Los Angeles. Per 100,000 population, Newton Street has some 9,500 crimes yearly, mostly offenses 'against the person,' as the police statisticians call them. Only Central Division has a higher overall rate.

Yet McQuown learned to respect the Negro for his bravery, humor, and kindness, and it bothered him that out of his frequent transactions with the police, the Negro had developed a persecution complex. Often when he was arrested, he complained that he was being charged only because of the color of his skin. To peace officers everywhere, the assertion is familiar, and most policemen ignore it. McQuown felt the charge had been ignored too long.

So he devised a patient explanation for every prisoner who raised the issue. Before knowing *who* had committed a specific crime, the policeman had known only that a crime had been committed. His sole objective was to catch the criminal, and if he happened to be Negro, that was just the way it turned out. Had he been white, he would have been treated the same. To Negro motorists, he explained the policeman hadn't known a Negro was driving. He had chased and stopped a speeding *car*.

The simple, sincere logic of the argument impressed Negroes throughout the Division and eased relations with the police. Once they felt assurance that they were not victims of discrimination, they were willing to accept justice. McQuown's philosophy interested various civic groups working for minority welfare, and soon he was addressing meetings all over town on the subject of the police and race relations.

Chief Parker spotted him as the man to handle a critical and growing problem. He sent McQuown to Chicago to take a special course in police-minority work and, when he returned, told him to revise the Police Academy curriculum.

Today LAPD emphasizes to its rookies that there are only two methods by which the laws and regulations can be carried out in the field. The first is to understand the people and the reasons behind their actions. The second is to try to enforce the Department's own standards on others. LAPD does not tolerate the second approach. Police can be neither judges nor prosecutors, McQuown says. 'We are *apprehenders* – and that's all we are.'

McQuown had been serving about a year as LAPD's No. One authority on race relations when he met his first serious test.

For some time there had been agitation over reported real estate discrimination against Negroes in nearby

Compton. McQuown knew that the bad feeling would probably spill over into Los Angeles in the homes bordering that town. The junior high school drew students, white and Negro, from the area, and was already a racial sore spot. In only eight years, the southern section of Los Angeles which it served had changed from eighty-five per cent white population to eighty-five per cent Negro. The remaining whites felt beleaguered and hostile to their new neighbors.

Under those conditions, almost anything, a schoolboy fight at recess, a rumor, even one insulting word, could touch off the trouble. Unfortunately for the school, three unrelated episodes which no one could have foreseen combined to give Los Angeles its worst experience with juvenile hate and prejudice.

First, a veteran official at the school who was aware of its background of racial tensions was promoted out of the district. The new administrator – on the job only two days – was unfamiliar with the situation. Second, after a long period of confinement in an institution, a mentally disturbed Negro boy was returned to the school and in his first two days back got into three fights.

Now gangs were formed on basis of race and extended challenges to each other for all-out combat. As they were preparing for action, a Negro boy playing on the railroad tracks was killed by a train. Rumor swept the school corridors that actually a gang of white boys had pushed him to his death.

That did it; and, before the new vice principal could act, gang fights broke out sporadically all over the area. When police patrol cars arrived, they found almost three hundred boys arrayed for battle. The area was close to a major race riot.

Quickly the officers scattered the youths in all directions and seized the ringleaders of both races. But it was only stopgap action, and McQuown moved in with both an emergency program and some long-range ideas.

To handle the immediate crisis, he persuaded school officials to stagger class dismissals at 1:30 p.m., 2 p.m., 2:30 p.m. and 3 o'clock. Both before and after sessions, he had five police cars assigned to patrol duty in the area. When strange youths infiltrated the neighborhood 'to watch the fun' (including one caravan of twelve cars), he asked all nearby schools to restrain their students.

But the underlying tensions persisted, and McQuown knew that these could be resolved only by the community and the students themselves. LAPD called a meeting of the ringleaders and laid it on the line. There must be no more violence. Further, it was suggested, some of the school's promising athletes might fail to win scholarships if the school became tabbed with a 'race' reputation.

Then LAPD officers visited the parents, asking their cooperation, and checked how many of their sons had previously got into trouble. Those with records were put back under the calming influence of their old probation officers.

McQuown also appealed for intervention by community organizations, which should have been the deciding factor. Unfortunately, because of the population upheaval, most of these clubs and groups had been badly weakened, and the job came back to the police. 'We were teaching these people to live with each other,' McQuown recalls.

But he got one break. The school's best athletes, worried about their chances of scholarships, began to talk openly against race hate. Their prestige carried weight, and soon other youngsters were anonymously tipping off LAPD whenever trouble loomed. To save face, they had to accompany their own gangs to the battlefields and then flee at the sight of the waiting police. But they wanted the officers to know that a lot of the fellows were sick of the whole thing.

At last the calls stopped. There were no more brawls, real or rumored. Negro and white were getting along with each other, perhaps better than before the trouble, because both sides were secretly ashamed. It had taken weeks, but McQuown had achieved success in the new variation of an old police function. He had kept the peace between the races.

III

For many years LAPD and the Los Angeles newspapers were joined in the trying bonds of Jiggs-and-Maggie wedlock. The police had to use the press to communicate with the public. Often publicity facilitated identifications of the dead, located the missing, and brought forth key witnesses. In turn, the newspapers relied on LAPD for some of the most fascinating stories in their news columns; and, in the robust old days of the circulation wars, a good police scoop meant thousands of additional street sales.

But by the very nature of the jobs, the partners were incompatible. To the policeman, the crime reporter was a ferret stirring up trouble, because police business was essentially confidential business. To this day, detectives in LAPD blame meddling by the press for their failure to solve the Black Dahlia torture murder. In turn, the police reporter, Headquarters man and district legman alike, charged that police stupidity and/or stubbornness deprived them of legitimate, public news.

Under Chief Parker, the press recognized, LAPD was conscientiously trying to root out many old inefficiencies and abuses; and yet, curiously, press-police relations dropped to a new low during the early years of the Parker regime. When the 'police brutality' scandal broke, all the papers lambasted him and, pointing out that the average Los Angeles Chief lasts two years in office, gleefully noted Parker had been in for nineteen months. The Los Angeles *Herald & Express* quoted 'well-informed politicians' as saying that Parker had become the favorite Los Angeles sport – 'They're shooting at him.'

An honest career cop doesn't make Chief by turning the other cheek, and usually Parker gave back as good as he got, which did not sweeten the relations. Once he even broke up the non-stop poker game in the City Hall Press Room which newsmen considered perilously close to infringing on the Bill of Rights. Parker blamed the intrusion of 'outside elements' into the game, but the press considered it petty reprisal. At two a.m. one day, they hung a funeral wreath on his office door and then decided to take photographs of it. But when a team of photographers returned, Parker's security patrol had already spotted and removed it. The press was more enraged than ever.

Actually, press relations (including radio and TV as well as the newspapers) should have almost top priority with any police department because they are essentially *community* relations. (The ex-newspaperman who handles press liaison for the New York City Police Department carries the title of Deputy Commissioner in Charge of Community Relations.) From minimizing stories of racial friction to withholding vital information during the search for a fugitive, the press can be, and must be, an invaluable police ally and helpmate.

In Los Angeles, it took a train wreck to salvage the almost broken marriage.

On an early January night, a sixty-one-year-old engineer was pushing the two-car San Diegan of the Santa Fe

Railroad south out of the yards. As he neared the six-degree bend in the track, he was doing almost seventy, but a strange optical delusion had seized him. Looking for the speed-limit markers, he saw 'orange trees' (they were really boxcars), and he didn't slam on the 'big hold,' the emergency brake, till the train was already shimmying. In the crash, twenty-nine persons were killed and one hundred and forty-six injured.

Through 'Sigalert' communications, LAPD poured everything into the thickly populated section south of the downtown district: doctors, nurses, ambulances, emergency vehicles, policemen, firemen, deputy sheriffs. Their job was threefold: save lives and care for the injured; isolate the disaster scene; remove unauthorized persons from the area.

Unfortunately, before a police command post could seal off the area of several square blocks, curiosity seekers by the thousands had swarmed in. They interfered with rescue work, delayed the righting of the overturned cars, blocked the traffic routes used by emergency vehicles. Ambulances loaded with the injured had to fight their way through.

But when the police did clear the wreck scene, reporters and photographers got the brush along with everybody else. 'You're just the press,' one reporter was told as the police shoved him back. Another newsman belted an officer on the jaw and yelled, 'If you want me out of here, you'll have to carry me out.' In the shoving confusion, reporters lost their hats and stories, photographers almost had their cameras broken.

Next day newspaper editorials denounced the police action, and some even demanded that Parker resign. Again, Parker fought back: in forty-five minutes, all one hundred and forty-six injured had been extricated and placed in ambulances. Their personal property had been safeguarded, and police had preserved the tachometer in the engine cab which showed the speed at the time of the crash.

'There were people all over the place with shiny sheriff's badges,' he said, defending the manhandling of the press. 'The place was lousy with them. Many times the officers had no time to stop and ascertain whether the wearer had the authority to have such a badge.'

But this time the press would not be turned aside.

As Los Angeles daily papers steamed with inflamed, accusing headlines of police inefficiency and maltreatment, the Police Commission waded into the battle. It stood as a buffer between public and police.

For several days, a stream of nearly seventy-five witnesses representing all law enforcement agencies in Los Angeles County paraded through the Commission's chambers to give testimony on the Santa Fe wreck hassle.

It soon became apparent that what had been sorely lacking was a steadying, coordinating hand between press and lawmen at the scene of the disaster.

At a reconciliation session, both sides agreed that a press liaison officer should be named to facilitate newsgathering at all hours, on all stories, under any circumstances. Further, he would have to appreciate the points of conflict between press and police and command sufficient departmental stature to assure the respect of the press and the obedience of the police.

From his own staff, Parker produced Inspector Edward Walker, a big, tough, soft-spoken, native Angeleno. He knew practically nothing about the complexities of newspaper operation, but after nineteen years on LAPD, he did know cops and newspapermen. And, as it turned out, he had some surprisingly uncoplike ideas about the handling of news stories.

Like race relations, LAPD would now recognize press – or community – relations at the inspector's level of command and permit one of its $12,000-a-year top men to give full time to bettering them.

In the new LAPD building, newsmen found they were being installed in large, airy quarters equipped with the same office furniture used by the police. Every newspaper and wire service represented on the police beat received its own desk, typewriter and six-way radio-phone. Thus, the newsmen were tied into all law inforcement radios in the county, plus fire and civilian defense communications and LAPD's own intra-departmental phone system.

Thus far, fine. But the skeptical reporters were still waiting to see how Walker would operate on the first big news break. Would all the nice promises be realized – or would he go cop on them?

When it broke, it was one of those cockeyed Hollywood stories that excite the reporters, delight the public, and harass the police. LAPD got the flash at one a.m., and roused Ed Walker. Before he had gulped down a cup of coffee, newspapers were calling him from New York, Toronto, London.

Walker groaned. From long experience, he knew how the reporters and photogs would roll on this one, and he raced to the early American home in San Fernando Valley to head them off. He had just two thoughts in mind: to placate the press by giving them as much leeway as he could, and yet, as a policeman, to protect the evidence, if any. The report said: Marie (The Body) McDonald has been kidnapped.

To this day, no one, including LAPD, knows exactly what did happen, but there is general agreement that Walker did his part. He allowed both reporters and photographers liberal run of the McDonald home, but to save the detectives on the case from utter distraction, emphasized that all police information would clear through him alone.

The following night, Marie turned up, bruised and hysterical, alongside a desert road about two hundred miles south of Los Angeles. She said two men had kidnapped her, apparently for an insignificant amount of ransom; had telephoned her mother reassuringly that she would not be harmed; then finally had released her. To quiet doubters, she agreed to a re-enactment in her home, and once again Walker had a problem.

To him, re-enactments were nothing new. LAPD had been filming them for more than a decade both to give detectives a better visualization of the case and to keep a permanent record. But when the reporters saw three investigators and two technicians enter the McDonald home with a tape recorder, a 16-mm camera, and twelve hundred feet of film, there was another outburst of excitement. They wanted in, too.

To keep them from interfering with the filming, Walker had a loudspeaker hooked up outside the house where all the press could listen. Inside, an officer with a walkie-talkie fed a running account of the re-enactment into the speaker. That worked fine till a friend of Marie, a local TV newscaster, phoned her direct and asked if he couldn't come in. Sure, Marie said, not clearing it with Walker, and the rest of the press revolted. Walker had to step in then on their behalf and get most of them into the house, too.

'It was a wild scene,' he says quietly today.

Next day there was another snafu. Reporters had just discovered that Michael Wilding, the actor, had been at the house during the re-enactment. Why, they demanded of Walker, hadn't they been told? Wilding had been available, Walker said tartly, but in their own excitement, they had overlooked him. The press accepted the rebuke.

Ed Walker knows that, like the police, the press are fundamentally interested in good police enforcement and, given the opportunity, will cooperate. Thus, LAPD radio code '20' was born. The number alerts news photographers to the locations where good crime or traffic photos can be made. 'We encourage the press to take spectacular pictures, especially in traffic accident cases,' Walker explains. 'It might help to slow down the next guy.'

So far as he is concerned, the press can enter into any dangerous police situation at its own risk, after being warned of the possible risks. Photographers have even been allowed into burning buildings. And since the Sante Fe wreck, where photos of the mutilated bodies were forbidden, police have been ordered to forego censorship of any kind. LAPD leaves it to the judgment and good taste of newspaper editors to pass on the photos considered fit to print.

After the Mecca Bar fire, the *Mirror-News* front-paged a photo of the burned corpse on the bar stool. The shot shocked Los Angeles, but more than anything else, brought home to the public the full horror of the tragedy.

As Walker sees his job, he is the middleman between crime and the public and, short of destroying evidence, he wants to let the press make its report in full. On one occasion, a second-hand dealer was found stabbed to death in his store, his body awkwardly jackknifed behind a narrow counter piled high with merchandise. Few detectives would have allowed the photographers inside. Walker directed that, one by one, the photographers squeeze into the tiny passage behind the counter, take their shots and leave. The evidence remained undisturbed.

Again, when an F-89J jet and a DC-7B transport, both on test flights, collided high over San Fernando Valley, Walker came through for his charges. Not only were five airmen killed, but the wreckage of the transport slammed into the crowded playground of a junior high school at the northern end of the Valley. Three students were killed, and more than seventy were injured.

Again, there was confusion, as at the scene of the Santa Fe wreck, as parents and passers-by by the hundreds stampeded to the playground. But this time Walker was one of the first officers to appear, and he ordered every policeman to refer to him, without any argument, persons without credentials who claimed to be from the press.

Walker did a fast screening job, separating the phonies from the legitimate newsmen, and arranged interviews with eyewitnesses, policemen and even some of the injured children. At one point, officials of the Civil Aeronautics Board asked that all newspaper men be cleared from the schoolyard; and that was when the press knew, beyond all doubt, that he was really one of them. Walker turned down the government men.

Bluntly he pointed out that representatives of the two aircraft companies involved as well as other outsiders were being allowed into the disaster area. As far as he was concerned, the press should enjoy the same privileges. The request, he said, was the 'stampede by government' which usually follows a disaster but is unnecessary and unfair to the public, which has the right to know.

So instead, he had a special section roped off for TV cameras and crews and provided floodlights for them. For the reporters and news photographers, he continued to supply leads and photo possibilities – and kept them close enough to the scene so that they could work.

Out of the coverage, two major gains, from the police point of view, were scored. First, the telecasts gave home viewers such a comprehensive picture of the disaster that the curiosity seekers stayed home and watched rather than jamming into the emergency area. And, through excellent photos and reportage, the press aroused a righteous public indignation against the folly of test flights over densely populated sections.

'I strongly feel that the press should cover *all* disasters first-hand and that there should be no hindrance whatever to such coverage,' Walker says.

In turn, the press is reciprocating. During the Mecca Bar investigation, they withheld much of what they knew at the request of the police. It was a painful responsibility, but they even passed up the page one story about the arrest of the first two suspects so the detectives could close in on the pair still at large.

That was just about the biggest bouquet a police reporter could hand Ed Walker.

THE DEPUTY CHIEF

When William H. Parker became Chief of LAPD, he closed the door marked Assistant Chief and re-distributed top administrative responsibilities among a handful of Deputy Chiefs. There have been unkind suggestions that Parker felt one assistant might be tempted to take over the department, whereas with several deputies he could divide and rule unchallenged. Actually Parker was dividing LAPD into its basic, semi-independent divisions and recognizing merit. At the top of each division, as its supreme boss, he placed a 'Chief' whose departmental record gave him clear title to the job.

All LAPD's Chiefs began as rookies, sweated out the exams, the eligibility lists, the promotion lists, and then gradually became specialists. All are now potential candidates for Parker's job; in fact one did serve as Chief before him and another lost out to Parker by the narrowest of margins. For a man who supposedly feared one assistant, Parker has rashly surrounded himself with no less than seven rivals. *And they are expert.*

Patrol Bureau. Half of LAPD's manpower, some 2,200 men, patrol more than six million miles yearly by car, more than one hundred thousand miles afoot. They roll on half a million radio calls and make two hundred thousand arrests. Their Chief: red-haired Frank E. Walton, a tough, determined officer who refused to let even the war hold back his police career. While serving as a Marine Intelligence officer in the Pacific, he wrote his exam for Lieutenant in a hut on Espiritu Santo and airmailed it back to Los Angeles.

Detective Bureau. Usually Patrol rolls first and makes the arrests, but it's up to LAPD's six hundred and fifty detectives to make them stand up in court. The record shows that they clean up ninety-five out of one hundred murders, sixty out of one hundred rapes, seventy out of one hundred aggravated assaults. Their Chief: Thad Brown, 'the detective's detective,' who has amassed forty-three official commendations during thirty-two years on the force. He is the Greenfield, Missouri, boy, ex-miner, ex-plasterer, who lost the No. 1 job to Parker by a squeaker.

Traffic Bureau. In a year, Angelenos drive the equivalent of four hundred thousand round trips around the earth. Their 1,300,000 registered vehicles would reach from Los Angeles to New York and back to Kansas City. They are probably the fastest drivers in the world because most of them live so far from work. And yet LAPD traffic men have made Los Angeles the safest big city in the country in movement of traffic. Their Chief: Harold W. Sullivan, a native Angeleno, amateur baseball statistician, who has been in Traffic since he was a sergeant.

Bureau of Corrections. Keeping the jails (a job LAPD doesn't like to be saddled with) consumes twenty per cent of its budget and more than eight per cent of police manpower. Corrections handles one hundred thousand drunks yearly, plus another hundred thousand assorted offenders, who cost the city more than $3 daily per man. They serve more than a million mandays (which means some three and a quarter million meals) and tie up three hundred and seventy officers. Their Chief: scholarly Roger E. Murdock, red-haired Scotch-Irish university graduate, who teaches a course in Investigation of Major Crime at Los Angeles State College.

Personnel and Training. Cops don't come off an assembly line. LAPD assigns eighty other officers to find them, sift them, mold them, fit them into the pattern. In a normal year, 3,836 will apply for the job of policeman. Ninety-seven make it. P-T's human obstacle course of eighty trips up the rest. Their Chief: Lynn A. White, forty-five, Purple Heart Naval Commander, whose baby face made him the undercover scourge of the Los Angeles dope rings for years. His pride in P-T is this: 'If we fail, the force fails. The department is only as good as the people we hire.'

Technical Services. It takes more than bone and tissue to run a police department. In LAPD's massive Administration Building it also takes twenty-one miles of conduit, seventy-eight miles of wire, thirteen separate radio frequencies, five hundred telephones. But the electronic miracle does not throb without the bone and tissue, either. The department's basic services are manned by a complement in blue of 179. Their Chief: droll, sage Arthur C. Hohmann, who at sixty-two looks back on thirty-four years of policing, including two years as Chief of Police. His epigram: 'I'm not one of those guys who goes out and gets trophies and medals.'

Bureau of Administration. Who helps the Chief be Chief? In Los Angeles, it takes 168 men. They are the eyes and ears of the Chief of Police. They are Intelligence, IA, Ad Vice, Business Office, Public Information, and Planning & Research. From the blast of an irate citizen to the daily atomic radiation reading, the job gets done by the men of BA. Their Chief: Richard Simon, fifty-four, burly whip of the annual police budget and bureau commander since its origin in November, 1950. In his spare time, he teaches minority and other special police problems to a college class of peace officers, including Negroes. He tells them: 'We ourselves are a minority group.'

These are the bones. Each Chief's-eye view of his own job is different, but all of them at their lonely command desks have a common problem. Unlike most top executives in the outside world, they can't just 'think big' and deal in abstracts. Statistics tell a persuasive story, but one officer goofing off or a suicide in the jailhouse carries greater impact with the public. A Deputy Chief's job is schizophrenic. He must see all divisions in his command together and separately.

Try these for specifics.

II

When Deputy Chief Frank Walton made up his mind that his career would be law enforcement, he swore off smoking. 'If you are on a stakeout and have a quick cigarette,' he explains, 'you can't hide the odor of the smoke. Your suspect will know you are around.' That's the specific approach to a police problem.

And his uniformed men deal in the specifics of crime. Detectives catch the headlines, but the patrolman catches the crook: the hoodlum prowling the quiet neighborhood, the stickup man backing out of a liquor store, the switchblade knifer standing over a body, the burglar leaping backyard fences.

The night Officers R. J. May and J. D. Reardon were riding radio in the Hollywood Division, the problem was specific. A bandit-rapist had been terrorizing young couples in lover's lanes, leaving behind only one clue. Two illuminated dials on his auto dashboard glowed red. Just after dark this night, police had stopped and examined more than one hundred cars looking for the telltale red dash lights, but without success.

Now a radio alert told May and Reardon that an eight-year-old green coupe, possibly a Ford, was believed headed toward Los Angeles from a stickup at Redondo Beach. Reardon was driving; so May jotted down a description of the car.

Two hours later, driving south on Vermont Avenue at the eastern fringe of Hollywood, they spotted the old coupe coming toward them. Reardon radioed for reinforcements and U-turned to follow. The coupe driver spotted them, too. He drove into a darkened gas station, then backtracked south on Vermont. The officers turned and followed.

For a mile and a half, from Sunset Boulevard to Beverly, the chase roared on, and then the green coupe broke right through a blockade set up by other police cars. Reardon followed, and when the coupe crashed, he and his partner collared two fugitives.

Very specific. One proved to be the so-called 'red-light bandit,' the notorious Caryl Whitman Chessman, subsequently convicted on seventeen counts of robbery, kidnapping with bodily harm, sexual perversion, and attempted rape. Chessman went on to make legal history by successfully staving off his death sentence for years through a prolonged court maneuvering.

Specifics.

In the dull and stately phraseology affected by policemen, the report begins, 'While on routine patrol . . .' And then are detailed the specifics that Frank Walton's men grapple with daily as each rides forty miles of street, three square miles in area, charged with the protection of fifteen thousand citizens and taxpayers.

Officers Jack T. Smith and Eugene Dossi question two

suspicious youths on the street, find they are carrying pliers, a flashlight, and a master key marked, 'Do Not Take From Office.' Thus, they end an outbreak of schoolhouse burglaries in the Harbor Division.

Officers Garth Ward and Warner Chinnis are routinely patrolling in University Division, but not too routinely to overlook the two cars which park side by side as the drivers engage in brief, whispered conversation. They tail one car – and then, before their night watch has ended, they serve warrants; search apartments; confiscate narcotics, needles, and burnt spoons used by heroin addicts; and arrest several men and women.

The placid routine of patrol may be interrupted by a teletyped All Points Bulletin from another city, or by the most ancient form of police communications, the anguished cry of 'Police!'

At roll call on the day watch one morning, Officers M. E. Buckner and S. Trypak memorized the teletyped APB from San Francisco, describing two men who had slugged a policeman there and fled by car. Five hours later, Buckner and Trypak bagged the pair five miles from downtown Los Angeles.

Officers J. M. Noonan and F. A. Sylvester dutifully stopped for a red traffic light about ten o'clock one night in the University area. From a nearby beauty shop, they heard muffled cries for help. They found an employee struggling with a stickup man. They captured him and got evidence resulting in two more arrests. In less than thirty-six hours, the gang had pulled five stickups.

Not all the patrol is routinely pursued by land. On night watch on LAPD's police boat, Officers Robert O. Ernst and John S. Gable received a radio command to find a twenty-seven-foot power cruiser reported operating erratically and without running or clearance lights.

Along with boats from the Los Angeles Harbor

Department, the Fire Department, and the Coast Guard, Ernst and Gable set off in pursuit. Two high-tonnage vessels were maneuvering in the harbor turning basin, and the pursuers had to pilot skillfully around them. The errant cruiser ahead poured on its power and tried to shake off the chase.

But the police boat pulled alongside, one of the officers leaped aboard the cruiser, and there was a tussle for control of the wheel. The pilot suddenly revved up his engine and veered sharply. He couldn't shake off the policeman. He was escorted to Harbor Division headquarters and held as a drunken boat driver.

Specifics.

As boss of patrol in the nation's third largest city, Frank Walton has his nose buried deep in such reports day after day. Yet, there is the other side of the job, too; the generalship, the staff work, which must place the men in the field where they are needed and when they are needed.

Walton was borrowed by the City of Chicago in the late 1940's to help overhaul its police department and then came home to revamp the training program of LAPD's Police Academy. After that, he got around to a revolutionary but scientifically plotted redeployment of every LAPD man in uniform.

Once policemen were shuffled around Los Angeles by rule of thumb. What this meant, in practice, was that the divisional captain who beefed the loudest, the civic representatives who pulled the most weight, got the most policemen for their districts. Some quiet neighborhoods beset chiefly by bicycle thieves were over-policed while areas roaring with mayhem remained badly under-manned.

With the help of LAPD's research specialists, Chief Walton amassed all the important crime and population statistics of Los Angeles and then broke them down by police divisions. The results were startling, even to Walton.

The Wilshire Division, covering a fashionable, well-to-do and peaceful neighborhood, policed an area with the second highest population percentage in the city. But, the crime statistics disclosed, Wilshire didn't require many uniformed men per capita. It rated only fifth in the amount of overall crime, so under Walton's reapportionment program, Wilshire got 123 men for patrol, which made it the fifth largest divisional force in the city.

On the other hand, Central, LAPD's incorrigible problem child, was jumping with trouble.

Though less than five and a half per cent of the city's six thousand miles of streets ran through the division, Central regularly piled up the highest percentage of injuries and fatalities in traffic accidents.

And though its population rated only sixth, its crime percentage figures led all other divisions in everything: in percentage of both adult and juvenile felony arrests; radio calls and time consumed answering radio calls; property loss from crimes, robberies, burglaries; felonious assaults; larcenies; murders; auto thefts; and burglaries, thefts from autos.

Chief Walton promptly beefed up the Central Division with 263 men, the highest percentage of the patrol force. Similarly, he allotted manpower to the other divisions on the basis of their qualitative needs, rather than by head count. No divisional commander or neighborhood leader could quarrel with percentage points.

Ideally patrolmen should spend seventy-five per cent of their time on patrol and twenty-five per cent 'off the air' in making arrests or investigating calls from citizens. But Los Angeles' enormous population increase has far out-distanced police manpower and cruelly increased every policeman's workload. In a city of two and a half million, LAPD is virtually a 'vest pocket' police force.

To combat the personnel shortage, Chief Walton has further refined his techniques for anticipating where his men will be wanted and at what hour of the day or night.

First, he studied the New York City experiment in slugging crime to death. In a saturation program, New York poured a task force of two hundred policemen into one small district and virtually overwhelmed the criminals. Within a short period, the crime rate plummeted amazingly. But the situation there was different. With a little more than three times the population of Los Angeles, New York had almost six times as many policemen. Walton just couldn't spare the men for such a frontal assault.

Instead, he again attacked with research and slide rule. LAPD analysts made a statistical examination of all divisions and ascertained for each the square mile – 'the crime mile,' they called it – which had the highest incidence of trouble. In addition, they pinpointed the period of high frequency along 'crime mile.'

In one division, trouble time was from seven o'clock at night until three in the morning. Ten two-man radio cars and two sergeants were then assigned during those hours to the 'crime mile.' They questioned suspicious characters, issued traffic citations, shook down vehicles. Most of all, they made themselves conspicuous. Trouble makers knew they were around.

Officers worked 'the crime miles' on a two-weeks' trial basis. After that, they might return for a few days or even a few hours. Because LAPD was under-staffed, they had to hit Hollywood for four hours, then move over to the Valley for the same amount of time. It was a sketchy, flying-squad assignment, but the results were immediate.

In one division, the area of high frequency crime cooled

down within days. In another, the mobile force of twenty-two men served $8,000 worth of traffic warrants in five days. A section of Hollywood which had become infested with purse snatchers did not record a single complaint for a month after the 'crime mile' operation.

Whatever the specific problem, the technique seemed to work, whether impulsive or planned crime was involved. Thus, in neighborhoods marked by street fights and ginmill brawls, the mere show of the uniform had a quieting effect. On the other hand, in a downtown loft district, the flying squads put an end to an outbreak of garment-factory burglaries and caught a 'phantom' second-story man who had long been pestering the division.

To Walton, 'crime mile' achieved two purposes. Divisional commanders received sudden, strong reinforcements in their fight against increasing crime. And the overall results dramatized what LAPD could really accomplish, given an adequate patrol force.

But Chief Walton operates under no delusion that he is going to get all the men he needs. He can't even get enough facilities. For example, the Patrol Bureau, which is also charged with control of juvenile delinquency, must on occasion turn loose young hoodlums because there just is no place to detain them.

In one instance, a patrol car from University Division brought in an over-sized sixteen-year-old, six feet, two hundred pounds, and roaring drunk. He had crashed a private party, started a brawl and then had brutally beaten up a smaller, younger boy. Obviously, even for his own protection, he needed detention.

But the city maintains no regular juvenile detention unit, and because he was under eighteen, he could not be booked into City Jail. The arresting officers tried Juvenile Hall, a detention facility operated by Los Angeles County.

Sorry, they were told; the Hall was already seventy per cent overloaded.

The watch commander at University had the boy's mother brought to the station, but even she had no place for him. 'He beats me up,' she said tearfully. 'I'm afraid of him.' Next the division called in the watch commander of the Juvenile Division. There was, he said, only one thing that could be done. Like it or not, the boy had to be released into the mother's custody, and she went home with the child she feared.

Sometimes, the overwork, the pressures, the tight restrictions on everything they do, on or off duty, become oppressive, and policemen just quit the job. In one case, a uniformed man became involved in petty difficulties with a neighbor, and though Patrol thought he was in the right, Chief Walton advised him that it would be more discretionary to move away.

'The policeman usually loses,' he says philosophically.

But as a man who must daily guard against the specific charge of 'civil rights violation' against any one of his 2,200 men during performance of duty, there is a dry note in his voice as he adds:

'A policeman gives up *his* civil liberties to a great degree – too much of a degree. People who shout about safeguarding civil rights don't appreciate the extent to which a policeman gives up his.'

Specifics.

III

'When did you go to the apartment?'
'Who, me?'
'When did you get there?'
'I wasn't there.'

215

'We found the scarf there. It's yours, isn't it?'

'Sure. That's my scarf. I don't know how it got there.'

'It didn't walk there, did it?'

'No, guess not. But I don't know how it got there. I didn't leave it there. I wasn't near the place.'

'Well, you must have been there. Now, try to remember. You did know Helen, didn't you?'

'Helen? Sure. I seen her a couple of times. Down at the drugstore. Nice kid. That's all. I hardly knew her.'

'The landlady said you visited her once, in the apartment.'

'Oh, no. Who, me? Naw!'

'Where were you last Monday night? About eleven?'

'Could have been anywhere. I'm usually out and around. Say, you got me wrong. This isn't my beef. Not at all.'

'Nobody said it's your beef.'

'No? Well . . .'

In the soundproof interrogation room just off the squad-room of the Homicide Division, the detective and the suspect with the familiar faraway stare of the guilty are momentarily quiet. Then it starts again.

'What do you say, Bill?'

'What?'

'Can you remember a little better now?'

'Why don't you leave me alone?'

'Let's have some right answers and we will.'

'Well, what do you want?'

'We found your scarf in Helen's place. You know where we found it, Bill?'

'Aw . . . Yeah, sure. I know where you found it. I know, I know, I know . . .'

'Why did you strangle her with the scarf?'

'She was a good kid . . . Helen. Too good. I had this crazy idea. I never had that idea before. You believe me? So I went . . .'

And there it is. He is talking. Another murder is being solved.

To Thad Brown, this is the specific he has known almost all his life now. The scarf, the clue; its owner, the suspect. Out of the specific, any damning little thing, come apprehension, interrogation, confession.

Thad has never forgotten the days when he was breaking in under Detective W. A. (Pappy) Neely, an Oklahoman with a sixth-grade education who could never quite master the sergeant's examination. But Pappy was a master of the specific.

Once Thad rolled with him on the investigation into the stabbing murder of a woman in her apartment. They found a few cigarette butts, some drinking glasses (without fingerprints) and a partially used book of matches that could have been picked up anywhere. Pappy studied it a moment and tucked it casually into his pocket.

Then they questioned all the murdered woman's boy friends, and all seemed to have good alibis. Especially one. During his interrogation, Pappy offered him a cigarette and a book of matches. The man struck the match with his left hand, and Pappy arrested him. The suspect then admitted the woman had been his mistress, and he had killed her in a jealous rage. The book of matches he had left behind in the apartment had been used from the left side, rather than from the right as a right-handed person normally depletes a book of matches.

In turn, Thad mastered the specific as he checked out on thousands of 'dead body' reports and saw murder close up in all its obscene and grisly forms. *Something* in the room, perhaps a wisp of hair because no two heads of hair are exactly alike, would give him his lead.

Once a woman's body was found dumped in the desert. She had been shot through the head at close range. There were odd-type powder burns on her cheek. They had to come from the muzzle of a strange and rare gun. That was all Thad needed because he remembered that gun. Once before it had been used in an unsolved killing. He traced the weapon to the woman's husband. The man had just fled, but Thad ascertained his direction, and when the fugitive stepped off the train at Chicago, the police there closed in.

Today, the specific is stretched almost into the abstract for Thad Brown. As Chief of Detectives, he has almost all sleuthing as his province and supervises detective divisions, which pursue investigations of auto theft, burglary, pawnshop, forgery, fugitive – bunco, narcotics, robbery.

And, of course, the Homicide Division whose sixty men are assigned to the almost fourteen square miles and some 160,000 residents of the turbulent Central Division. Outlying divisions have their own detective staffs, but often Homicide helps them on an important case. And the word 'Homicide' is a bit of a misnomer because the Division is also charged with investigating assaults, bigamies, suicides and other 'dead body' reports, rapes, abortions, kidnappings, and train wrecks.

Thad Brown doesn't concentrate on the specific as much as he used to do. That's the job of his detectives. He coordinates the action in the field, accelerates the investigation through his enormous personal file of contacts and informants, and counsels on the preparation of the evidence for presentation in court.

Sometimes, because of his close personal friendships with police in distant cities, he cuts red tape with a single long-distance call. Once during the tedious Black Dahlia murder investigation, there was a 'confession' (one of the dozens that distinguished that peculiar case) in faraway Lansing, Michigan.

Thad Brown doubted the suspect knew anything about

the murder and didn't want to tie up one of his detectives in the time-consuming formalities of taking over responsibility for the prisoner. So he phoned a friend in the Lansing police department. Without delay, the suspect was brought to Los Angeles, cleared after a few questions and returned to Lansing. The whole thing took a few hours, instead of several days, because Thad Brown had a personal contact.

And sometimes it works in reverse. When a bad check artist fled Honolulu by plane, one of Thad's friends, Chief of the Island police force, Dan Liu, telephoned ahead. A LAPD detail was waiting at the airport, grabbed the fugitive, fed him, and put him back on the next Honolulu-bound plane.

In a way, Thad Brown's career is a microcosm of LAPD itself. When he joined the force, Los Angeles was struggling under the Volstead Act. Before the shine had worn off his rookie badge, Thad was cracking nine to ten whisky stills monthly and making thirty to fifty felony arrests in the same period.

He spent a dozen of his first fourteen years on the force in Detective Bureau assignments; and, right after Pearl Harbor, he was named LAPD's liaison officer with the armed forces in the defense of Los Angeles Harbor. His mission was primarily to help guard the area's huge shipyards and refineries against sabotage. As a trained detective lieutenant, he spotted and plugged many holes in the security wall. In one instance, he discovered that the power unit which fed an entire shipyard was left exposed and unguarded. He changed that.

When Japanese aliens, the Nisei, had to be rounded up and sent to relocation centers in the desert, it was Thad's squad that accomplished the job with lists supplied by the FBI. By 1942 the Nisei had been cleared from the city, and LAPD grappled with a more dangerous wartime problem.

As the aircraft, oil, and shipbuilding industries boomed, the war workers flooded the city by the tens of thousands, and so did the criminals looking for an easy buck. In that first year of war, the population skyrocketed by 70,000, and arrests increased by 11,000. There were more murders and rapes; and six hundred more persons were reported missing than the year before. It was getting far more dangerous just to walk across the street. Traffic citations doubled to half a million compared to about a quarter of a million in the last prewar year.

Thad Brown was holding down an assignment in the Administrative Vice Squad, but now he was needed in a hotter spot. Reported crime surged upward another thirteen per cent during 1943; and, with the department weakened by men absent on military service, there were 17,000 fewer arrests. Los Angeles seemed to be moving toward wartime anarchy, when Thad Brown was made captain and put in command of the catch-all Homicide Division.

That year there were seventy-eight murders in Los Angeles, and Thad particularly remembers two as symptomatic of the mixed-up adults who had jammed into Los Angeles from all over the country.

One gray November morning, John Valentine,* a six-foot-five war worker, was up by six o'clock to go to his job. A friend, Raymond Boyd, spoke casually to him, but Valentine didn't like his tone. So, instead of going to the plant that morning, he shot and killed his friend. Just like that.

And then, Thad remembers, there was the fumbling little hood with the impressive name of Farrington Graham* who finally fumbled his way to Death Row at San Quentin. Beginning at the age of ten when he stole a

*These are fictitious names.

bike, Farrington Graham built up a mediocre but uninterrupted police record for theft, robbery, burglary, possession of weapons, and jail-breaking.

Then Farrington Graham went on a long holdup kick in Los Angeles. At first he was lucky, but he really had neither the brains nor the nerves for the job. When a hotel clerk seemed about to resist, Graham panicked, poured four shots into him and fled with his loot – $3. He went to Las Vegas and repeated his mistake. He tried to hold up the cashier at the Frontier Club, panicked again and killed him.

Graham was returned to Thad who prepared the evidence, a confession buttressed by ballistics findings, which convicted him. Then Graham devised a novel appeal, claiming he resorted to crime only after taking drinks and hence was not guilty by reason of intoxication. But the California high court found that voluntary intoxication is neither an excuse for crime nor a defense. And thus belatedly Farrington Graham made a constructive contribution to society. To this day, he stands as a musty precedent in the law books barring that possible loophole of escape to any other killer . . . drunkenness.

Specifics.

All that Tuesday in mid-June, the mercury had bubbled above the one hundred mark through the San Fernando Valley, but tonight in the $200,000 hilltop mansion of Lauritz Melchior, the opera singer, there was the whisper of relief. Melchior and his wife, Klinchen, had entertained two couples at dinner, and, just before half past ten, they left.

Melchior's property was well-secured, and he had to press a button inside the house to open the electrically controlled gate for his departing friends. It opened and closed in a matter of seconds. With his wife, Melchior sat down to watch the 10:30 news on TV while Klinchen's invalid mother, Mrs. Maria Hacker, seventy-five, sat in the patio beside the pool, seeking relief from the heat.

Melchior's two German hunting dogs barked suddenly, but the tenor quieted them. And then four strangers, their faces grotesquely masked in silk stockings, were confronting Melchior with guns. With them they had the housemaid and caretaker. 'Don't try anything,' the leader said, 'and nobody will get hurt. We want the money and the jewelry.'

Melchior tried to sidetrack them by opening a wall safe which contained mostly record albums. 'Quit stalling,' the leader commanded, jabbing his gun into Melchior's back. 'We know there's a big safe.'

Fearing for her husband's safety, Klinchen told them its location, and the tenor grudgingly opened it. The intruders scooped up more than a dozen pieces of jewelry, including a diamond ring and two bracelets which had once been among the crown jewels of Denmark. They seized five costly fur pieces: three sables, a leopard, and an otter; $518 cash and a hundred dollars' worth of imported cigars. One couldn't even resist stealing five packs of cigarettes.

Except for Klinchen's invalid mother whom they ignored, the quartet then bound their victims with Melchior's expensive ties and his wife's lingerie. They tore out the phone lines and pressed the gate button. They had been in the house thirty-five minutes. They now had fifteen seconds to get through the gate before it closed again, and they made it – with $100,000 worth of loot.

Quickly Melchior broke his flimsy bonds, called the police from a hidden phone and ran into the yard with a high-powered .270 hunting rifle. The getaway car was racing down the hilltop road beyond gunshot range.

Obviously the raid had been based on inside information. The stickup men had seemed to know how

222

much jewelry was in the house and practically asked for one piece by name. They knew Melchior possessed a prized hunting pistol and took it. They realized Klinchen's mother was confined to a wheelchair. They understood the mechanics of the gate.

But, except for a few tire tracks, that was all Thad Brown had to go on. By morning he had twenty detectives checking all M.O. cards, questioning and requestioning the Melchiors, searching and researching the grounds. And that was it till Robbery Lieutenant Ed Jokisch picked up a lead from possibly the oldest police source of all – the informant. For a price, he would divulge the identities of the four holdup men.

Once police would have rolled instantly on such 'information received,' but police work is more complicated and intricate these days. It is LAPD's policy not to deal with informants on their terms. Further, the courts had been getting increasingly severe with the police on their methods of obtaining evidence, and it had been made plain in more than one case that there must be no tampering with the civil rights of criminals.

Lieutenant Jokisch had to wake Thad Brown in the middle of the night for authorization to deal with the informant. Go ahead, but only on a 'clean hands' basis with no entanglements, Thad ordered. That meant that if Jokisch could wangle the information without committing LAPD to 'a price,' fine.

Somehow, Jokisch did it; and, just forty-eight hours after the robbery, two of the quartet were seized in separate downtown hotels. The other two (one of them a former butler for the Melchiors) were also identified, and an alarm went out for their capture.* Best of all, from the

* One suspect was convicted of robbery and kidnapping. Two suspects pleaded guilty to robbery. One suspect turned state's evidence, and was released after the trial. No appeals are pending.

Melchiors' point of view, Thad Brown found where the loot had been stashed throughout Los Angeles County, and detectives retrieved $90,000 worth of the valuables.

When Thad Brown and LAPD observed their pearl anniversary, the Police Commission cited his forty-three commendations in every rank and assignment and formally thanked him for 'the thirty years of his life he has dedicated to the service of his fellow man as a law enforcement officer.'

Getting back to specifics, Thad Brown says the job just boils down to 'hard work and common sense' in finding the pattern and then finding the man that fits it. 'It takes a persistent man and a suspicious man to make a good investigator,' he explains.

Specifics.

IV

To most Americans, our only personal contact with the police comes when the motorcycle appears out of nowhere and the officer writes a ticket. If we had been really speeding instead of just doing maybe ten mph above the limit, it wouldn't be so bad. But clearly we are being made a martyr to the police quota system. The cop hands out so many tickets a day or they take his shiny bike away from him.

On almost any highway anywhere in the U.S.A., you can get into quite a brisk argument on this topic with the arresting officer. Most policemen piously deny that there is any such thing as the quota system; but, surprisingly, LAPD makes no bones about it. 'They write tickets, or they don't ride bikes,' Chief Harold W. Sullivan says frankly.

Furthermore, as far as he is concerned, his men will

continue writing some thirty-three hundred citations daily, more than 1,200,000 yearly. Almost half a million are for illegal parking, but nearly all the rest are for the 'moving' violations which range from speeding to running red lights and stop signs. And these are what cause accidents.

In Los Angeles, where the populace lives and often dies on rubber, there are more than 130 auto crashes daily and an injury toll of about ninety-four, some eight of them pedestrians. During the week eight of the victims die.

Yet, by comparison with other metropolises, the carnage is restrained. One survey shows that the Los Angeles rate of traffic injuries per 10,000 vehicles is 27.7 – only a third to a half that of comparable cities (Detroit, 55.9; Chicago, 75.9; Philadelphia, 90.6). And the death rate of 1.6 contrasts with 2.3 in Detroit, 3.4 in Chicago and 3.0 in Philadelphia.

'There is a direct relation between the number of tickets issued and the accident rate,' Chief Sullivan says in defense of the quota. 'We have charts to prove it and surveys to back up the charts.'

Once, for example, Traffic set up a speed check on one of the city's fastest thoroughfares and stopped scores of drivers. They were given three types of treatment: a mere warning, a ticket, or a ticket and a short talk on the dangers of speeding. Then motorcycle policemen tailed them to see what the effect would be on their driving habits.

Of those who had escaped with the warning, two-thirds were blithely speeding again after a mile. But in the two ticketed groups, only a third were speeding after *five* miles. Sadly, Traffic is convinced that tickets talk louder than words.

At least since 1873, when unhitched horses were first recorded as a problem, traffic has been a major headache to Los Angeles. In its rambling length there is practically no mass transportation, and the average Angeleno is forced to drive farther and faster to work than city drivers anywhere else in the world. He logs 10,000 miles yearly on his speedometer, and travel of thirty to forty miles daily to and from work is not uncommon.

Mostly he rides the freeways which were threaded through southern California only a few years ago to serve both as inter- and intra-urban facilities.

At first the congestion and pile-ups were spectacular, and out of the Hollywood TV studios came a spate of gags that on them you were either 'quick or dead.' 'Driving the freeways is like going into combat.' Between neighborhood cars, inter-city drivers, and coastwise transports, the chances seemed excellent for either a multiple-car crash or bumper-to-bumper waits while an overturned alfalfa transport or a burning oil tanker was towed out of the way.

The first city to do so, Los Angeles quickly met the problem by using its own motorcycle corps for large-scale patrol of the freeway system. Uniquely, the freeway within the city limits was deemed part of the city streets and the same traffic regulations applied with one exception. Theoretically the state speed limit of fifty-five miles per hour applied, but in practice LAPD's motorcycle officers have tolerated whatever speed the traffic will bear. Within reason.

To avoid bottlenecks caused by accidents, Traffic relies on 'Sigalert,' an electronic town crier devised by Lloyd Sigmon, now a Los Angeles radio executive. When a major traffic problem (or any other emergency) develops, LAPD throws a switch in its radio network which sets off a sub-audible tone. The tone actuates a relay at all the local radio stations and, as the policeman broadcasts instructions to the driving public, receivers in the radio station record the message.

A red light tells station personnel that a Sigalert has been received, and it goes on the air immediately, taking precedence over any program in progress. Speed in reaching the motorist is the secret of Sigalert's success because a delay of only five minutes in diverting traffic can over-fill a paralyzed sector of the freeway with thousands of additional cars.

During one disastrous flood, thirty Sigalerts were aired in a single day to warn motorists of road hazards and brief them on new emergency routes. In fact, Sigalert has been so helpful as a sort of super-traffic cop that LAPD uses the system in all kinds of public-communications situations. Once a Sigalert 'want' resulted in the capture of a murder suspect, and an explanatory Sigalert broadcast while civil defense tests were being conducted reduced the usual number of alarmed inquiries to police by ninety per cent.

Specifics.

The man behind the man who writes you a ticket in Los Angeles was born in a house which now nestles alongside one of the freeways he polices. Chief Sullivan was in the class of forty which joined the force in 1937. During their winter of training, Los Angeles almost froze over, and in the department they were nicknamed 'the penguins.' It wasn't very prophetic. Sullivan and one other rookie of '37 went on to make Deputy Chief, four of their class-mates became Inspectors, two rose to Captain and there is a good sprinkling of Lieutenants and Sergeants. No other Academy class has produced so many departmental leaders.

The year war broke out, Sullivan was transferred from the Harbor Division to Traffic as an accident-investigation Sergeant. During the war the police shortage prevented LAPD from adopting a number of traffic suggestions made by the International Association of Chiefs of Police. 'But traffic looked like a good future for a young man,' Sullivan recalls now, and LAPD's postwar traffic progress has borne him out. From almost total reliance on the man on the bike, Traffic has mushroomed into a four-division Bureau known cryptically as TED, PIC, AID, and TSD.

TED (Traffic Enforcement) does the dirty and hazardous job of patrol. With six thousand miles of street and only 324 men, the task is almost frightening; especially since Traffic has been forced to reduce its street patrol personnel by five per cent in a period when vehicle registrations increased by almost half a million cars.

Only with the help of his other divisions has Chief Sullivan been able to avert an accident-injury break-through. The 190 PIC officers (Pedestrian and Intersection Control) are especially chosen on the basis of youth, manners, and prepossessing appearance. 'Everybody is an expert when it comes to pedestrian control,' Chief Sullivan says philosophically. 'They all have the answer. But unfortunately there is no panacea. We need the thinking of all elements of the public – and then daily cooperation in day-to-day problems.' It is the handsome young PIC officer in direct contact with the public who tries to win this cooperation and break down the old American distrust of *any* regulations and particularly traffic rules.

TSD (Traffic Services) propagandizes on a broader scale, presenting more than 1,400 traffic safety programs yearly and distributing pamphlets with such titles as 'How Far Behind Are You?,' 'Accidents Don't Happen!' and 'So You Have a Motor Scooter.'

As a matter of fact, TSD drops to its knees to implore the Angeleno to drive more carefully. In saturation educational campaigns, the division borrows department store windows for safety exhibits which often include life-size replicas of a LAPD motorcycle policeman and offers driver-aptitude tests under laboratory conditions. In city traffic, the division preaches tirelessly, regularity in driving rather than bursts of speed gets you there sooner as well as safer. As a matter of fact, under such driving conditions, tests show, *thirty miles an hour more often than sixty mph is the quicker way between two points.*

An uncomfortably large proportion of Los Angeles drivers seem determined that their community will live up to its name – *the City of Angels* – and that is when AID (Accident Investigation) rolls.

With traffic camera, special slide rule, distance measuring devices, sketch pads, flares, and recording equipment to take statements at the scene, AID men make scientific investigations into almost all accidents, even when fellow policemen are involved. They are called out some one hundred and twenty times daily, and their reports not only fix responsibility, but also provide the raw meat for future accident-prevention work.

Thus, with colored pins and enormous wall-sized maps, Traffic follows the shifting locale of accidents, plots the time and cause and then readjusts its motorcycle beats accordingly. If, in a given street, failure to signal turns has been the chief trouble, the man on the bike there is quick to hand out tickets to such offenders. With a scrap of legal paper instead of a gun, he cleans up his variation of 'the crime mile' which is the careless mile.

Fortunately for the undermanned patrol, most Angelenos are cooperative when they are caught and submit passively to the citation. A few try to challenge the ticket in court and, of these, only about three per cent are successful. Some may try to square the ticket, but Los Angeles has made its system as fix-proof as is humanly possible.

Now and then, just often enough to keep the bike men edgy, something will happen. One April midnight TED Officers Blass N. Skvicalo and Lloyd Thomas ticketed an aircraft worker in the Wilshire district for having followed the car ahead too closely. The man accepted the citation without protest, and the TED men drove off on their cycles.

Three blocks farther on, the motorist rammed them from behind, hurling Skvicalo fifty feet and Thomas twice as far. Both received internal injuries, and only their white crash helmets saved their lives. The motorist drove on till passers-by forced him to the curb. He protested that it had been a pure accident, but he was ordered held for assault with a deadly weapon – an automobile.*

An open-minded man, Chief Sullivan will experiment with *anything* that promises to save lives or facilitate the movement of traffic on four wheels or two legs.

One innovation was 'Scramble,' the pedestrian control system used in a few cities. At the proper signal, walkers can cross an intersection any which-way instead of just one way.

In a large city, LAPD had established, there are sixteen variations of traffic movement which must be anticipated for effective control. Hoping that 'Scramble' would simplify this pattern, Traffic installed the system at twenty-two intersections. While it solved some of the eternal conflict between auto and pedestrian, in other ways 'Scramble' has seemed to slow car movements. It works best when traffic is light, poorest when it is heavy. It was found, however, that because of Los Angeles' distinctive traffic problems 'Scramble' was not feasible. Early in 1958 the city's Traffic Commission voted to abandon the plan after a trial of nearly a year.

Traffic has also tried to persuade the motorist to help himself by lightening the load on the freeways. On an

---

*He was later convicted for hit-and-run felony.

average day of the week, the freeway system criss-crossing through the heart of Los Angeles hauls 600,000 cars through the downtown area. So a 'park-and-ride' service was offered motorists from the San Fernando Valley. They were given a parking area near Hollywood Bowl and bus service to carry them downtown from that point. Only a thousand fainthearted drivers weekly patronized the buses, and the service had to be dropped. The average Angeleno is just too game to accept that kind of solution.

However, in most ways, Traffic has conquered its freeway problems. Accidents are being kept to a minimum, and congestion is reduced by a helicopter patrol during peak hours. LAPD was the first American police department to utilize the whirlybird in traffic control. Its three-place Hiller is manned by a crew of Korean War veterans who spot bottlenecks and potential hazards which they relay by radio to surface police units.

In fact, the way things have worked out, Traffic is a little annoyed that the stale jokes about the 'quick or dead' still persist, especially among visitors. Their mathematicians have calculated that the odds against getting killed in a freeway accident are twenty-to-one, compared to five-to-three in a crash on the streets.

Now and then, to get away from it all, Chief Sullivan himself takes to the helicopter, and there his problems seem reduced to little multi-colored bugs darting in various directions. But, like the other Deputy Chiefs, he is never permitted to relax long in the abstract. The specific is always close at hand.

There was, for example, the telephone call that had to be answered politely when Traffic utilized Sigalert to avoid serious congestion on the inbound Hollywood freeway.

'I just heard Sigalert about that accident,' a woman said worriedly. 'Would you please tell me what color car that

231

is? I'm worried about my husband. He was going to Los Angeles on the freeway and . . .'

Specifics.

V

Of all LAPD's Chiefs, Roger E. Murdock suffers the most occupational conflicts. He stood No. 3 on the last eligibility list for Chief Parker's job itself, and yet he runs the department's Siberia. He feels what he is doing is extremely important, and yet he feels the proper concern of policemen is crime, not correction.

He says bluntly, 'We policemen are not glamorous and we're not missionaries.' And yet, as part of his job, he administers LAPD's four and a half million dollar experiment in trying to dehydrate drunks.

In his more than quarter of a century with LAPD, Murdock has served with distinction in detective, juvenile, traffic, personnel, and patrol work. Now he heads the Bureau of Corrections and, like his three hundred and seventy subordinates, feels that a lot of police manpower, chosen, trained, and paid for more complex work, is being wasted on jail keeping.

Chief Parker thoroughly agrees, but so long as LAPD is stuck with the job, a big one and an expensive one, he needs a top administrator to do it. Sometimes the daily population in the city jails exceeds 4,500, and the care and feeding of the inmates approximates four million dollars yearly. Murdock operates the biggest, if not the most popular hotel in Los Angeles.

Despite LAPD's monumental reservations about the whole thing, the police go out of their way to make jail a clean place. Thus, the department believes, prisoners can be encouraged to cling to their self-respect while repaying

232

society. They must shower daily and keep their cells immaculate.

They eat good food and sleep on comfortable beds. As LAPD sees it, good food is not only humanitarian but also practical penology. Complaints about the food have sparked more jail and prison riots than any other cause. Even in the outlying divisions, each of which has its own jail, the city's Health Department supervises the menus.

In cooperation with city and county health authorities, all prisoners are X-rayed for tuberculosis, and in a year more than three hundred active TB cases will thus be spotted. They are sent to a sanatorium for treatment. All newcomers are also screened for other communicable diseases, and physicians are available around the clock in case of emergencies.

Murdock runs good jails and clean jails, but the interesting thing about Corrections – and the project the bureau should be *least* concerned with – is its drunk farm. Forty miles from downtown Los Angeles in the northwest mountain-desert country, LAPD maintains a 581-acre rehabilitation center for the chronic drunk.

'Nobody seemed to be helping the alcoholics in Los Angeles, so the police had to try it,' Murdock says a bit defensively.

The venture was launched early in the war when Los Angeles' Skid Row suddenly became the No. 1 Bowery of America. Because of the climate, more and more homeless men drifted into the city, and police found that the 'alcoholic recidivists,' or common drunks, were being arrested over and over again, some as many as two hundred times. They clogged the jails and courts, and a few days or weeks after doing their routine sentences, they were back again. Of the almost one hundred thousand arrests yearly for drunkenness, some sixteen thousand individuals account for about seventy per cent of the total bookings. Thus, for each wino who can be reformed in a year, the police will have to make four fewer arrests.

From an original fifty-inmate capacity, the rehab center has grown into ten dormitories which house about six hundred men. Each week, in batches of thirty-five to forty, they are sent up by the courts to do 120-day sentences at LAPD's 'mountain mission,' and enough come out new men to make the cost worthwhile.

The average arrival is white, forty-two years old, divorced, jobless for about six months and last employed at unskilled labor. Only one in six is currently employed, and one in ten has not worked for four years or even longer.

An analysis of some 3,100 men passing through the center during a two-year period disclosed that whites led Mexicans by more than seven-to-one, Negroes more than ten-to-one and Indians by almost twenty-five-to-one. (There was one Japanese, one Filipino and one Eskimo during the period.) The divorced outnumbered the married by almost five-to-one, but there were only half as many widowers as married men. Agewise, the years between thirty-six and fifty were disclosed as by far the most dangerous alcoholic years for men.

Therapy at 'mountain mission' consists of a daily, 3,500-calorie menu, eight hours of sleep, a shave, bath, and change of clothes every twenty-four hours, and supervised recreation. While the inmates are being physically rehabilitated, police social workers start a 'package' looking toward a new design for living after the men's release. Relatives and former employers are interviewed, unions and fraternal associations notified in the hopes they can ease the readjustment.

Little by little, the six hundred receive religious help, medical attention, and trade training. In most cases, they respond. For security, there is just a fence and a bicycle patrol, yet escapes average only fifteen yearly. And when they do leave legally, almost nine in ten don't come back again. So far as LAPD knows, they have put together the shattered pieces of their lives.

One derelict, once an expert radioman, had drunk himself out of a job and while he was on Skid Row, the progress in electronics had passed him by. He couldn't have held a job if he had wanted to.

At the center, he was assigned to the radio shack, and there he not only brushed up on his rusty knowledge of radio repairing, but also learned TV techniques. In four months he was released and rehab has not heard of him since.

In turn, the inmates do things for LAPD. They have produced 600,000 pounds of produce, most of it for the jail system, and they operate K6QFI, the police short-wave receiver and transmitter at the center. During the Geophysical Year they maintained twenty-four hours a day monitoring of scientific data being shortwaved home by scientific explorers and forwarded the information to the American Radio Relay League, West Hartford, Connecticut, for transmission to federal authorities.

Very practically, one inmate devised a tool to extract the burned-out vibrators from police car radios. Previously, they had been replaced at a cost of $2 each. Now the rehab inmates extract them, repair them, and replace them at a cost of twelve cents apiece.

And all this is done *without* the services of a professional therapist, psychiatrist, or psychologist in the entire program. It is done entirely by police officers.

And yet for Murdock, too, there is always the jarring specific. In two weeks three prisoners under his charge hanged themselves. One was a transient, another a young drunk with family troubles, and the third an attractive woman airlines clerk. That was the one that caused the most trouble because an official report said she was known to have had suicidal impulses and yet had not been relieved of the cord on her dressing robe.

Murdock's investigation established that the police had not known of the woman's suicidal tendencies. She had been drunk and wearing only the robe (to which the cord was sewn) when she was arrested.

Since the cord could not be detached, matrons went to get jail clothes for her; and, during an unguarded five minutes, she managed to tie one end around her neck and the other to the cell bars.

Such tragedies, even though Corrections is exonerated, increase Murdock's distaste for a job that doesn't properly belong to the police. And Chief Parker agrees.

'The identification of police with the processes of punishment works to destroy the ideal of a non-judging, non-penalizing police,' Parker says. 'The detention of sentenced prisoners by the police is a dangerous violation of the democratic theory of law enforcement.'

Specifics.

THE CHIEF

Somehow, by the very nature of his work, whether it is a warning, an arrest or a death notification to a home, the policeman is always an intruder. Always, it seems, he makes the last knock on the door, the last phone call, the last command. As the fortieth Chief of the Los Angeles Police Department, William Henry Parker symbolizes all of this – the intrusion, the authority, the finality – which distinguishes the peace officer from the civilian, and on behalf of his 4,400 men he bears the brunt of the fears and resentments which the public feels toward the policeman.

In his first seven years in office, the newspapers prematurely buried Parker seven times; and he has been verbally attacked by politicians, minorities spokesmen, and civil liberties defenders. He has twice been marked for assassination by gun and bomb. For years his wife has been subjected to anonymous, harassing phone calls at their home. Attempts have been made to 'get' him legally through lawsuits; at one time he and LAPD faced a variety of damage actions totaling almost fifteen million dollars.

Chief Parker is not the kind of civil servant who complains about the hours and pay, though it is generally accepted that he could do twice as well in private industry. For twenty-three years and one day, an honest and efficient officer in a department that was often notoriously dishonest and inefficient, he worked toward his goal, and no distraction, threat, or temptation, is going to dislodge him now.

In a momentary mood of frustration, he will say that no policeman in his right mind should accept the job of Chief unless he is ready to retire, but immediately dismissing the distasteful thought, he plunges back into the counter-attack. He has fought the newspapers and politicians, harassed gangsters and Communists, opposed racial pressures on the police, and tangled with his own district attorney. Recently he has broadened his target range to include the California State Supreme Court and the California State Legislature. Whether his views are asked or not, he expresses them bluntly on any controversial subject involving law enforcement which may range from proposed legalized gambling to the increasing legal restraints on police activity.

For the most part, those who opposed him in the past now respect his utter dedication to his job. Though they may question some of his approaches, they acknowledge that he is cop, pure cop, twenty-four hours a day; and they worry not so much about Parker as about the precedents Parker sets.

Thus, a lawyer suing as a taxpayer asserted that the Department's use of listening devices to record conversations was a 'shocking trespass' when done without search warrant. He thought taxpayers should be permitted to sue the police, explaining:

'Chief Parker, the respondent in this case, is doubtless acting in good faith when he orders installation of electronic machines to obtain evidence. But Parker won't be Chief forever. If we do not give the citizen greater powers to protect himself, future police enforcers might conceivably misuse these devices.'

Though he is a lawyer himself, Parker reacts with the baffled frustration of an honest layman caught in legal toils when such arguments are advanced against him.

Under attack, he knows how to counter-punch. When he is enmeshed in legal niceties involving wire taps and search-and-seizure, he chafes impatiently: 'The voice of the criminal, the Communist, and the self-appointed defender of civil liberties cries out for more and more restrictions upon police authority.'

If attacked on the sensitive minority issue, particularly for tagging criminals by race, color, and creed, he answers back: 'We are all members of some minority group.' Such labels, he insists stubbornly, are the very basis of identification, and identification is an indispensable police tool. At Louisville, Kentucky, he once encouraged the Southern Police Institute to resist 'undue pressures' by minority groups. 'Such demands are a form of discrimination against the public as a whole,' Parker said bluntly.

Considering that at various times he has incurred opposition from almost every vocal group in Los Angeles, Parker's survival is a comforting example of municipal intelligence. Despite their individual grievances, his critics have had to accept him as a first-rate administrator of a first-rate department.

LAPD, says the International City Managers Association, is 'probably the most soundly organized large police department in the country.' It has, adds Chief H. J. Anslinger of the Federal Bureau of Narcotics, 'the only adequate narcotics squad in the nation.' As a result, Los Angeles stands 'well in the forefront in the battle against crime,' says Senator Estes Kefauver.

Parker is an essentially simple man who believes with all his soul that crime and Communism are the twin scourges of America and their suppression, by almost any means, the greatest challenge of our era. Some legal and social philosophers may question his simplifications, but he has built a record that demands from them a simple answer:

either accept Parker and the LAPD he has fashioned or make a grave and weakening concession to the hostile elements.

Through inheritance and early environment, Parker absorbed the direct-action philosophy of the Old West. He was born in Lead, a town in the Black Hills of South Dakota, where an imaginative boy could still detect the six-shooters' aroma in the air. His grandfather, William Henry Parker, had been one of the great frontier peace officers when there was no middle ground between right and wrong. After the gunslingers had been quieted, he had gone on to Washington as a Congressman; so the boy knew that, though the fight may be dangerous, courage and honesty win out in the end.

From old-timers he heard stories of outlaw and Sioux, showdown and massacre; and he knew the Valley of the Little Big Horn, Hay Stack Butte, Sundance Creek, Buffalo Gap, and the Belle Fourche. Though the frontiersmen were now old and garrulous, he caught their tough, impatient spirit; and it was to mark him for life.

In his early teens, he was subjected to more softening influences when he served as an altar boy at little St. Ambrose's Catholic Church in Deadwood. But even religion had its pioneer austerities. Many a dark, bitter-cold Sunday morning during the Dakota winters he had to walk to church and light its furnace before donning his cassock and surplice.

Like his forefathers, he felt the call of the West, and when he was twenty, he migrated to California, settling in Los Angeles. Even then he was drawn to the law; and, after he got a job as a taxi driver, he bought legal tomes and studied them between fares. His interests focused on criminal law; from that he developed an interest in police work. On August 8, 1927, Parker joined LAPD.

Today, police legal scholars are not a rarity, but in Parker's rookie days the sight of a young policeman with his nose in Blackstone caused considerable squadroom comment. Parker ignored the hecklers, and three years later obtained his law degree and passed the state bar examination.

For a time, he considered leaving LAPD and making law his profession, but after the '29 crash, more shingles were being taken down than tacked up. 'As I dimly recall,' Parker explains today, 'there was a depression, and thus fate decided that I should remain with the Police Department.' He settled down to attack the departmental promotion exams with lawyer-like thoroughness, later married a policewoman, Helen Schultz, and gave his life without reservation to law enforcement.

On merit, on the unassailable results of the exams, he was a first-rate officer and he slowly advanced. But those were the days of blatant corruption within the department; and, as a policeman who was both intelligent and honest, Parker was one of the most feared men in the top-brass offices. He got so far and could go no farther.

For years he stood first on the civil service promotion lists for Inspector and Deputy Chief; yet he was always ignored. 'I was the most passed-up officer in the history of the Los Angeles Police Department,' he says now. Resolutely he recalled the example of Grandfather Parker and held to his courage and honesty.

Finally, in the late 1930's when Parker had completed a rough ten years with LAPD, the decay in the department exploded.

Those were the days when some policemen paid for their appointments, when the vice officers collected weekly 'juice' from bawdy houses and gambling joints, when madams and bookies could get the honest men transferred out of harm's way. But tough, wise Harry

Raymond, an ace detective and former chief of the San Diego police, knew too much about their operations and other corruption pockets within the city administration.

That was dangerous for everybody. Raymond had worked on such celebrated cases as the Mary Pickford-Douglas Fairbanks kidnapping and the kidnap-murder-rape of twelve-year-old Marian Parker, daughter of a banker, by William Edward Hickman. Now the rogue cops in LAPD suspected he was after them, and they subjected him to counter-surveillance. LAPD's 'Special Intelligence Unit' under Captain Earle E. Kynette took over the job. The unit consisted of some eighteen to twenty policemen assigned largely to conducting extensive espionage on persons suspected of being politically opposed to the Shaw administration. Kynette's so-called 'eye squad' rented a house across the street from Raymond's home, and a dictaphone was planted in his house.

Every waking hour he was under surveillance; and, being a pretty shrewd detective, he promptly realized it. But courageously he went on gathering evidence of malfeasance against the city government. Then one January morning, he rose, breakfasted, and went out to his garage. As he stepped on the starter, an explosion shattered the car and wrecked the garage. Raymond's body was riddled by 150 fragments of shrapnel; but, after a long series of operations, he miraculously recovered.

The murder attempt backfired on the administration and led to the election of Mayor Fletcher Bowron on a reform ticket. Captain Kynette and his Lieutenant, Roy J. Allen, were sent to prison for both attempted murder and malicious use of explosives. Allen died in San Quentin, and Kynette was finally paroled in the early 1950's. Despite his wounds, Harry Raymond lived to the ripe age of seventy-six.

Feeling the shame and frustration of a good cop, Parker

vowed two things. If he ever were in the position of authority, he would revitalize LAPD by driving out the rogue cops and by rewarding the good ones with promotions right off the top of the civil service lists. That alone would stamp out most of the inefficiency, favoritism, and corruption. Further, to keep scandal from creeping in through the back door of the Department, he would button up vice as it had never been buttoned.

Then the war intervened, and Parker went overseas for the Army to organize police systems in Sardinia, Normandy, and Germany. When he returned, he found himself again in exile and again a helpless spectator as another vice scandal blew up in LAPD's face. But this time LAPD's shame and heartache were a minor price because real reform came to the department.

Mayor Bowron persuaded William A. Worton, a hardbitten administrator, who was a retired Marine Corps general, to take over as Chief. With military vigor, Worton stamped out scandal from the halls of Central Division to the shores of the Pacific. He re-shuffled his men, rewarding the good and disciplining the bad, and brought back the almost forgotten element of morale.

This writer remembers attending a dinner meeting shortly after the General took over the Chief's desk. The occasion: A minor milestone in my life – our then nebulous radio program 'Dragnet' had garnered its first sponsor. In attendance were two NBC executives, the program's writer, Jim Moser, and a great many policemen of all ranks and title.

When the General rose to address the gathering, we all settled back expectantly, awaiting great words of encouragement of our radio project.

He made a cursory remark that if the program continued its present course, it might someday be of value in accurately depicting law enforcement.

Then he turned to the policemen in the room:

'You're cops. You're damned good ones. When you walk down the street, I want to see those chests out a mile; those heads carried high, and be damned proud when someone says: "There goes a cop".'

Good officers, including Parker, came out of the nooks and crannies where they had been tucked for safekeeping. Parker was assigned to the organization of an internal affairs unit to police policemen. Other top men established a planning office to chart the city's trends and habits. Worton even introduced a military-style intelligence squad to scout the underworld and keep abreast of mobsters' plans.

The renascent LAPD seriously alarmed rackets leaders, and the 'Big Five' of vice and crime supported a recall movement against Mayor Bowron, according to intelligence reports that reached Headquarters. But Worton's spit-and-polish police administration had made too favorable an impression on the electorate. The recall plans and the 'Big Five's' wistful hope for an 'open city' administration collapsed.

And then, after a year of prodigious work, General Worton asked to be relieved of his interim appointment. A new Chief had to be chosen, and the underworld optimistically regrouped its forces in the expectation that it would soon be doing business again at the old stand. LAPD stood at the crossroads.

In any town there are three ways to become Chief of Police. You pay somebody, you know somebody, or you earn the job. In Los Angeles, at least in recent years, you earn it.

In March of 1950, two dozen LAPD officers of the rank of captain or higher began the civil service exam for Chief. When the results were in, the competition for the top police job in the West had resolved into a two-man race, odds even and take your choice.

One was the rugged, uncompromising Parker who at last had achieved the rating of Deputy Chief under Worton and headed the Patrol Bureau.

The other was the experienced, unrelenting Thad Brown, Chief of Detectives.

In every way, the race was a standoff. Parker was then forty-seven years old and had twenty-three years of service. Brown was forty-nine and had been with LAPD for twenty-four years. Both were nationally known police officers with their own devoted followings in and outside the department.

Parker had achieved a brilliant administrative record overseas for the Army, but Brown had served just as impressively on the home front in security and anti-sabotage work.

Parker made top score in the written examination and Brown beat him in the oral test. Overall, Parker had a 5.06 edge and was No. 1 on the eligibility list. But the final decision was still odds even and take your choice. Detective versus Patrolman.

In such a neck-and-neck race, it seemed, a dark horse could slip ahead to the wire. There was talk that Roger Murdock, No. 3 on the civil service fist, might be chosen as a compromise appointee. Under the rules, the Police Commission had to make its choice from among the top three candidates. However, if a candidate withdrew, the men below would move up. For a time, No. 5, Bernard R. Caldwell, also looked like a comer in case any two men above him dropped out. But the list stood pat, and Caldwell eventually became head of the California State Highway Patrol.

In one of the stormiest, behind-the-scenes political battles ever known in Los Angeles, supporters of Parker and Brown argued and caucused for months. Late in July, four months after the exams, the Police Commission slowly resolved, by a three-to-two margin, in favor of Thad Brown.

Then fate stepped in.

Mrs. Curtis Albro, one of the commissioners who supported Brown, died on the eve of the vote, and the commission was deadlocked again.

Now the controversy boiled to a climax that had all the city watching. In the newspapers, it was a bigger story than baseball or the heat wave, and the reporters smoked out secret meetings all through City Hall. Meetings between the Mayor and his police commissioners; between the Mayor and the candidates; between the commissioners and the candidates.

Finally the Mayor, the commission, and ex-Chief Worton, who had brought Parker out of departmental limbo, sat down together. One pro-Brown commissioner swung over, then the holdout conceded, and the commission announced Parker's victory by unanimous vote.

Thad Brown gracefully accepted the crusher, and Parker's grin looked as though it could stretch from San Diego to Seattle. He had served as aide to three Chiefs, and he had seen one underling after another jump him. Now, though it had taken a little while, Grandfather Parker's old-fashioned reliance on the virtues of courage and honesty was justified.

Despite the protracted bitterness of the controversy, Parker's appointment was accepted inside the department and out with surprising unanimity. Punning gracefully, the Los Angeles *Times* ran an editorial cartoon depicting the outstretched hand of Public Cooperation over the caption, 'Park 'er There, Chief.' The *Times* expressed the hope that the new Chief had 'a carapace sufficiently durable to shed the slings and arrows of self-seeking politicians.' . . .

248

'Perhaps the very heat of this controversy,' the *Times* added happily, 'indicates the serious attitude adopted by the commission – that here was a decision which must withstand the years.'

Importantly, labor, which had often collided in the past with LAPD, and various minority groups also approved. Parker was the first Catholic ever to become Chief in Los Angeles, and a religious publication said the city's 600,000 Catholics were particularly pleased by the appointment. 'Chief Parker's background indicates a wise choice,' commented *The Southern California Teamster*, official organ of AFL Joint Council No. 42. During the honeymoon, Parker could almost have been elected Mayor.

Exactly one week after the announcement, the badge was placed in his hands, and he announced somewhat deceptively, 'It is now time to quiet down the department and get down to policing.' Whereupon, he plunged into the job as though LAPD had been sleeping the previous eighty years of its existence and now had to make up for the long nap.

Down through the years, Chief Parker has tried to live up to the threat-and-promise he made on assuming office. The threat, tireless war on the underworld: *'We will not tolerate the many parasites who drain thousands of dollars yearly from the citizens of Los Angeles.'* The promise, reasonable and unoppressive law enforcement: *'All ills and evils cannot be cured by law, but a great many social evils can be mitigated by proper enforcement.'*

The underworld moved first, making four attempts during Parker's first month in office to 'reach' him so that a gambling czar could be set up in Los Angeles. Parker retaliated by exposing the plot before a meeting of Los Angeles County peace officers that included thirty-five chiefs of city police. 'Now they're plotting to frame me because I stand as an obstacle to their plan,' he further charged.

By way of counter-attack, he persuaded the peace officers to pool county-wide resources and form a central intelligence bureau against the threatened invasion of organized gambling. Parker has always had the knack of drawing the issue boldly, and he told his somewhat startled fellow officers:

'This plan goes deeper than a means of saving Los Angeles from the stigma of vice. We are protecting the American philosophy of life. It is known that Russia is hoping we will destroy ourselves as a nation through our own avarice, greed, and corruption in government. Hence, this program has a wider application than in the Los Angeles area alone.'

Parker was convinced that the underworld was making a serious and violent re-alignment in preparation for infiltration of Los Angeles. From a police standpoint, he told a group of businessmen, the city represented 'the last white spot among the great cities of America.' But he added bluntly, 'I do not know how long this can be continued. There are men here ready to get their tentacles into the city and drain off large sums of money through gambling activities of various kinds.'

To those who thought their new Chief talked grandiloquently on his favorite subject, there were three startling developments within the first six months of the Parker regime.

Sometime late on a December night, a man carrying a cheap, sawed-off, double-barreled shotgun slipped through an unlocked boulevard gate into the rambling grounds of a $50,000 mansion in Laurel Canyon. He made his way up the drive and settled behind a hedge, as heavy impressions in the soft earth later disclosed.

250

At half past one in the morning, Attorney Samuel R. Rummel returned home. As he walked from the floodlighted garage up the steps of his home, the twelve-gauge shotgun roared, and all the writs of habeas corpus in the world, all the notices of intent to appeal, couldn't have saved him. He fell dead with seven slugs in his body. He was 46 years old.

By coincidence or deliberate timing, the assassination took place just one day before the county grand jury was to open its investigation into the connection between county law officers and a large bookmaking ring. Parker swore, somewhat rashly, that he would get the killer, and assigned scores of his best plainclothesmen and intelligence aides to the case.

Two days later, LAPD's Gangster Squad seized eight members of the Jack Dragna mob, but the detectives couldn't crack their wall of silence. Other leads petered out, too. A year later, twitting Parker on his promise that the murder would be solved 'if it takes every man on the force,' the Los Angeles *Mirror* observed deadpan, 'Today, Parker begins the second year of trying to solve the underworld assassination . . .'

The Rummel case was a defeat.

Somewhat paradoxically, the Los Angeles Breakfast Club was holding a banquet at eight o'clock at night with Parker as the scheduled speaker. A few hours before, Captain Jim Hamilton, commander of the Intelligence Division, received a whispered tip from such a reliable source that plans had to be changed drastically.

At a well-secluded spot on the road between Parker's home in Silver Lake and the Breakfast Club building, underworld gunners would be waiting to ambush him as he drove by. The area was hastily surrounded by police; and, while Parker went ahead and gave his talk, he remained under continuous guard for forty-eight hours.

Later, police were tipped off on another plot to bomb Parker's home, and again a sizable cordon of guards frustrated the attempt. For added protection, Parker acquired two giant dogs.

But, by telephone, his harassers did get through with almost daily 'poison phone' calls aimed particularly at his attractive wife, Helen. Often on weekends women would call, demanding to speak to Parker 'as a matter of life or death.' Shrewdly he suspected entrapment. Recording equipment was being used on the other end of the wire in an effort to get his voice after which the conversation could be cut misleadingly. He avoided the pitfall. And Helen Parker, being an ex-policewoman, knew how to handle the anonymous callers who tried to torment her with false information about her husband's activities. Thoughtfully she continued target practice with her Detective's Special.

Parker survived, and this was victory. But the phone harassments and even death threats still continue. 'They're coming in by way of Syracuse now,' he said recently.

The third development was a *Mirror* 'exclusive' that representatives of five powerful syndicates had met in a Hollywood hotel suite to 'cut up the town' and apportion the various rackets, bookmaking, open gambling, bingo, prostitution, and all the rest, among themselves. The conferees were said to have included the late Sam Rummel; Jimmy Utley, a figure in the old bingo mob and abortion operator; Max Kleiger, bookie and gambler; Robert J. Gans, former slot machine king of Los Angeles County; and C. A. (Curly) Robinson, reportedly active in the coin machine field.

The reason its story was so specific, the *Mirror* explained, was that the authorities had been able to 'bug' the suite ahead of time. The whole conversation, including talk about another recall movement directed against Mayor Bowron, had been relayed to listening detectives from Los Angeles, San Francisco, and the California Crime Commission.

Significantly Chief Parker did not throw off the story. He conceded that such a meeting was possible and confirmed that there certainly had been a plot to 'cut up' Los Angeles for the vice rackets.

That was victory, too. Law enforcement had gotten *inside* the enemy.

The *1-2-3* developments during Parker's first six months in office amply justified his often colorful language in depicting the shadowy forces of evil that threatened Los Angeles. When a lawyer is murdered, a Chief of Police marked for assassination, and an executive mob conference called to discuss taking over City Hall and splitting the 'take,' strong and colorful language seems indicated. More and more through the years, the public has listened respectfully when Parker talks.

Unfortunately, the rackets leaders shine in the usually praiseworthy virtue of stick-to-it-iveness; and, when muscle and corruption fail, they resort to other techniques. Once they knew Parker had them blocked in Los Angeles, they tried a long end run, hoping to ram through a state constitutional amendment which would create a *legal* gambling setup.

To Parker, purely from a policeman's point of view, licensed gambling might be even worse. 'The proposition is reprehensible,' he cried to an investigating committee of the State Senate, 'and will lead to other crimes involving narcotics, alcoholism, and juvenile delinquency. The police department is not equipped to handle the attendant crimes with the opening of licensed gambling establishments.'

Already, he disclosed, Eastern mobsters had penetrated as far West as Las Vegas; and 'the Cleveland mob,' was poised specifically for an invasion of Los Angeles. Dryly he added, 'Our department is trying desperately to dissuade these individuals from enjoying our climate.'

By now, most Californians realized that when Parker cried wolf, the wolf was somewhere nearby, but nevertheless he was forced to read a letter which the committee had received from an assistant police chief in Las Vegas. The communication praised Nevada's fine gambling laws.

'Of course he's for it,' Parker snapped. 'He works in Nevada – for Las Vegas! But I'll tell you about crime in Nevada!

'The last time I was in Reno, someone pulled fire alarm boxes all through the city and turned in a lot of fake police calls. While police and firemen were all answering the false alarms, bandits swept through the gambling district and robbed five or six casinos before anyone was the wiser!'

And then, with a sudden turn of phrase that a philosopher could not have polished, Chief Parker said:

'*No social structure founded on the weakness of its people can hope to survive.*'

The amendment proposal died.

As J. Edgar Hoover has demonstrated so brilliantly, a top enforcement authority must be more than just Superman with a badge. Somehow, in a nation weaned on traditional Anglo-Saxon dislike of police authority, the policeman must communicate a sense of urgent mission. And the more honest and unreachable he is, the more necessary is his task. Even to many law-abiding citizens, blindly impartial authority that cannot be influenced by a friend at City Hall is a little frightening.

Before Kiwanians, Legionnaires, any other group who would listen, Chief Parker has been LAPD's best press agent. As he once ruefully observed, Los Angeles 'is probably more conscious of its constitutional rights than any other place in the nation. They are constantly indicting policemen. Our men are instructed not to tap wires even if the place is running wild with criminals.'

Against this particular symptom of public distrust – fear of electronic eavesdropping by the police – Parker has argued for years. In big crime or little, the phone is indispensable to the criminal – and listening in is almost indispensable to the policeman. Big mobsters transact most of their business by long-distance. Punks work out of corner phone booths. Bookies and prostitutes couldn't operate without the help of Alexander Graham Bell's invention. Both to obtain leads and evidence, the policeman must run taps on them. Parker cites the case of a notorious confidence man who, his detectives knew, was in the process of fleecing a new victim. Without listening devices which recorded their conversations, there would have been no evidence against him.

Yet the use of such machines is curtailed in spite of Parker's campaign, and he says ruefully: 'The police organization, heavily shackled by legal restrictions, is little match for a well-organized and extensive underworld.' He has carried this fight up to the California State Supreme Court and sooner or later, he thinks, he will achieve victory through court rulings or new laws.

In his book now is the time for a critical re-evaluation of the statutes protecting individual rights which the underworld has distorted into legal licenses to steal. 'Since internal crime is jeopardizing American freedom,' he argues, 'we must re-examine the balance between the criminal army and society, lest a misconception of individual liberty result in the destruction of all liberty.'

It is this kind of talk which distresses civil liberties defenders and makes them fear that, in a blind dedication to law enforcement, Parker would repress traditional rights. No such thing, the Chief argues back. He merely thinks the policeman should get as much help and comfort from the law and the courts as the criminal now does.

Inevitably, between the cop who has to do the dirty work and the legal scholars who sit back in quiet prosecutors' offices and more quiet courtrooms to ponder guilt and justice, there is this clash of opinion. Having brought in a mug at the risk of his own life, the policeman is outraged when the case dissolves in seeming legal involvements and quibbles. He sees the specific – the quick shakedown that *did* disclose the gun or the heroin – and why all the big talk now? The court sees the *general* – the precedent that may allow the police to start searching everybody – and where is the Bill of Rights then?

Temperamentally, Parker is not the man to submit quietly. Largely on their contrary views about methods of obtaining evidence, the Chief and his own district attorney, the late S. Ernest Roll, broke openly. Roll wanted policemen to sign 'rejection of complaint' slips when the DA felt that there was no ground for prosecution. Parker ordered his men not to sign the slips, and for a long time Los Angeles law enforcement went forward in a curious atmosphere. Police and prosecutors were almost as cool to each other as both were to criminals.

The worst blow to Parker – and to date all his vigorous pleading has not been able to change the situation – is the adoption of the 'exclusionary evidence' rule in California courts. In a bit of irony which the Chief does not at all relish, the decision grew out of his own total war on Los Angeles bookies.

Charles H. Cahan, known as the 'boy bookie,' was among fifteen asserted gamblers rounded up by police and convicted largely on evidence obtained by the planting of secret microphones.

Cahan appealed, and the California State Supreme Court ruled that the 'bugging' had violated the Fourth Amendment guaranteeing 'the right of people to be secure in their persons, houses, papers, and effects against unreasonable searches and seizures.' The four-to-three decision exonerated Cahan and upheld the 'exclusionary evidence' rule. In practice, this meant the police could not break down a door to arrest a bookie because if he were subjected to illegal search or seizure, the case would be thrown out. Suspected dope peddlers or even child molesters could not be jailed on suspicion; they would have to be caught in the act.

Parker direfully predicted that criminals would run wild, and LAPD's statistics bore him out. In the eight months following the decision, robbery and auto theft each increased more than thirty per cent, burglary rose almost fourteen per cent, larceny more than eleven per cent. And, despite the rising tide of crime, prosecutors hesitated to issue complaints against known criminals. The courts threw out what formerly were routine cases – all because of the Cahan decision.

In one instance, an LAPD motorcycle officer chased and caught a speeding car containing two youths. He shook down one youth and found a bindle of heroin on him. He arrested him and also turned in a typewriter which he had found in the car. Checking stolen property records, police found an All Points Bulletin from Bakersfield reporting the theft of the typewriter.

So the motorcycle man went to the preliminary court hearing with a pretty good case, he thought; a speeder who had been carrying both heroin and stolen property. What happened next, at least to the officer, was something like a court proceeding in Alice's Wonderland. The policeman had been justified in making the speeding arrest, the judge said, but that was as far as he should have gone. The cop had *not* had any probable cause to believe the prisoner had committed a criminal offense, and hence the search of the defendant had been unreasonable, even though it did disclose heroin and a stolen typewriter. Evidence excluded, charges dismissed. The suspect was fined for speeding. Nothing more.

In another instance, 'With grave and utmost reluctance,' a judge freed a prisoner whom he himself described as 'a dope peddler and smuggler.' The police, he explained, had raided the defendant's home without warrant or *legal* reason to believe that a felony had been committed. Hence, under the law, the judge was forced to throw out the case although the search had turned up 140 bindles of heroin and a batch of barbiturates.

Parker was not alone in his distress over the Cahan decision. As he freed the aggrieved owner of the heroin, the judge pleaded for new laws 'so that our policemen can effectively and legally perform their duties in apprehending these criminals.'

Under the 'exclusionary evidence' rule, Chief Parker says, the plight of the policeman and, more particularly, the society he is protecting boils down to this: *'The question of the conduct of the officer in obtaining evidence is paramount to the question of the guilt of the defendant.'*

For example, since the first boatload of Chinese disembarked inside the Golden Gate, Oriental gambling dens have flourished in California. The Chinese players of piquet, pi-gow and fan-tan have become exceedingly copwise over the years, and the ancient games of chance are pursued behind modern barred doors guarded by lookouts. Under the most favorable conditions, raiding parties with battering-rams had difficulty gaining access and evidence. Since Cahan, elaborate, expensive, time-consuming undercover surveillance has been forced on LAPD.

Or take the crime in progress, like a juvenile dope party. The police cannot crash in unless they first go for a warrant, by which time the offenders may have fled. On the other hand, if they knock politely on the door to obtain entrance, they hear scurrying feet and a toilet flushing away the evidence.

Twice in a year men died because the police did not make a thorough search for weapons. Policeman Leo Wise, thirty-four, father of four small children, hauled a belligerent, sawed-off cop hater out of a bar near Pico Boulevard and Figueroa Street where he had been causing a disturbance.

Wise didn't know that his prisoner, Marion Linden, forty-three, had a record of arrests dating back for twenty years, and he searched him only casually. As Wise was asking for prisoner transportation from the nearest callbox, Linden pulled a nickel-plated, .32-calibre revolver and fired twice at point-blank range. His liver and heart pierced, Wise fell, fatally injured.

In the Westlake District, Robbery Detectives Robert Peinado and Jim Brady picked up a tough young hood whose description fitted that of a holdup fugitive. They, too, gave him a casual shake and missed the snub-nosed, .38-calibre pistol tucked into his shorts. As the three started to enter the detectives' car, the hood suddenly stepped back, pulled out his .38 and pointed it at Peinado.

Brady, who had just opened the car door, spun around and fired twice. His first shot pierced Peinado's coat sleeve and hit the suspect's gun arm. The second ripped into the youth's stomach, and he died a short time later in the Georgia Street Receiving Hospital.

In view of these cases, not to mention the thousands of times when shakedowns do disclose the weapons, Chief Parker feels his men have a good probable cause to make searches in the field. Yet if they find any criminal evidence, they face a dilemma: Will the courts say they have again overstepped their authority?

To Parker, one solution would be adoption of the Michigan plan which exempts cases involving narcotics or deadly weapons from the corset of 'exclusionary evidence.' Urging this proposal before a State Senate sub-committee, he told them of the breakdown in enforcement after the Cahan decision and said:

'I think it is important that you have a statement from the "workers in the vineyard." It is easy for the courts and prosecutors to criticize because the police, not the courts and prosecutors, are liable to civil suits for errors in judgment.

'The breakdown came when the police were unable to bring criminals before the bar of justice. You can't blame the police. You must blame the high court of this state and the prosecutors who favor the Cahan decision and the legislators who have failed to do something about it.'

II

'At the present time, race, color, and creed are useful statistical and tactical devices. So are age groupings, sex, and employment. . . . If persons of Mexican, Negro, or Anglo-Saxon ancestry, for some reason, contribute heavily to other forms of crime, police deployment must take that into account.'

– CHIEF PARKER

Probably no other city in the country, even New York, presents the racial admixtures of Los Angeles. The largest Japanese group in the nation, the third largest Chinese population, the largest Mexican-descent colony outside of Mexico City itself, all live in Los Angeles. There are

300,000 Negroes, more than the number of white and Colored combined in most Southern towns.

All told, one hundred different races are represented in the West Coast's melting pot, and the non-Caucasians probably comprise more than forty per cent of the people. To Parker it seems as plain as his badge that LAPD's Modus Operandi cards and other records should note the race and color of the criminal as well as his nickname, hangouts, associates, and other identificatory detail. If LAPD is pursuing a Chinese rapist, it's because he has violated a woman, not because he is Chinese, Parker feels; and a radio broadcast of his race and color does help to narrow down the search.

The minorities, particularly the National Association for the Advancement of Colored People, do not see it that way. NAACP has charged Parker with racism, persecution, and discrimination. An unsigned communication on its letterhead to the police commission demanded his removal. Alter a truce meeting between Parker and NAACP leaders in Los Angeles, which had been arranged by neutral sources, the Negro leaders discarded their suspicion that he is an intolerant man, but they still fear his seemingly blind absorption in law enforcement. And Parker still says doggedly:

'From an ethnological point of view, Negro, Mexican, and Anglo-Saxon are unscientific breakdowns; they are a fiction. From a police point of view, they are a useful fiction and should be used as long as they remain useful.'

Unfortunately perhaps for the cause of sweetness and light between police and minorities, Parker's candor goes further. He cannot resist saying (a heresy in some circles!) that the minorities can be wrong, too. Thus, at the Institute on Police-Community Relations at Michigan State University, sponsored by the National Conference of Christians and Jews, he insisted:

261

'The fact that minorities have received intolerant and discriminatory treatment does not automatically lend justice to all of their demands. They are as prone to error as majority groups, and the wiser and calmer citizens within those groups recognize this fact. Thoughtful citizens expect the police to stand their ground when they believe they are right. They expect the police to criticize as well as be criticized.'

Against this impolitic statement, against the sporadic charges that an arrest was made or a crime complaint ignored because of the color of the skin involved, Parker points to the records. During his regime, there has been no major racial strife in the city. Much as the many community agencies have helped toward this end, he feels that it is the *professionalization* of the police that has been the key factor.

During his thirteen weeks of training, the Los Angeles police cadet must absorb about a year's learning. That means cramming a prodigious amount of basic technical information on everything from weapons to law. But Parker also insists that the cadet learn the emotions and drives of racial groups, their movements, and the tensions that arise from such movements. There are courses in Police Sociological Problems, Ethics, Human Relations, Professionalism, Civil Disturbances, and Public Relations. Even in the purely technical courses like Interrogation, Patrol Tactics, and Investigation, human relations also are emphasized.

During his thirteen weeks, the cadet is closely observed for any symptoms of prejudice which might make him a poor police risk. Unknown to him, conditions of tensions are deliberately created to test his reactions. And finally he is briefed on the racial composition of the various police districts in Chief Parker's own words:

'It must be made clear that there are no "Jim Crow"

areas, no "Ghettos." Every police division has everything found in all divisions, differing only in proportion.

'The aim here is to correct stereotyped impressions that the city is divided into clearly defined groups and areas and that law enforcement differs accordingly. The Police Department's policy of *one* class of citizenship, *one* standard of police technique, then becomes readily understandable.'

Those who profess concern about Parker's attitude on individual rights acknowledge one strong point in his favor. Whenever those rights are threatened by an outsider, he moves promptly with all the facilities of LAPD. The outsider may practice blackmail and extortion ('the big underquoted crimes of our day,' Parker says), or he may operate in the gamey world of the private eye and the scandal magazine. The latter is in the twilight zone of legality, and Parker has had to think up new procedures to carry his attack.

Thus, when the California State Senate decided to investigate private detectives, Parker quietly assigned his best Intelligence and Bunco men to the inquiry. For months one Lieutenant did nothing except run down the tie-ins between scandal mags, private eyes, and strongarm collection agencies. He turned up the scabrous story of *Confidential* Magazine's dirt-collection system in which gossip fed by prostitutes was double-checked by private investigators.

One admitted having hidden in the bushes and secretly shot fifty feet of colored film of an actress at her Bel Air home. 'I would have taken indiscreet or embarrassing pictures,' the peeping eye confessed, 'but I just had no chance to.' He surrendered his film to the committee.

Another divulged *Confidential*'s technique for printing all the dirt possible and still escaping reprisal by libel:

'Say that movie star "X" has committed adultery with some girl. I am given a memo as to what phases of the story they want checked. Say that movie star "X" drove a white foreign-made car and was working on a movie and his wife, also a movie star, is on location in Arizona.

'Say he went to this girl's apartment and they saw the landlady on the way in. I will be told to check whether he has a white sports car and whether he is working in a certain movie, whether his wife is in Arizona and if the landlady saw the couple in question. That's how it works.'

The undercover work which had been done primarily by Parker's men led in turn to a grand jury investigation and even further disclosures about the love-and-tell-for-pay activities of call girls and bit actors. One notorious Hollywood party girl admitted to the jury that she fed stories to *Confidential* by allowing a private eye to tap her phone while she was talking to an actor. She even sold the magazine intimate details of her marriage, involving her husband and a movie actress. The grand jury returned indictments which led to the successful prosecution of the slick-paper scandal rag and a considerable toning down of its editorial content.

Parker would love, almost above all, to stamp out blackmail and the twin crime of extortion (which carries with it violence or threat of violence). These ancient, un-American crimes flourish increasingly in Hollywood, detectives believe, but the victims will almost never testify, even when police know what is going on. Therefore, from Parker down, they were delighted to receive a brave complaint from Victor Berke, a thirty-nine-year-old tax consultant.

In the process of moving from Chicago to Los Angeles, Berke stopped off briefly in Las Vegas to try his hand at the gaming tables. He dropped $11,000. Berke paid off $10,000 and wrote a check for $1,000 which later bounced. Soon after, he was summoned by telephone to a Hollywood hotel and given an ultimatum.

He was now to pay $3,300 – or else. The 'or else' was violence.

When Berke told his story to the LAPD Bunco Squad, it was the first documented exposé in Los Angeles of extortion growing out of Las Vegas gambling losses. Parker had the case sped to the Los Angeles County Grand Jury. One night while Berke was dining with a client in a Hollywood café, three men paused briefly at his table.

'You're dead!' one of them muttered.

Then came further threats to keep him from testifying against the strongarmers. LAPD retaliated by giving Berke round-the-clock security protection. Three suspects involved in the case threw in the towel and pleaded guilty to attempted extortion.

Certainly in all such threats to private rights Parker is vigilant enough to satisfy even the American Civil Liberties Union.

According to Section 199 of the Los Angeles City Charter, 'The General Manager of the Police Department shall be known as the Chief of Police.' So, in addition to crusading for what he considers right and denouncing crime on the grand scale, Chief Parker must administer what is essentially a *service* organization. Ten thousand times daily the bulbs light on the communication system, and each is a service call. The taxpayer may demand relief from a barking dog, report a murder, or ask for a radio car to fill in a week-old minor accident report (because an insurance company requires police action on the form).

Obviously Parker has to take the big view and work from the top down in an organization which is handling seven calls a minute. He holds a tight personal rein on what he considers the key activities of big-city police work, but trusts his subordinates to carry through on detail.

On the key jobs, internal discipline, intelligence, public relations, vice control, and planning, the field forces are given responsibility to carry through. But administrative divisions with both staff authority and line responsibility double-check their work – and so does Parker. On vice, for example, he is taking no chances on fresh scandals that could upset him as other police administrations have been upset in the past.

The Administrative Vice Squad maintains a constant survey to determine that vice officers in the field do their job and, if necessary, do it for them. In turn, through reports on volume and direction of vice activities throughout the city, Ad Vice is directly responsible to Parker.

He is the only Chief in modern Los Angeles history who has survived a change in city administration and he is determined to keep it that way.

For the average police officer, he has fought to keep the politicians out of the department. He has made good his early promise to himself that promotions would be on merit, 'off the top' of the civil eligibility lists. He has cut dead wood, raised recruiting standards, and pleaded at City Hall for higher salaries. He wangled half the raise he wanted from the City Council, but he keeps coming back. 'Professionalization' of the police, his dream of dreams, requires men of superior backgrounds, and they can be attracted only by decent salaries and working conditions.

For a restless man of action, he puts almost touching faith in the value of paper work. For example, he made permanent the Intelligence Division which had been set up by General Worton to infiltrate, reconnoiter, and provide advance information on the plans of the criminal syndicates. Properly, this is police activity on the federal level, but Parker gave Intelligence carte blanche because no federal agency was supplying the information to local law enforcement bodies.

From one end of the country to the other, Intelligence amassed detailed dossiers on every important mobster in the U.S., many of whom never had seen Los Angeles and probably never would. Parker felt that in an airplane age when cities are only minutes apart, the long job of interviewing and corresponding with police and crime commissions from Maine to Florida was worth the time and expense. And from this file has grown a federation of fifty-two law-enforcement agencies west of the Mississippi dedicated to the exchange of vital statistics on the existence and movement of the nation's criminal network.

Similarly, Chief Parker has thoroughly supported the Planning and Research Division which he calls 'possibly the most interesting development within the police department in some years.' What a riot control expert can do with tear gas P&R does with slide rules and graphs to predict where and what time how many policemen will be needed.

To achieve this, the scholars of crime digested population figures, family size, income, education, ages, census surveys, uniform crime reports, local social and economic studies, standard reference works like the Municipal Year Book, and any other Los Angeles statistic they could lay hands on. Their findings have brought about new and exact re-deployments of LAPD's under-manned field forces.

In Planning's statistical unit, more than two million police reports have been studied and more than four million IBM cards coded. If you wonder why, here is an example.

When detectives in San Fernando Valley seized a theft-and-burglary gang, its members began confessing crimes by the dozens which stretched from Los Angeles through cities along the Southern California coast as far south as

San Diego. The crimes were not committed at definite times, and three separate M.O.'s were used.

Sometimes the gang (so they said) carried safes away from service stations; other times they burglarized the places without removing the safes; and still again they stole money from vending machines in the stations. Skeptical detectives turned to the Stats unit to pinpoint and verify their story, if possible, from the thousands of burglary-theft complaints on file. The Stats office machines quickly picked out 200 cards, of which 198 were traced to the gang.

In P&R's legal section some 1,500 questions asked by department members are researched and answered yearly. Recently the section saved the city a sizable $40,000. That amount had been claimed for the maintenance of city prisoners committed to county jail, but LAPD's detailed legal report in opposition was sustained by the City Attorney.

Even the *Department Manual*, a prosaic-looking book in a three-ring loose-leaf binder, represents a formidable task of research. To compile it, P&R made abstracts from some 4,600 departmental orders, teletypes and bulletins, as well as bureau manuals and numerous police commission resolutions dating back for a quarter of a century.

Whether it is the recognition of the imminence of childbirth or the proper report to be used when a consul is arrested, *Department Manual* is the 'how-to' of LAPD procedure. Down to disposition of dead animals found on the street (notify Dead Animal Dispatcher, Refuse Collection Division, Department of Public Works), no problem is too humble to be excluded.

In this division of paper work, there is even a section which studies paper work to combine, simplify, or eliminate police forms. During one year the section studied 282 different forms, eliminated 109, revised 113, and added 60 new forms.

More than the public realizes, investigation and apprehension of criminals depend on the recorded knowledge of their habits and methods; but, at the same time, a department can become 'paper-bound.' When Parker became Chief, he introduced the latest business and government techniques in paper handling. As a result, he reduced the number of forms by over one hundred in his first year in office and with simplified design saved up to thirty-five per cent in time needed for dictating, typing, and filing them. The changes enabled him to use civilian help and free one hundred and eight policemen for field duty.

In looking to the future, Parker hopes that there will be deeper public awareness of the dangers presented by organized crime. In fact, he says, the two major political parties should formulate policies for dealing with the problem nationally. At the same time, he feels that crime is also an intimate, local affair demanding *your* personal support of your own crime fighters.

'It is physically impossible for the Los Angeles Police Department to eliminate lawlessness, vice, and corruption from this city if the citizens do not honestly want such things eliminated,' he emphasizes. And he has pleaded with his fellow Angelenos, 'Give the nation the leadership for which it is looking by starting the old-fashioned habit of being honest in government!'

Essentially Parker is a moralist. While full adherence to Scriptural ethics would abolish crime overnight, he fears we have become 'a confused nation' and too many of us have adopted double standards 'adjustable to private and business life.' Of necessity, the policeman represents the 'thin blue line' which protects the truly law-abiding. Not, he adds quickly, that LAPD lays claim to perfection.

'Mistakes will be made, perhaps serious mistakes,' he

says. 'We do not claim perfection within our ranks. But they will be made in good faith.

'We have attempted, within the limits of our authority, to enlist the finest personnel available. However, since the City Charter limits us to selecting mortal human beings, we may continue to experience some mortal weaknesses.'

THE COMMISSION

Behind Chief William H. Parker are five men who also wear badges. They also have taken the policeman's oath to support the Constitutions of the United States and California and faithfully to discharge their duties 'in and for the city of Los Angeles to the best of their ability.' Yet they are civilians serving, by mayoralty appointment and City Council approval, on the Police Commission. They are cops by courtesy, but mighty important cops.

Even a first-rate Chief like Parker couldn't survive without the support of the Commission. Especially a Chief like Parker, as a matter of fact. The Commission is the shock absorber between him and the public, protecting the one and reassuring the other that in spite of LAPD's 'professionalization,' mufti still controls the uniform.

In choosing Parker in the first place, the commissioners knew that they were getting a peppery, tenacious, dedicated man, and that thereafter their weekly Wednesday meetings would never be routine. Nor have they been; but the Commission, without degenerating into a rubber stamp, has not wavered in its support.

When Parker vowed, 'With all the fiber of my being, I will see to it that crooked rats who would change the City of Angels to the City of Diablos will not do so,' the Commission backed him – and no fingers were crossed under the table. A politically-minded commission could have given lip service and then cut him down with backstage sabotage.

In the first two months of his administration, there was the opportunity to get rid of him if the commissioners already regretted their choice.

In a routine traffic shakedown, a police reserve officer shot and killed an unarmed, eighteen-year-old college honor student. Parker was caught between public indignation and the strong, 710-man reserve corps which serves without pay. Parker promptly ordered that thereafter no reserves could patrol except in the company of a regular officer. Dozens of old-time reservists turned in their badges, lambasting Parker as a political grandstander. The Chief stood firm and the Commission backed him up. And it has done the same time and again in petty matters and Los Angeles *causes célèbres*.

This support is especially significant because the Commission is bipartisan and biracial and includes followers of the three great religions. Thus, when the representative of some minority group seeks a favor or lodges a protest, he knows that across the table are men who sympathize with the motives, tensions, and hopes of minorities. He cannot complain that the deck is stacked against him.

Its own diversity has given the Commission the courage and assurance to act firmly in delicate matters. Very few political appointees anywhere in the country would think of turning down routine requests from any religious group, for example. Yet LAPD's commissioners rejected a permit for a religious parade on the common sense grounds that the guard duty would take up too many LAPD manhours and 'interfere with its ability to cope with crime.' 'Fringe' prayer groups have been denied the right to broadcast services from sound trucks because it would constitute an infringement of the public welfare. And the Commission has risked the wrath of California's many left wingers by forcing Communists and Communist front groups to register with LAPD.

Big names do not particularly impress the five quasi-cops. When the city outlawed discharge of firearms within its limits, Clark Gable asked for an exception for his Encino estate in San Fernando Valley. Gable requested the right to shoot coyotes, blue jays, and ground squirrels which would have given him a sort of miniature shooting lodge. Chief Parker protested that any exception would retard LAPD's program against use of firearms within the city. Parker was upheld, Gable refused.

'The Commission is the servant of the electorate in police matters and is the means by which the voice of each citizen may be heard,' LAPD's annual report states, and the commissioners take their own department's words to heart. In behalf of the people, they even collided head on with the Los Angeles City Fire Department.

The situation arose when Fire Chief John Alderson disclosed to the Fire Commission that the racial-integration program had been eliminated by moving all transferred Negro firemen back into all-Negro stations. Before that, he asserted, there had been danger of riots and bloodshed because of 'carloads of Negroes who follow fire trucks to fires and try to create dissension and trouble.'

Promptly the Police Commission rapped the Fire Chiefs knuckles for failing to notify it of any situation which 'might have led to riot and bloodshed.' Alderson, the Commission said bluntly, had been remiss in his duty 'as both a public official and a citizen.'

The Commission has backed up Parker in his unending harassment of gamblers and contributed one or two harassments of its own. With its support, the Chief obtained a ruling from the City Attorney that bookies who serve felony sentences in the county jail can be classified as ex-convicts like the offenders who go to state prison.

Thus, by city ordinance, the gamblers had to register with the police as ex-criminals. Two weeks after their registration got under way, more than a thousand had complied with the order, and the police department ran out of registration blanks.

The Commission went Parker one better in a manner which only civilians could accomplish. Through Commissioner Michael Kohn, the anti-gaming law was strengthened to include as a violation even a *visit* to a gambling establishment which operates behind barricaded doors. Whereas police often deal lightly with the citizen who patronizes the gambler, Kohn's aim was the bettor who makes the games possible.

'The barricaded nature of these joints makes their purpose obvious,' he explained, 'and it would be a fair assumption that visitors to such places are there to gamble.'

And, when valid complaints are lodged against LAPD, the Commission follows through as the representative of the public. Thus, motorists who complained that motor-cycle policemen were taking fifteen to twenty minutes to write out traffic tickets received a sympathetic reception from the Commission. It was bad enough to get a ticket, the Commission agreed, without also being unnecessarily delayed.

As a matter of public relations, LAPD's five bosses ordered that the officers speed up the procedure to five minutes flat. 'The only contact most residents have with the Police Department is through traffic tickets,' the Commission observed.

Often there was deeper concern about issues of public relations, too. A few years back, the word 'race' was eliminated from the traffic ticket issued by the policeman to the public. Minority races resented receiving a ticket which indicated the color of a man's skin. They felt, also, that many times this was the reason for getting the ticket in the first place. So LAPD erased the word and closed the gap a little more.

Similarly, the Commission signed the death warrant of the annual LAPD police show so that businessmen would not feel obligated to buy tickets and program advertising. Further, there was a growing Commission objection to lowering the dignity of the police officer by making him sell the Police Show ads and tickets.

Though Parker runs his department as 'the pro' who knows where and when he wants to deploy his men, the Commission doesn't hesitate to give him advice when it hears from the public.

For example, burglary, which occurs some 27,000 times yearly, hitting one home in every hundred, is LAPD's worst headache because it strikes the average householder. As a taxpayer, he is quick to protest.

During one serious outbreak of burglaries in the San Fernando Valley, the Commission received so many protests that it asked Parker for an emergency patrol in the area and the assignment of extra men where needed. Parker obeyed and the outbreak subsided.

By and large, it's difficult to understand why a civilian accepts the largely thankless task of worrying about LAPD's problems. Certainly it isn't the handsome salary of $10 a week. Nor is it the prestige.

'Sometimes you figure maybe it *is* a thankless job, being a police commissioner,' admits Herbert A. Greenwood, the Negro member of the board. 'That is, people think it's a picayunish appointment.'

'The average person doesn't know that the Commission is the head of their Police Department,' adds Commissioner Kohn.

Nor is it 'politics.'

Chief Parker is remarkably unskillful at 'playing

politics,' and far from dictating to him, the Commission is usually in the position of explaining or defending Parker to the public. The only answer seems to lie in that often-suspect phrase 'public service.' The commissioners are genuinely concerned as citizens with law enforcement in their city.

Consider them, one by one:

Michael Kohn, who has served as President and Vice President of the Commission, is a native son of a Jewish produce merchant who migrated from Hungary. He is forty-eight. Thirty years ago Mike Kohn was an office boy in the powerful Los Angeles legal firm of Loeb and Loeb. Today he is a senior partner. He knows Los Angeles, and Los Angeles knows Mike Kohn.

One of the big passions in his life has been Los Angeles and its youth. The father of two sons, he has worked hard for such groups as Hillel and the Big Brothers in LA. In addition, he has ranged into every facet of communal life which emphasizes youth programs.

Most of all, he believes the public must understand that the Commission is part of the public, too, and that *together* their job is to encourage a constantly stronger LAPD. In one optimistic message to the Mayor, written in behalf of the Commission, Commissioner Kohn sees that awareness growing steadily. There has been, he says, 'a remarkable upsurge of active public cooperation in all phases of law enforcement,' and he points out joyfully:

'The Los Angeles citizen has not only accepted the progressive efforts of the Los Angeles Police Department, but is coming to insist upon this type of police work as a public right. Without question, such a right exists and a continuing public demand for it is the best guarantee that professional law enforcement will prosper and grow in our city.'

John Ferraro, the son of an Italian farmer-macaroni manufacturer, was twenty-eight years old at the time of his appointment and thirty-two when he served a term as Commission president. His age seems unnecessarily young for such an important body, but there is a good reason.

Unlike the old days, Los Angeles now is a city of youth. About a quarter of the population still is in grade or high school, and seven in ten Angelenos have not reached their fortieth birthday. Hence, when Norris Poulson became Mayor, he felt that youth deserved representation on the Police Commission and Ferraro looked like the right man. A former all-American tackle at the University of Southern California, and a wartime Navy ensign, he had become a successful executive with his own insurance business.

Poulson proved right. 'A lot of my contemporaries took interest in what we in the Police Department were trying to do,' Commissioner Ferraro says. 'They began to wonder about the operation of LAPD. They asked a lot of questions. It was a healthy, creative interest; and it has proved good for the city and for the Police Department.'

Though in civilian life he is executive vice president of one of the fifteen largest advertising agencies in the world, Commissioner Emmett C. McGaughey is the only board member with professional police experience. For eight years, he was an FBI agent. Since he did most of his federal sleuthing in Los Angeles, his law enforcement contacts are valuable to the Commission.

On one occasion, from a source which he won't divulge, he received a tip that a LAPD officer had been guilty of malfeasance. High brass in the department refused to believe the report, but McGaughey persuaded them to put the man under surveillance. He was shortly dismissed from the department.

As a former FBI man, McGaughey, like Parker, firmly believes that in the preservation of the American way of life, it is law enforcement which carries 'the greatest challenge and the greatest burden.' And, as a father in his mid-forties with three small boys in public school and a girl ready to enter, he feels a personal responsibility to face up to the task.

'I want to help make this city as good as I can for them to live and grow up in,' he says.

When you are a police commissioner, the job may call you back from Seattle or Salt Lake City, or wherever you happen to be at the time on private business. It's happened any number of times to Bill Lucitt. Or the job may mean working nights in your own garage to repair toys for underprivileged kids. Or counseling potential delinquents. Or helping policemen themselves who are in difficulty. That's the kind of Commission work that appeals to Bill's Irish generosity.

A simple, friendly man, he still lives in the seven-room Hollywood bungalow where he and his wife, Mary, began raising their own four children thirty-five years ago. Though he has never been a sworn policeman, Commissioner Lucitt knows more about thieves than anyone else on the board. For twenty-eight years he has directed internal security for one of the nation's largest retail and mail-order chains throughout the Pacific Coast, Hawaii, and Canada. That means he isn't home very much of the time, but Bill always flies back for the Wednesday meetings.

Only once, the other commissioners recall, has Bill ever been abrupt in any Commission matter. That was when he summarily opposed the granting of a junk dealer's license to an applicant. It developed that three years before, the man had been a porter in one of the stores Bill polices –

and Bill had caught him stealing $500 worth of credit coupons.

On several occasions, Lucitt has been loaned to the Federal Government as an investigator in connection with Congressional Investigations. During his career, he has worked closely with the enforcement agencies on the federal, state, and local levels.

He has worked in cooperation with the U.S. Marshal's Office, the Secret Service Agencies, the Department of Justice, and the Postal Inspection Service.

Through his work he is widely known by law enforcement agencies throughout the seven western states, particularly the police and sheriff's departments of cities and counties of the Pacific Coast.

With all of these contacts, as well as traveling throughout the United States on special assignments and through seventeen foreign countries on pleasure and observation, Bill Lucitt feels qualified to make the proud assertion: 'The Los Angeles Police Department is the finest and most efficient Police Department in the World.'

Lucitt subscribes to Chief Parker's philosophy that the major requisite in curbing juvenile delinquency and preventing crime is a re-education in self-discipline and a return to the recognition of moral absolutes.

Herb Greenwood was born into a big family, six girls and four boys, counting him, in Atlanta, Georgia. His father, a letter carrier, never made too much money to support a family of that size; and, when Herb was only twelve, his father died.

Nevertheless, working 'every job in the book,' Herb Greenwood put himself through school. Back in 1923, when he was still only twenty-four years old, he won his law degree from Western Reserve University, Cleveland, Ohio, and the next year passed the exam for the Illinois bar.

Like many a young lawyer, he got his start by defending the needy and poverty-stricken who seemed to file in a shabby, unending, often uncomprehending line through the halls of justice. He developed a warm understanding for the underdog that has never left him.

A quarter of a century ago he moved from Chicago to California; but, in the depths of the depression, there was little legal work for a Negro newcomer from 'the East.' Herb Greenwood went to work for the state, serving first as social worker and then as a liquor control officer for the State Board of Equalization. But he kept up his legal studies and later was appointed an Assistant United States Attorney in Los Angeles. When he received his LAPD commissionership, he gave up the federal post and returned to private practice. He was then in his fifties, and it was a serious decision.

'Yes, some people take it as a picayunish appointment,' he says. 'But I didn't. I felt it was an opportunity for service – if I tried. If I did try, and did give service, then it was not at all picayunish.'

As the representative of Los Angeles' 300,000 Negroes, Herb Greenwood has been in a particularly trying spot at times because of the impasse between Chief Parker and the National Association for the Advancement of Colored People. More than once, Herb admits ruefully, he has felt 'like a sitting duck,' but this was his special opportunity for service and he refused to close his eyes to it. He has worked hard to convince the NAACP officials in Los Angeles that Parker is a sincere and unprejudiced official. When the commotion arose over integration in the Los Angeles Fire Department, Commissioner Greenwood could say proudly that it had been long since achieved and taken for granted in LAPD.

But then there is the other side. A Negro railroad porter who reported late for work in Chicago blamed the delay on his brutal and unjustified detention at the hands of Los Angeles policemen. Not only NAACP but also the porter's company joined in the investigation. Once again, Herb Greenwood was in the middle.

But, the investigation showed, the porter had been involved in a barroom disturbance and arrested only after the bartender had called the police. He later received fair, routine handling and while his court appearance delayed his return to Chicago, he could hardly blame LAPD for that.

'Being a police commissioner has been an education,' Commissioner Greenwood says. 'You hear criticism of the police; and you, as a member of the department, are criticized yourself.

'When I was in Chicago years ago, defending in criminal cases, I used to wonder about policemen. That was in the Twenties. I learned. There's nothing wrong with policemen that public interest and public cooperation won't cure.'

But he believes that, like himself, the public has to be educated. 'You have a certain, small element which claims continually that enforcement isn't strict enough. They forever want more enforcement. But they don't understand that more enforcement means more policemen. And they just don't understand how much enforcement they *are* getting – they're lucky to be getting – with the number of men we have.'

Despite dwindling LAPD manpower, Greenwood says, the constantly increasing number of yearly arrests shows what LAPD is accomplishing. For seven straight years, he points out, the productivity of the individual officer has gone up, and as proudly as Chief Parker, he adds: 'Nobody can tell me that LAPD isn't doing a good job! I just show them the figures.'

*

If in the peculiar nature of your business you wear disguises, take out ladies for pay or offer a retreat where couples can walk around together without any clothes on, your activities are of immediate importance to the Police Commission. Through licensing, the Commission controls any business which possibly poses a public risk, an opportunity to defraud, or an encouragement to unethical business practices. In Los Angeles these are deemed to include the following:

Advertising posting, auctioneering, auto parks, baths, bowling alleys, dancing clubs, escort bureaus, junk collecting, massage parlors, merry-go-rounds, nudist colonies, night clubs, pawn shops, pool rooms, rummage sales, sidewalk hawking, and used-car sales.

And quite a few more. In all, the Commission must police more than 10,000 businesses in fifty-two categories.

From its quarters in the new seven-million-dollar Police Administration Building, the Commission thus directs a sort of super Better Business Bureau. With a staff of seventeen LAPD policemen, the board checks the character and background of every applicant for a police permit, determines whether he has an FBI or other police record, sends out a field investigator to ascertain whether the proposed business would adversely affect the neighborhood.

Once the permit is granted, the Commission investigates any complaints and spot-checks against lax operations. During World War II, constant vigilance was maintained against Hollywood clip joints suspected of feeding knock-out drops to servicemen and then robbing them. Though police in the divisional stations help in the field work, the Commission's own probers make more than 2,000 investigations and almost 10,000 personal calls yearly.

Sometimes the sleuths find that junkyards are acting as receivers of stolen property. They ferret out the clip artists employed to fleece customers in cheap night clubs.

Particularly, since Los Angeles lives on wheels, they war against the used-car swindler and the gyp garage which charges $300 for the advertised '$49 motor overhaul.'

On one occasion, a motorist drove into the lot of one of the biggest used-car dealers, a firm with assets of almost two million dollars, with a very simple request. He wanted to trade in his three-year-old Cadillac sedan on a newer Cadillac club coupe. The salesman agreed to accept his old car as a $2,000 down payment against the $3,664 price of the coupe. The customer was told he could make up the $1,664 difference in monthly payments that would run 'somewhere between $108 and $110.'

With a big, successful company like that, he saw no harm in signing a blank contract because he was in a hurry to drive off in the new car. Two weeks later, the company told him he would have to pay $630 cash on the deal. When he protested that his old car represented the down payment, the manager told him firmly, 'The salesman wrote up the deal erroneously.' He refused to pay, and the company promptly repossessed the car.

The motorist complained to the Police Commission and then, a few days later, in an apparent change of heart, returned to the dealer, agreeing to pay the $630. Two friends waited casually as the motorist signed a new contract promising to pay $230 at once and the rest of the $630 in biweekly $100 payments – all in addition to monthly installment charges of $117 (rather than the $108 to $110 the salesman had cited).

Then the two friends stepped forward, identified themselves as Commission investigators and opened a full study into the company's other sales, trade-ins and contracts. They found eighteen similar cases where the blank-contract racket had been worked. The firm was closed.

When permit applications are questioned or protested,

civilian examiners conduct hearings on behalf of the Commission. They receive $25 per diem (which means that any day they work they are making two and a half times what a commissioner makes for the whole week). The Commission can approve or reject the examiners' findings, but even its adverse ruling is not the last word. Appeal can be made to the courts.

In one instance, the hearing examiner had ruled against a young Negro who wanted a junk dealer's license. The examiner cited his record as both an ex-convict and former dope addict. Since junk dealers ordinarily come into private homes, he added, the youth was obviously a bad risk.

On appeal to the Commission itself, the Negro admitted his record, but he pleaded that during his last jail sentence, and in the four months since, he had been off narcotics. He liked handling junk, he said, and he thought if only he was allowed to go into the business, he could straighten himself out forever.

Almost in tears, his sister, an intelligent girl with a responsible job, backed him up. Until his teens, she said, he had been industrious and considerate, and then there had been a falling out between him and his father. After that, he just drifted for several years between 'fixes' and jail. But now she *knew* his reform was sincere, and she was lending him the money to start the business.

The youth's probation officer confirmed his story of apparent reform, but naturally, he said, he could not guarantee that he had completely conquered addiction. The decision was up to the Commission. 'We try to do what is right and fair for all,' says Commissioner Ferraro, but what *is* fair in the classic contest between society and the individual?

Finally the Commission decided to take the risk and grant the license. As the youth stood before the board, tears in his eyes, Commissioner McGaughey said slowly:

'We have a duty to the City of Los Angeles. We take our obligation very seriously. If you don't live up to the spirit of this permit, you'll be letting a lot of people down. *You'll be letting the City of Los Angeles down.*'

'Oh, I won't sir!' the boy promised. 'I won't!'

And thus far he hasn't. He's making it.

In its dedication to the job, the Police Commission reflects a hardened public opinion that the mistakes of the past must not happen again. There were the corruption scandals of 1938 which sent two officials to prison for the almost-fatal bombing of an honest detective. Then in 1947 two women, one The Black Dahlia, were gruesomely murdered and a man disappeared, and the police didn't seem able to solve any of the three. There was the vice scandal of 1949 when the red-haired madam Brenda Allen charged that she had paid in both cash and kisses for protection of her one hundred and fourteen courtesans.

In those dreary days, the honest policeman felt ashamed to come home nights, the taxpayer jeered, 'Where's his next dollar coming from?' and the Commission fought a rearguard action for LAPD. During the '47 furore over the murders, the Commission supported then-Chief C. B. Horrall against public clamor for his ouster. 'People who read mystery books and listen to foolish radio programs expect magic solutions almost at once,' the board observed tartly.

In the Brenda Allen scandal, the Commission again supported LAPD because, it said, a few bad cops shouldn't besmirch a whole department. But this time the board could not save Chief Horrall, and General Worton moved in as interim Chief. From then on, LAPD slowly gained ground and the Commission was no longer fighting the rearguard fight.

Ever since, LAPD and the Commission have been on the offensive, but it is a wary offensive. Historically Los Angeles was a violent, sinful town right back to its birth. There can be no complacency lest the bad old strain assert itself again.

To the visitor, the Barbary Coast still is a tourist stop; a quaint, subdued relic, they think, of the wildest, most sinful days of the old Far West. Actually, at the same time that San Francisco was making a red name for itself, cutthroats from Mexico, thieves from the East were flocking into Los Angeles, too. In fact, the city even got the spillover from San Francisco when the Vigilantes began to ride.

Los Angeles' Barbary was a sump in the heart of the city, where four hundred gambling joints and all the deadfalls known to sin were crammed into an area of two square miles. The only law in the town was a volunteer force of one hundred men. Despite the constant crackle of gunfire and at least one fatality from violence every day, they made few arrests.

The first show of enforcement was the mass hanging of five assorted horse thieves, cattle rustlers and no-goods following a trial by 'representative citizens.' Though admirable, the affair was perilously close to mob lynching, and thereafter matters were entrusted to several vigilance groups and the Los Angeles Rangers with which the Mayor and the responsible business-professional element rode.

In 1869, when the population was something under 5,000, a paid police department was organized with six men and a city marshal. As an afterthought, the Police Commission was created the next year, consisting of the City Council Committee on Police and the marshal.

Uniformed according to their individual tastes, the seven-man force was identified only by white ribbon badges which warned, in both English and Spanish, 'City Police – authorized by the Council of L.A.' Such malefactors as fell into their hands labored on chain gangs at $2 per day, fifty cents for Indians.

No sooner were the police firmly organized than mob action exploded against the Chinese. For months the community leaders had blamed them for aggravating Los Angeles' considerable vice problem and then a tong war developed over the theft of a Chinese girl. With the support of citizens, police moved in to break up the dispute.

Officer Jesus Bilderrain was shot in the right shoulder and wrist, and his fifteen-year-old brother caught a pistol ball in the leg. From behind iron shutters, Chinese marksmen cut down several more of the group and then an Oriental brandishing two guns, shot and killed Robert Thompson, an enlisted deputy.

That night a mob of one thousand men, described as 'the scum and dregs of the city,' descended on Chinatown with guns, knives, and ropes. Doors, windows, and furnishings were smashed, and nineteen Chinese, many of them innocent, were hanged on an improvised gallows. Though a special grand jury later handed up forty-nine indictments, twenty-five of them for murder, only six of the lynchers were punished with brief jail terms.

In this stormy period, the Police Commission was a docile creature of the Mayor. With more social than police consciousness, the members regulated the saloon trade, periodically scolded Chinatown for its morals, and debated the temptations to youth provided by the curtained alcoves then popular in the city's public dining rooms. But Los Angeles had entered the Gay Nineties before the Commission acted decisively on a real police matter.

In his annual report to the board for the year 1890,

Police Chief J. M. Glass plainly put it up to them that something should be done in a city which boasted:

'Nineteen hotels; 212 lodging houses, of which twenty-seven have a doubtful reputation; seventeen pawnbrokers, four of whom are Chinese; twenty-seven second-hand dealers; 171 saloons; sixty-five poker games, exclusive of those places where an occasional game is allowed; ten houses of prostitution; eighty-nine cribs; 104 prostitutes known to police; twenty-five maquereaux (French pimps better known as "Macks").

'In Chinatown, there are twenty-six fan-tan rooms; nine lottery companies; seventeen Chinese poolrooms and 138 Mongolian prostitutes.'

In addition, there was the continuing problem of the highbinders, criminal gangs associated with the Chinese section, who hired out for assassinations and lesser crimes.

With unaccustomed vigor and some political acumen, the Commission ordered LAPD to launch a campaign against vice – to start with Chinatown. Again the hapless Orientals saw their section dismantled, practically board by board, but this time there were no lynchings. Having forced their incontestably higher moral standard on the heathen, the police and the Commission sort of lost interest in the rest of the vice campaign.

Actually, it was Chief Glass rather than the Commission who did something with LAPD. He established physical standards for recruits, banned smoking, drinking, and pool playing while on duty and prudently ordered that police hats be hard instead of soft. 'You will,' he commanded his mustachioed regulars, 'keep your coats buttoned, stars pinned over the left breast on the outside of your coats – and hold your clubs firmly.'

By the early 1900's, with a population of almost 320,000, Los Angeles had outgrown the approach of the Nineties, gay as that had been. In 1911 the Police

Commission was changed so that two independent citizens, appointed by the Mayor with City Council approval, could serve four-year terms without pay. Though the Chief still dictated police policy and operation, subject only to mayoralty veto, there were at least two inside observers who had the taxpayers' interest at heart.

In the wake of World War I, the Chinatown and Metropolitan Squads had to double their lockup activity, the number of arrests equaled more than one-in-ten of the total population, and in a year the amount of stolen property recovered quintupled. The postwar crime spree was immediately followed by labor violence and public indignation forced the revision in the City Charter which is still followed today: Thereafter, there were to be five men on the Police Commission serving five-year terms on appointment from the Mayor – but *they* were to name the Police Chief and he was to be responsible to *them*.

At last, democratic control of the police by the people had been achieved in Los Angeles.

Looking back on the development of LAPD, the police historian would be hard put to single out the one decisive moment where the upturn began. Very probably, it was that day in the late 1940's when Chief Parker, then a deputy chief, and Captain James E. Hamilton, then the lieutenant who acted as chief investigator for the Commission, decided that bingo would have to go.

Offhand, bingo (bridgo, beano, keno; call it what you will) is an innocuous, sociable game that has charmed even the Russians. At the same time violent anti-Communists were playing it in Los Angeles, Muscovites by the hundreds were piling into No. 3, Kropotkinskaya Naberezhnaya, Moscow, the 'American House,' for a turn at the cards and beans.

It was cheap (only ten cents a card), and it didn't take any brain power. As the pit boss called out the numbers, the players covered the corresponding numbers on their cards with beans, discs, or squares. The first player who covered a full row of numbers, horizontally, vertically, or diagonally, yelled, 'Bingo!' He was the winner. It seemed such an innocent pleasure that the police were narrow-minded meanies to stop it.

But bingo was a vice. Welfare officials in Los Angeles had long since classified it as such. Four out of five players were women – housewives who should have been home instead of gambling the grocery money, elderly widows frittering away their retirement money – and all chanted the nonsensical refrain of the bingo addict:

'Money, marbles, or chalk! Never mind the prize! How's the gamble?'

Parker and Hamilton had long since resigned themselves that the policeman cannot save man (or woman) from self-determined folly. But bingo had grown so big and blatant that the underworld had moved into the operation and complaints had multiplied. Entire pension checks were disappearing, rent money was vanishing, and one husband filed a missing persons report, telling his wife had vanished, too. (She later came home in a taxi which the bingo parlors provided for some of their better customers.)

Worst of all, millions of dollars yearly were pouring into the underworld coffers. One police investigator who followed the play for two weeks, noting down everything on graphs and charts, estimated that the games brought in $200 income hourly, and they ran from one o'clock in the afternoon till midnight. The yearly take had to be at least four million dollars and possibly as much as twelve millions.

The poor man's Monte Carlo of Los Angeles was, appropriately, located on the sea side of the city, in Venice.

Here Abbot Kinney, multimillionaire manufacturer of Sweet Caporal cigarettes back around the turn of the century, had transformed one hundred sixty acres of sand and marsh, some twenty-five miles from downtown Los Angeles, into an American city on water. There were homes, hotels, connecting canals, gondolas, and even two dozen Italian boatmen brought over from Venice on the Adriatic.

Kinney had dreamed of a Chautauqua resort by the Pacific, but the dream died with him; and in 1925 Los Angeles annexed the little community. As part of the deal, it was reported, immunity was promised for so-called games of skill along the beach.

The bingo operators had devised a clever stratagem to get around the law and still promote gambling. For a 'skill' game which involved tossing a ball at a series of numbered holes, they charged and awarded prizes. At the same time, contestants played bingo; but since this game was free, the operators claimed to be within the law. And, on one occasion, the District Court of Appeals had supported their stand, ruling that there was no evidence of gambling and setting aside a lower court injunction.

At 9:40 o'clock one August night, Lieutenant Hamilton and Policewoman Rita Holmes strolled casually into the Clover Club to see whether they could make a case against 'Venice-type' bingo.

As the policewoman played five 'skill' games and simultaneously enjoyed five 'free' games of bingo, Hamilton watched the players. In one case, he noticed, the balls in the 'skill' contest were never in play, and yet the pit boss collected from the player after each game. Obviously he was collecting for *bingo*.

In the Palace Club, operating along the bingo strip, Policewoman Holmes played five successive games of bingo, four cards per game, which cost her ten cents per card. 'In spite of the fact,' her report added, 'that I did not throw any balls or participate in any way in the respective games of skill and science.' In other words, bingo was *not* a free adjunct of the ball-type game. You were being charged for bingo cards.

To nail down his case, Hamilton decided to come back with twenty-two officials, men and women, who would work all eleven clubs in teams of two. For two months, they pounded the bingo beat, surreptitiously jotting down their observations every fifteen or twenty minutes till they had amassed an overwhelming amount of evidence.

'Twice during the game I took one bingo card in excess of the number of blue balls I had paid for,' reported Policewoman Estella R. Wallen. 'The first time the attendant said, "You owe me another dime." I paid. The next time I said, "The announcer said that the cards were free so I thought I would just take another one." The attendant smiled. "But you owe me a dime," he said. I paid.'

The experiences of the undercover officers disproved the Neon signs: 'ATTENTION! The Public Is Invited to Participate in All Relaxation (Bingo) Games FREE OF CHARGE!' Every time you took another card it cost you another dime.

But even this didn't satisfy the painstaking Hamilton. He decided that he also would prove no skill was involved in the 'skill' games. The police constructed a ball 'bin' exactly like that used in the bingo parlors and from the same firm that supplied the gamblers obtained the same kind of balls.

Methodically a team of seven officers then tossed balls hundreds of times at specific holes. Of 756 balls thrown, there were exactly nineteen hits, four of them direct and fifteen just happened to go in. In a so-called game of skill, the odds thus were about two hundred to one. In one instance, a policewoman even found that she did better if she threw while blindfolded.

Breaking down the odds and take with their slide rules, police experts calculated that the overall bingo operation was giving the suckers a payoff of *one dollar on every six dollars wagered*. It was a bigger steal than slot machines.

With Hamilton's evidence to go on, and Deputy Chief Parker's hearty recommendation, General Worton, then Chief, padlocked every bingo parlor in Venice. The Police Commission followed up by lifting their permits. The gambling interests fought back with a temporary court order under which they reopened and also produced new supporters at another Commission hearing.

Businessmen from Venice protested that $10,000 of the weekly bingo payroll was spent right in Venice, plus another $5,000 weekly for maintenance, various other services, and rent. All would be lost, they argued, if the games were closed. But the Commission remained adamant, court decisions elsewhere went against bingo, and the gamblers finally surrendered.

Venice is a nicer place today.

THE ANSWER

The Badge . . . how do you judge the men who wear it . . . ?

In Chapter One, the question was posed.

This book has been an attempt to depict a modern police force in its planning, execution; yes, and in its personalities because the police as human beings have a personal impact upon their communities.

Once you appreciate that the complicated machinery of modern law enforcement merits study more than headline-deep, a second problem arises. It is easy to get lost in the intricacies of LAPD, and you have to keep reminding yourself of the goals: honesty and efficiency; and the tools: honest, intelligent, well-trained policemen.

In any town, *your* town, those are the goals and the tools and everything else from pay raises to a new crime lab are important but subordinate parts of the picture. To the extent *you* want good tools and good goals, your town will have a good police department.

Will you work for them?

Will you pay for them?

Will you abide by the result – honest, efficient, impartial law enforcement?

Even Chief Parker admits that lawlessness, vice, corruption cannot be eliminated by the police *'if the people do not honestly want such things eliminated.'*

Thus the final chapter of LAPD – or of any other department – cannot be written by its Commission, its Chief, or its force.

It must be written by *you*.

Appendix

GLOSSARY OF POLICE TERMS

ADW	Assault with a Deadly Weapon.
APB	All Points Bulletin.
DR Number	Division Record Number.
ID Card	Identification of Police Officers.
LOCAL	A teletype to local police divisions and sheriff's department.
MO	Method of Operation.
PV	Parole Violator.
TT	Teletype.
WMA	White, Male American.
WIC	Welfare and Institution Code.
211	Robbery – Penal Code Section 211.
240PC	Assault.
311	Indecent Exposure – Penal Code Section 311.
390	Drunk – Penal Code Section 390.
390W	Drunk Woman – Penal Code Section 390W.
415	Disturbance, i.e. disturbing peace, etc. – Penal Code Section 415.
459	Burglary – Penal Code Section 459.
484	Theft – Penal Code Section 484.
484PS	Purse Snatching – Penal Code Section 484 PA.
488PC	Petty Theft.
502VC	Drunk Driver – Vehicle Code Section 502.
510	Investigator's Sheet containing all information about suspect.
4127A	Drunk in a Public Place – Los Angeles Municipal Code 4127A.

4127B	Drunk on Private Property – Los Angeles Municipal Code 4127B.
F CAR	Felony Car – Driven by plainclothesmen in the field.
K CAR	Detective Car.
M	Motorcycle.
R CAR	Radio Car.
T CAR	Traffic Car.
CODE 1	Acknowledge.
CODE 2	Proceed with Traffic.
CODE 3	Red Light and Siren.
TO QUALIFY	Police Officers must qualify in shooting each month.
$6 SHOOTER	Officer who shoots exceptionally well and $6.00 is added to his payroll. There are also $2.00, $4.00, $8.00 and $16.00 shooters.
HOT SHOT	Telephone connected with Communications where emergency calls are relayed to proper division.
KMA367	Radio Identification.
BADGE	Policeman.
BIG TIME	Time served in any state penitentiary.
BINDLE	Container for Heroin.
BLOW JOB	Where explosive is used on a safe.
BOOSTER	Shoplifter.
BUNCO	A crime where money or other valuables are taken from victims under misrepresentation.
CAP	Container for Heroin (Short for capsule).
CARRY AWAY	Where safe is carried away before being worked on.
CLEAN	A person not carrying a weapon.
CON MAN	Confidence Man (referring to Bunco).
CRIME REPORT	Complete report of a crime, containing Method of Operation or information furnished by victims or witnesses.
DIP	Pickpocket.
FBI KICKBACK	Answer from the FBI to request for information on suspect (may include fingerprint classification, etc. and also all arrest information throughout the U.S. and its possessions).

FINGER	Informer.
FINK	Informer.
FISH	New man in prison.
FIT	Narcotics – Hypodermic needle, syringe, etc.
FIX	Taking Heroin.
FUZZ	Policeman.
GAFF	Gimmick of confidence game.
GRIFTER	Confidence man.
'H'	Heroin.
HANG ON CITATION	Parking citation issued without signature of driver.
HEAVY	Suspect who is known to be armed.
HEAVY SQUAD	Robbery.
HIGHPOWER TANK	Where prisoners (such as murderers) are kept under heavy bond.
HOP SQUAD	Narcotics Division.
HOT CAR	Stolen car.
ISO CELL	A single cell where prisoners (usually narcotics addicts) are kept individually to prevent them from communicating with each other.
JAIL PROWLER	Officer assigned to the jail who makes rounds checking.
JOINT	Any state penitentiary.
JOLT	Taking Heroin.
MAKE	Identification of suspect or car.
MUG SHOTS	Photos of criminals taken at time of arrest.
MUSCLE HAPPY	Prisoner who belongs to prison gym team.
ODDITY FILE	Special file maintained of physical oddities.
PACKAGE	Criminal record of defendant (suspect).
PAPER	Container for Heroin to be sold.
PAPER HANGER	Check forger.
POP	Taking Heroin.
PRECIPITANT TEST	Test determining if human blood or not.
PUNCH JOB	Punch dial out on safe.
PUSHER	Narcotics peddler.
QUEER	Counterfeit money.
REPEATER	One who has offended before.
RIP JOB	Rip safe or peel.
RUNDOWN	Bringing up to date on a crime.

STAKEOUT	Fixed post of surveillance either in anticipation of a crime or in anticipation of arrival of person who has committed a crime.
STEERER	Confidence man's accomplice.
STRIP CAR	Parts taken.
TEA	Marijuana.
TILL TAPPING	Hitting a cash register.
VAG CHARGE	Vagrancy – no visible means of support.
WANT	Check warrant section and find out if there are any outstanding warrants on the suspect.
WHEELS	Automobile.

POLICE DEPT. DIVISIONS –
IDENTIFICATIONS & FUNCTIONS

A.I.D.	Accident Investigation Division.
AUTO THEFT	Division handling any theft involving an automobile.
BUNCO-FUGITIVE	Division handling theft from person by misrepresentation.
BURGLARY	Division handling theft from premises.
BUSINESS OFFICE	Division handling all detective business between the hours of 12 midnight and 8:00 a.m.
COMMUNICATIONS	Division handling Locals, APBs, radiograms, etc.
CRIME LAB	A section of Scientific Investigation Division which handles blood classifications, ballistics, pictures, plaster molds of marks left by suspect, etc.
C.I.I.	Criminal Investigation and Identification. (Sacramento, Calif.)
D.M.V.	Department of Motor Vehicles.
FORGERY	Division handling felonious forging of a document.
GUN RECORDS	A section of Records and Identification which maintains files listing serial number and makes of all registered weapons and information necessary for a permit to carry a concealed weapon.

304

HANDWRITING	A section of Scientific Investigation Division which compares and evaluates handwriting exemplars.
HIT & RUN FELONY	Division handling automobile hit and run cases.
HOMICIDE	Division handling any unattended death or any attempt on a person's life.
I.A.D.	Internal Affairs Division.
JUVENILE	Division handling any crime (burglary, homicide, robbery, narcotics, etc.) in which a person under 18 years of age is involved.
LATENT FINGERPRINTS	A detail of Scientific Investigation Division which obtains fingerprints at the scene of an investigation and files same.
MISSING PERSONS	A detail of Homicide Division which handles reports of disappearance of people.
NARCOTICS	Division handling any narcotics manufacture, sale, distribution or use.
POLYGRAPH	Section of Scientific Investigation Division which administers lie detector tests and evaluates evidence received.
R & I	Records and Identification.
ROBBERY	Division handling thefts from persons.
SCIENTIFIC INVESTIGATION	Division handling correlative, scientific information received as a result of an investigation of a crime.
SOUND LAB	A section of Scientific Investigation Division which installs and maintains communication equipment. The department works closely with the Crime Lab.
STATS OFFICE	A section of R & I which compiles and maintains Crime Reports on all solved and unsolved crimes with like M.O.s.
VICE	Division handling prostitution, gambling, etc.
WARRANT	A section of R & I which maintains a filing system for keeping track of warrants issued on various suspects.

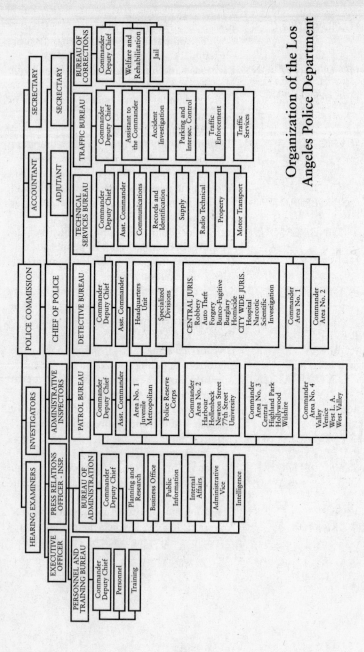

Organization of the Los Angeles Police Department